# GunDigest

# TACTICAL SHOTGUN

## SCOTT W. WAGNER

Published by

Gun Digest® Books, an imprint of F+W Media, Inc.
Krause Publications • 700 East State Street • Iola, WI 54990-0001
715-445-2214 • 888-457-2873
www.krausebooks.com


To order books or other products call toll-free 1-800-258-0929
or visit us online at www.krausebooks.com, www.gundigeststore.com
or www.Shop.Collect.com


Cover photo courtesy Yamil R. Sued/Photoworks, www.hotgunshots.com


ISBN-13: 978-1-4402-1553-7
ISBN-10: 1-4402-1553-7


Cover Design by Tom Nelsen
Designed by Dustin Reid
Edited by Corrina Peterson

Printed in the United States of America

# DEDICATION

This work is for my late father, Charles Wagner, who took me shooting for the first time when I was age eight. This experience led to a lifetime of shooting enjoyment and employment as a law enforcement officer, police trainer, criminal justice professor and writer.

It is also for Clifford Wagner, a neighbor of no blood relation and friend for life, who took me and my dad and brother skeet shooting with his personal shotgun collection for the first time when I was 14.

And it is also for Sgt. John Groom of the Columbus Ohio Police Department SWAT team, who was kind enough to share his staff, equipment, knowledge and skills with me and my tactical team at the Union County Sheriff's Office. It was this additional training that helped me to write this book.

Special thanks to Ms. Mandy Hughes for her photographic assistance.

Finally, for Bobbie Hughes, my fiancee, who supported me throughout this work.

# TABLE OF CONTENTS

# INTRODUCTION

**READY FOR ENTRY,** Benelli M4 Tactical works well for SWAT entry missions. Here it is backed up by a Beretta M92 with Crimson Trace Lasergrip Sights and a Blackhawk Serpa Holster.

"I'm gonna grab the shotgun!" How many times have those five words struck fear into the hearts of those on the receiving end of them since the shotgun was invented? Bad guys hearing it from cops, cops hearing it from bad guys, burglars hearing it from homeowners, robbers hearing it from storekeepers, guys who are in the need of an immediate wedding due to their personal and poorly planned activities…the list goes on and on. Yes, the shotgun in all its various guises and permutations is the stuff of legends, especially when it takes the form of a short-barreled model, such as the very first tactical shotguns – the "sawed-off" double barrel. The short double was used for home, store, and stagecoach protection and law enforcement duty in the west. Stagecoach protective use added the term "riding shotgun" to our common vernacular.

## WHY CHOOSE THE SHOTGUN AS A PRIMARY DEFENSIVE ARM?

I started shooting shotguns at age 14. We didn't have any shotguns in the family "armory," but the other Wagner family that lived down the street from us did. The father, Cliff Wagner, a WWII B17 co-pilot, was an avid shooter, hunter and reloader. He took us out to an area gun club where me, my brother and my dad all learned to shoot 12 and 20 gauge guns at clay birds thrown off a hand-operated thrower. We even had some home-loaded tracer rounds to play with. I seemed to take to it naturally, hitting 17 out of the first 20 thrown. Great stuff.

From there I continued my shotgunning career at the Boy Scout Camp. Back then, in 1971 or so, there was a shotgun game called "Mo-Skeet-O" which used half size clay pigeons and .22 caliber shotguns, actually .22 rimfire bolt guns with smoothbore, choked barrels and bead sights. The cartridge was the standard .22 LR crimped brass birdshot round. The birds flew around 50 or more feet as I recall, and I spent the summer paying for cartridges and blowing up clay birds. I went on the get the Rifle and Shotgun Merit Badge on the Mo-Skeet-O range.

I didn't do much else until my law enforcement career began in 1980. Already familiar with the Remington 870, I found my training and qualification time with it very enjoyable. In 1986 I got my NRA police firearms instructor certification which included shotgun instructor certification, then in 1987 I obtained the Ohio Peace Officer's Training Commission certification as a police shotgun instructor. I continue to train regularly with it as a deputy sheriff at the Union County Sheriff's Office in Marysville, Ohio, as well as during police academy training time at our college police academy. Working with the shotgun has always been an enjoyable part of my police career, and something I have never dreaded, but fortunately I had early and proper exposure to it. I wish more officers felt the same way about the shotgun; perhaps this book will help.

The shotgun is a legendary arm, and rightfully so. It has a tremendous amount of close range power, as suggested by the very large hole in the end of the barrel – a hole which, in the 12 gauge, measures a whopping .72 caliber! Even so, it is not difficult to shoot with the right training, attitude and equipment. It is versatile and useful for a wide range of tasks. If you purchase a gun that allows for the use of different length/type barrels and chokes, you can use it for anything from hunting birds or clay pigeons to hunting bear and everything in between, for home defense, law enforcement and military situations, including lethal and less-than-lethal interactions. Ammo is still relatively low cost, and was still available during the great 2007-2008 gun sale. In the proper configuration, it is extremely reliable and can feed shells in its gauge with the proper chamber ranging from 2-1/2" to 3-1/2" inches in length. Ammo is abundantly available, even in the now mostly anti-gun Walmart stores. I would speculate that 80-90% of the jobs that need to be done can be done with some form of the shotgun.

Even with the predominance of the AR-15 platform these days – and I have to admit, I love AR-15s – the tactical shotgun still rocks. It's true, you can't conceal it well legally unless you get the $200 federal tax stamp for a 14-inch barrel model (why bother), at best it holds only a total of nine rounds in an extended magazine (okay, so normally how many shotgun rounds do you need in the average self defense situation?) and it kicks a little bit depending on the setup. But it is still the best game in town, and one worth having access to. Remember, if you have a handgun, its only purpose is to allow you to fight your way to a big gun, or as a backup to the big gun, no matter how big that handgun is.

One of the best reasons this day for selecting a tactical shotgun is the cost. Clearly, you get more "bang for the buck" with one of these as opposed to the cost of a quality handgun or especially an AR-15. As a matter of fact, as I write this, my favorite gun emporium, Vance's Shooter's Supply in Columbus, Ohio, has Remington 870 Express Tactical Shotguns that feature an 18-1/2" barrel, the very cool looking if not functional Tactical Rem Choke, a full seven-round magazine capacity with 2-3/4" or 3" shells, XS® Ghost Ring Sights, XS blade front sight and sight rail (which is fully adjustable for windage and elevation), and the receiver is drilled and tapped for scope mounting. (With the rail rear sight, I would go for a scope with a quick detach rail mounting system on sale.) The price? $299. I could buy three of those babies for the price of one middle priced AR: one for the front door, one for the bedroom, one for the car.

Price any 1911 pistols lately? Yep, also more expensive. In fact, the new Remington 887 Nitro Mag tactical I purchased for this book – a brand new model with many features, and perhaps one of the best tactical pumps out there, was on sale for $439 in the same store!

Why are they so much cheaper? There is a lot less work required to make one. Smooth-bore barrels, no need to build it with the same attention to detail to wring every last bit of accuracy out of it such as with most AR-15s (you just need to hit within "minute of felon" with it). There is no finely polished blued finish (and no need to polish out any but the largest tool marks when parkerizing or tactical finishes are applied) and an overall ease of assembly. What's easier to completely field strip than the average pump shotgun? Couple all those practical aspects with the fact that, for right now, the AR-15 is still in the biggest demand, and you get sale prices like I just described. Finally, add an almost universally-available selection of ammunition and you start to see the practicality of the mighty shotgun as a primary defensive/offensive weapon.

## WHAT IS A "TACTICAL SHOTGUN"?

Webster's online dictionary defines "tactical" in part as, "of or pertaining to the art of military and naval tactics." That means we are talking about shotguns that are capable of being used in military applications in one regard, and of course we can extend that definition to law enforcement, since we in that field are often performing paramilitary type operations. However, the Webster definition is a very limited one and doesn't fully cover the modern usage of the word. These days, all things "tactical" – guns, lights, clothing, knives – are the most popular items for sale in any gun store. So I will expand upon the Webster definition of tactical by outlining three qualities of the modern word usage to qualify something as tactical. Remember that my definition is not the "be all-end all" definition and involves three different requirements.

If a product is to be considered truly "tactical" (and not just an average everyday product just spray painted black- such as a "tactical sledgehammer" originally purchased at Home Depot) it must:

1. Be reliable and of high quality-after all we are talking about products designed to be used in person-to-person fighting situations. It must work each time, every time.

2. Be of such a configuration that it is currently useful in combat type operations, whether that means military, law enforcement or civilian "operations." The configuration of the item cannot, due to complexity or poor design, impede the basic reason for which the product was designed.

3. Possess features that give it an advantage in use over the standard version of that product. Why pay more for something that is marketed as being "tactical" when the standard version will suffice?

So now that we know generally what "tactical" means in this context, we can examine how that applies to the shotgun. While later chapters dedicated to home defense and law enforcement applications will go into more detail, the basics of a modern tactical shotgun are as follows:

1. It must be of compact configuration. For civilian use it should have an 18 inch or shorter barrel. For law enforcement the barrel can be much shorter. 14 inches is a common length. It should be cylinder bored or improved cylinder in terms of the choke. Benelli's M2 Tactical comes with a set of interchangeable chokes to make it multi-use (field or farm). I like that.

2. It must be fully stocked. The pistol-grip only models look way cool, but are difficult to handle and their effective range is limited. The pistol grip models do have a very

**POLICE ACADEMY** cadets receive initial instruction with dummy ammo in order to safely learn the operation of the Remington 870 pump shotgun.

limited application for SWAT entry teams, but not for general law enforcement or civilian use. Don't use them; they don't shoot as cool as they look. And, while I prefer the traditional stock layout for shotguns, the shoulder stock models with a pistol grip do work, although I find the length of pull (length of the stock which should position the gun for optimal use) to be too long. These models also feel a little more ungainly than a standard stocked model, they don't seem to swing as fast or as smooth, nor do they carry as well.

There are some folding stock models available, but avoid the old-style Remington folding stock for their 870 shotgun. It's solid steel and will beat you to death in short order, and you will be too tempted to use it with the stock folded (it folds over the top of the weapon), which makes the sights useless.

3. It needs to have a high-visibility sighting system, no simple bead sight. Brightly colored front sights or even red dot optical sights are a must.

4. It should have either a high magazine capacity or a spare ammo carrier.

5. Color doesn't matter, although dark colors are to be preferred. Black or OD green work great. Wilson Combat's OD green finish on their Scattergun Technology pieces are great indoors and out. There is, however, a train of thought

that says a bright chromed double barrel shotgun at close range is the most terrifying close range weapon on earth, and I can see their point. So would a homebreaker.

6. It should be capable of mounting a carry sling.

7. It should be capable of solidly mounting a weapons light.

We will go step by step in examining what types work best in home defense or law enforcement applications (of course there will be overlap), makes and models that qualify as a tactical shotgun, the features the make one type stand out from another, and what might work best to meet your needs. It is to these shotguns and their users that this book is dedicated.

**IN TERMS OF HOME DEFENSE**, there is nothing more formidable than a mother defending her children, in this case with a Remington 887 Nitro Mag with BLACKHAWK! Xiphos light attached to the barrel band picatinny rail.

# CHAPTER ONE

# THE TACTICAL SHOTGUN
## FOR HOME DEFENSE

Home defense is probably one of primary uses of a shotgun. From the days where farmers once loaded shotgun shells to fire "rock salt" to irritate and scatter interlopers on their property, hopefully without killing them, to 21st-century defense against home invaders where some form of lead shot is the load of choice.

Even though its popularity is being supplanted by the meteoric rise of the AR-15, the shotgun still has a place in self-defense. Really, the shotgun exists outside of the basic self-defense arena, which is dominated by the handgun. Because of its legendary reputation and brute power, the shotgun is more of an offensive weapon. It has been used in warfare since the invention of the powder which powers it, and the military is not usually in a defensive mission. I believe it was Clint Smith who said that the handgun exists to allow you to fight your way to a bigger weapon, and that's the shotgun.

The shotgun is also the most versatile weapon out there. While it's not always the best for every purpose, it can serve nearly every purpose requiring a firearm. For home and property defense, at close to moderate range, it is hard to beat the right type of shotgun. Also, the shotgun may be legally obtained more easily than a handgun (as in Canada or Australia). But before we look at the guns of this type, it is time to dispel some common myths.

Myth #1: The shotgun, or "scatter gun," is an "alley cleaner." Fire one shot at a group of people and they all go down. Well, at least in the movies. Shot pellets in most choke configurations spread at a rate of one inch for every yard traveled. Seven yards is the standard assumed distance in interpersonal firearms combat. A seven-inch hole at that range means that you can miss your target or its vitals if you don't aim. Remember that seven inches is an average for all shotgun barrels and ammo types. Depending on our choke and load, many combinations will shoot even tighter than that.

Myth #2: The shotgun is easy to use and fire. In an old police training film from the late 1960s, the instructor, with his best John Wayne/Clint Eastwood attitude, says, "The shotgun doesn't need to be aimed. With the shotgun, you can whirl, fire and blow the guy away." This statement sounds cool, but now brings a laugh from police cadets when they see the tape. The fact is, you can't go out and buy one of these wonder weapons, load it, and leave it in a corner or close at hand ready to go without practicing with it. The shotgun requires work to master, and it is not for the recoil sensitive, at least in its 12 gauge configuration. You cannot fear or dread this weapon. You have to embrace it and make it an extension of yourself – zen-like but true.

If you are using a shotgun for home defense (or any kind of defense), you must be able to hit the target you are facing without endangering others.

If you can't handle the recoil of a shotgun, then perhaps its configuration and setup is wrong for you. There are simple things that can be done so that you can handle it better, and we will discuss these in later chapters.

You have got to be familiar with your shotgun and take it out to shoot at least a few times per year. The shotgun is far more of a precision weapon than you might realize. If you are using one for home defense (or any kind of defense), you must be able to hit whatever target you are facing without endangering others.

Myth #3: The shotgun is an infallible "stopping weapon," guaranteed to take down the largest attacker with ease. Many people think that if you hit the bad guy with a shotgun round, it's gonna kill him instantly and blow him six feet backwards to boot. Well, no. Remember, your shot pattern may be no more than an inch wide when it hits the intended threatening target and can easily miss the vitals, which would fail to stop determined opponent. Shotguns can fail to stop the aggressor – it's happened. This also means that a shotgun hit is not always fatal. Many people survive. Sure, it's way better than a handgun in a fight, and usually a better choice, it just isn't guaranteed. Nothing is.

> **If you are using a shotgun for home defense (or any kind of defense), you must be able to hit the target you are facing without endangering others.**

Now that we have dealt with some of the myths, let's look at some of the facts and discuss which shotguns will work best for home defense.

A home defense shotgun can take several forms, and also serve as a multi-role tool, especially if one lives on a farm or ranch, where it can serve animal control duties as well. When we talk about defending the home, we can also mean defending the camper trailer or RV. Traditionally a standard hunting shotgun is used for this purpose, such as a Remington® 870 Wingmaster, loaded with hunting loads, since the concept of a tactical shotgun is relatively new. While a weapon like this can suffice, there are some better shotgun configurations to work with.

**AUTHOR DEMONSTRATES** visually clearing a room with a Remington 870 Police Magnum while using the Surefire Forend Tactical light. The rooms behind him have already been cleared.

**A HOMEOWNER** confronting intruders presents an imposing threat when armed with a Remington 870 Police Magnum Tactical. Shotgun is held in a tactical low ready position, ready to be brought to bear for firing. Note Surefire tactical forend.

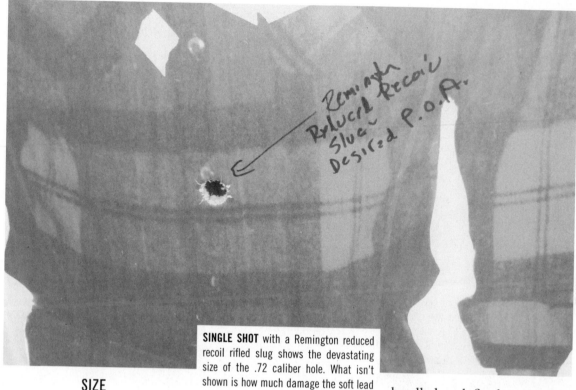

SINGLE SHOT with a Remington reduced recoil rifled slug shows the devastating size of the .72 caliber hole. What isn't shown is how much damage the soft lead slug causes on impact. The point of aim is about ideal for a shotgun.

## SIZE

Yes, size does matter, but sometimes the biggest isn't the best for everyone. A shotgun can be too heavy, kick too much, or penetrate too much. Some people can handle it and some can't. Also, abilities change over time, for better or worse. In my case for instance, I have lost a lot of shoulder functionality through deterioration and heavy use (abuse, my doctor would say) over time. I simply don't have the strength that I used to when I extend my arms. Despite the fact that I still engage in weight training on a regular basis, I find that holding and operating a pump shotgun with standard length stock and forend difficult or uncomfortable. Because I have lost some of my reach, most pump shotguns feel overly long and cumbersome. In researching this book, I have found ways around these problems.

That said, let's talk size. Like a law enforcement or military shotgun, the home defense shotgun should have a short barrel, 18 inches is the shortest civilian-legal length. The gauge of choice for the tactical shotgun is almost universally the 12 gauge, but other gauges can work as well. For example, in the 1980s I once handled and fired a compact law enforcement version of the old Ithaca Model 37 pump gun (once a major police favorite) in 20 gauge. It was designed for law enforcement and had the manly name of the "Stakeout." It was parkerized and had a stockless pistol grip-only configuration with provisions for a carry sling. Very maneuverable in a car on a stakeout, hence the name. The gun I handled had high "chicks dig it" factor and, in 20 gauge, it was much easier to handle than a 12 gauge version of the same style.

Twenty gauge shotguns for home defense (excluding single shots) are something to be considered. The 20 is not a 12, but being on the receiving end of a load of 20 gauge buckshot or slug will certainly ruin your day. There is the added side benefit of being much more user-friendly than a 12 gauge for smaller-framed members of your family. A 20 gauge tactical or home defense shotgun is a great idea from the standpoint of maneuverability since, in home defense situations, you may be using your shotgun to check the interior of your home (room clearing).

**THE VISUALLY IMPAIRED** are capable of defending themselves with a firearm. Here the author's fiancée, totally blind since birth, wields a Stoeger 12 Gauge Coach gun in a hallway. A would-be attacker would be foolish to advance any further.

**SINCE SHOTGUNS** were developed, many homeowners have stood guard over persons and property with a trusty double barrel. Few civilian legal handheld weapons are as intimidating.

A short-barrel gun of whatever action type (double, pump or auto) or gauge, allows for increased "swingability" or maneuverability as you move from room to room clearing an area of threat. It also allows you to maneuver and fire the shotgun one-handed if you need to use your support hand for other duties. Yes, the shotgun can be effectively fired one handed, even in 12 gauge. More about that later. The home defense tactical shotgun doesn't need to be expensive, or even expressly designed for or limited to short barrel home defense configuration. At the time of this writing, the Remington® 870 pump can be purchased in the low-priced Express Combo package, which features a 26-inch field barrel with ventilated rib and a 20-inch fully rifled barrel with Remington's® excellent rifle sights, for under $600.

Mossberg® also markets their excellent 500 Series pump shotgun in the same type of configuration for $441. The barrels can be easily changed in 20 seconds or less. I've used the Remington® combination for some time in multiple roles – home defense and training with the 20-inch barrel, and sporting clays with the field barrel. The Remington® 870 Express with the 20-inch un-rifled barrel is also the basic training shotgun we use in our police academy. Its Parkerized finish protects the shotgun somewhat better than blued versions of the 870s or other models, but definitely not as much as stainless

## Your significant other should be able to use the gun to defend hearth and home if you are not available or, worse yet, down.

steel or some other dedicated, truly protective finish like Wilson Combat's® Armor Tuff™.

While the Remington 870 Express package currently comes with a fully rifled 20-inch barrel, I would switch that out for the available smoothbore 20-inch Express Barrel with rifled sights, which gives you the most versatility with slugs, buckshot or field loads. And yes, you can do well for home defense using a shotgun that was originally set up for killing deer or other large animals. It doesn't have to have the word tactical as part of its name, or a bunch of bells and whistles, to make it valuable for that purpose.

Speaking of barrels, don't leave the double barrel side-by-side out of the picture. Stoeger® markets an excellent side-by-side double barrel for home defense called the Double Defense™. It is set up with a single trigger, Picatinny rail below and above the barrels for lights or optics, and a fine, very visible green fiber optic front sight (but no rear). The double barrel gun really excels with buckshot, and usually isn't the best choice for rifled slug use. A variation of Stoeger's Coach Guns for Cowboy Action Shooting, the Double Defense is tactical black in color (stocks are painted wood and not synthetic), but it is the addition of the rails that really qualify it for the tactical title. Available in 12 or 20 gauge, the 20 gauge is a great choice for multiple family member use. Your significant other should be able to

use the gun to defend hearth and home if you are not available or, worse yet, down. The double is simple to operate, especially in this single-trigger style. What could be scarier for a would-be rapist entering a home than to find himself facing his anticipated victim pointing a double barrel equipped with a tactical light and/ or laser sight, or heck, even without one?! Believe me, two 20 gauge barrels laid side by side is still very scary. The Double Defense is in very high demand; I couldn't obtain one at the time of this writing. A very formidable home defense gun indeed!

### AMMUNITION CAPACITY: HOW MUCH IS ENOUGH?

While a single-shot shotgun can, like its single-shot muzzleloading ancestors, be used for home defense, your home defense shotgun should be capable of firing two rounds without reloading. In a home defense situation, you will be scared and nervous, you may miss with that first shot or, in the case of a home invasion, have multiple suspects to shoot (or shoot at). Reloading in the middle of a gunfight is something no one relishes. Two rounds is the minimum. Most standard Remington 870s or Mossberg 500s have a magazine capacity of four rounds, which really should be enough. If you want a larger magazine capacity, that's fine, but realize that the extra weight forward of an extended magazine tube slows down your swing and makes the weapon decidedly muzzle-heavy, as well as just heavy in general. For the average homeowner, four rounds in the mag tube, or the old style double barrel, should suffice.

### TACTICAL WEAPONLIGHTS

Do you need a tactical light on your home defense shotgun? Yes and no. No, you don't really need one if you are only using your home defense shotgun inside your home. If you are also planning on using it for defense on your property then, yes a weaponlight would be a nice addition.

There are several ways of attaching a tactical light which don't necessarily require the use of a Picatinny rail, commonly found on the AR-15 system, which more and more tactical shotgun

**THE TLR1 AND TLR2** are both excellent, strobe capable lights, with the TLR having the advantage of an additional laser sight module below the light. The light on both the TLR1 and TLR2 can be used in a momentary, constant on or strobing mode. They can be affixed to shotguns like the Stoeger Double Defense or the Remington 887 Pump. Although originally designed for pistols, at 130 lumens and with solid aluminum construction, they are capable of working fine on shotguns with rails. The TLR2 can be set for light only, laser only, or both light and laser.

manufacturers are starting to add. There is the option of using a light-bearing forend such as the one offered by Surefire. These forend units, which are model-specific for pump or semi-auto, replace the original forend on the weapon and hold the tactical light and operation switches. The switches allow for thumb operation by both right- and left-handed users. There are models available in LED or incandescent bulb systems, with the LED versions far outnumbering incandescent versions. The LED is going to stand up to shotgun recoil much better than any incandescent bulb, and the lumen power is now right up there with the formerly dominant xenon incandescent systems.

In addition to dedicated forend mounts, there are universal mounting systems available that can be affixed to the magazine tube to hold your light system of choice. These however, usually require the use of a light that has an external wire leading to a pressure switch adhered to the forend by Velcro. This wire can catch on things. This may not be the best system available, but it is less expensive than the Surefire system and, since we are talking home defense here and not dynamic entry on a SWAT team, the external wire mounting might not be an issue.

## SIGHTS

For many years, the basic single front bead sight, first seen on hunting weapons, has sufficed for most purposes, both defensive and hunting. For ten years of full-time policing, my department issue shotgun was the blue steel Remington 870® with an 18-inch barrel and single front brass bead sight. Sighting was accomplished by placing that brass bead on top of the receiver and, "voila", sight picture. Well, a sight picture of sorts. A single bead works okay for ranges of 15 to 20 yards when using buckshot on a full size silhouette target. But for accurate fire using rifled slugs (and I mean accurate in terms of head shots in a hostage rescue-type situation not normally encountered in home defense), you are missing out on the precision capability of the weapon when you use a bead-sighted shotgun.

Shotguns can be very accurate with slugs, and shots if you equip them properly and train with them. Remington's rifle sights mounted on their shotgun are among the best I have used. The front sight is a brass or white bead, and the rear sight has a white triangle in the center of it, below the square notch. The rear is also fully adjustable for elevation. It is a very precise system and has been around for a long time. Call me old fashioned, but I still favor them over the modern ghost ring style.

There are other sighting options that come already installed, including red-dot electronic sights, and we will discuss those other sights later. In any event, a home defense tactical shotgun should have both front and rear sights, just like a rifle, as you may want to use both shot and slug loads, especially in exterior defense situations on larger properties.

**PROPER TRAINING** with a combat shotgun like the Wilson Combat Standard Model is critical to your effectiveness with it, whether you are a civilian or someone in the law enforcement field.

**THE REMINGTON SP10 MAGNUM SYNTHETIC** is the Remington Version of the old Ithaca Mag10 Roadblocker 10 gauge magnum shotgun. This model is set up for hunting. A 10 gauge magnum is a bit on the overkill side for tactical use. The 12 will work just fine.

A rear "ghost ring" with a tritium/white front, such as those from XS sight systems, works very well. However, you don't really need tritium on the rear sight, you can pick up on the front sight without it. Call me funny, but I'm a little nervous about having radioactive tritium vials right by my eyeball. Not that there's any known danger, I just think rear ghost ring tritium sights are more "chicks dig it" cool than they are practical.

The ghost ring rear sight is simply too close to the eye to have tritium be of value. Everything blurs with it anyway – hence the term "ghost" ring – because it becomes hazy while the front sight remains sharp. That is where the tritium is of value.

XS also makes express rifle-style sights (the same configuration as they use on their pistol sights) for the Remington 870 rifle sight systems. In that system, the rear sight is a shallow "V" shape with a white stripe in the center. To align the sights, you simply set the front white/tritium bead on top of the stripe making a "lollipop," as I tell new shooters. If I still had that basic 870, those are the sights I would mount on it if I wanted tritium sights. The rear express sight can be had with or without a plain white stripe or a tritium/white stripe.

Of course, in addition to XS, there are all sorts of fiber optic styles available as well. Fiber-optics sights are great in low level light, but obviously not in total darkness. On the Mossberg 590 there is a nice set of non-adjustable open white three dot sights, simple and solid, and of a style familiar to most semi-auto pistol users. They don't have tritium lamps in them.

One final thing you should expect about tritium sights: They normally only will be good for that first shot. After that, your muzzle flashes will wash them out, but it is that first shot that is going to be the most important one anyway.

## AMMUNITION SELECTION

Load selection for your home defense shotgun will depend on where you reside, or rather, what type of structure you reside in. Interior construction and location may even determine if a shotgun is a viable home and self-defense option. If you live in an apartment with paper thin walls, or even a house or trailer with this type of contruction, the shotgun may be totally out of the question due to over-penetration risk.

## GAUGE

Let's discuss shotgun gauges and what shotgun "gauge" actually means. The term gauge is an old form of measurement that is only indirectly related to barrel diameter. Shotgun gauge is actually the number of lead balls, the diameter of a particular bore, that it takes to equal a weight of one pound. Therefore a 12 gauge diameter would take 12 bore diameter lead balls to weigh a pound, a 20 gauge, 20 and so on. The 12 gauge would actually be about .72 caliber. The only exception or anomaly here is the .410 gauge, which is actually a measurement of bore diameter – nominally .410 inch. Actually more like .45, as those of you who own or shoot a Taurus judge know, .45 Colt cartridges and .410 shotshells are interchangeable in the gun without modification, and the .410 is the smallest true shotgun round in common use.

Mossberg chambers their 500 series of pump shotguns in 12, 20 and .410 gauge. For those interior home defense situation where overpenetration is a factor to consider, the .410 gauge loaded with field shot may be just the ticket.

## SHELL LENGTH

Next comes shell length. The most commonly-used shell lengths, regardless of gauge, are 2-1/2 (.410 gauge only) to 2-3/4 (20 and 12 gauges) inches. These shells, depending on powder charge and shot type, are adequate for most any shotgun duties that the particular bore is capable of handling, from clay targets to deer, or larger close-range game when slugs are used. Magnums can be overkill both on the giving and the receiving end in most defensive encounters.

There is a 2-3/4-inch magnum load (same velocity, slightly heavier payload) but it is not commonly encountered. Beyond that is the 3-inch magnum round. A round is generally considered a "magnum" charge for the given gauge when it provides longer range, more power, a heavier payload, and/or, you guessed it, more recoil. For example, the standard 2-1/2-inch 12 gauge shell loaded with 00 Buckshot holds nine pellets. In the 3-inch magnum load, it packs 12 pellets and begins to become unpleasant to shoot. I had to fire some 3-inch magnums for "familiarization" (torture) when I went through police shotgun instructor school many years ago, and, I can tell you, my "fun threshold" was reached and exceeded in short order. Even bigger is the newer 3-1/2 Magnum, which is about the equivalent in power and payload of the old 10 gauge round. Talk about overkill. At one time the 10 gauge enjoyed some law enforcement popularity for specialized, not general, purposes.

As a young Ohio deputy sheriff, it was suggested in my first academy training class that when chasing a fleeing automobile we should try to chase the car across the Indiana border, then back off a little. According to our instructor, the Indiana State Police carried Ithaca Mag 10 "Roadblocker" semi-automatic shotguns, and they would blow the car (and the driver) to smithereens. It may indeed be true that fewer people would consider fleeing the police as an option if they knew a Mag 10 awaited them down the road.

The rights to the Ithaca Mag 10 were purchased by Remington when Ithaca went out of business, and it is still produced in various hunting guises as the SP10. It really won't do anything more than a 3-1/2 12 gauge magnum, but it is certainly a cool concept if you can stand the recoil. Also, it is not available in a dedicated law enforcement or home defense configuration.

## RECOIL

Speaking of recoil, here is a chart comparing recoil energy for various 20 and 12 gauge loads and how they compare. For load selection, this may help some of you who are a little overzealous with the "biggest is the best" mindset. Yep, you can handle the big loads for a few shots, but not for long term practice, and you must practice with the rounds, or their direct equivalent, that you plan on keeping in your weapon.

## RECOIL IN FOOT/POUNDS

| Gun weight (lbs.) | Gauge | Load | Comments | Recoil (ft./lbs.) |
|---|---|---|---|---|
| 8.4 | 12 | 2-3⁄4" | 1⅛ oz. shot | 12.5 |
| 7.5 | 20 | 3" Mag | Factory Load | 13.0 |
| 6.0 | 12 | 2-3⁄4" | Heavy Game Load | 16 |
| 5.5 | 12 | 1 oz slug | Duty Load | 17 |
| 5.5 | 12 | 2-3⁄4" Mag | 1 ¼ oz shot | 24 |
| 5.5 | 12 | 3" Mag | 1 1/4 oz shot | 33 |
| 6.0 | 12 | 3" Mag | 1/14 oz slug | 45 |
| 6.25 | 12 | 3-1/2" Mag | 2 oz shot | 55 |
| 6.25 | 12 | 3-1/2" Mag | 2 ¼ oz shot | 70 |

This is kind of a "beating" chart – it shows what kind of beating you will take based on gun weight and load. To understand foot pounds, the measure of free recoil energy, we will use this definition: one foot pound is a unit of work equal to the work done by a force of one pound acting through a distance of one foot in the direction of the force. In other words, one foot pound is the amount of energy required to move a one-pound object (not including calculations of friction) a distance of one foot. 12.5 foot pounds of energy is the amount of energy required to move a 12.5 pound object one foot and so on.

12.5 has always been given as the standard amount of free recoil energy for the 12 gauge, but, as you can see, when you change gauge, payload and shell length, you boost the amount of foot pound recoil energy. The other factor involved in felt recoil in this list is the weight of the gun. What is not included in these calculations is action type, which is important, since a gas-operated semi-automatic shotgun (not a recoil operated semi-auto) has reduced recoil over that of a pump or double in most cases.

Okay then, how much of a thumping do you want to take on the butt end of your defensive weapon system? How much can you take, while still being proficient and not developing a horrible flinch? How effective will your shots be? A 3 or 3-1/2 inch magnum in a six pound shotgun for home defense in suburbia or Midwest rural areas? No. While traversing or living in grizzly country in Alaska? Sure, no problem, but in my house or on my property – no way. I want my shot to hit the first time, every time. I don't want stray pellets or slugs endangering others. I don't want a flinch developing. And maybe most importantly, I want to have fun shooting my guns. I don't buy guns to collect them or seal them in a safe never to see a shooting range because of their value. I buy them to shoot. How many of us take our .375 H&H Magnum or .458 Win Mag out plinking? Nope, before the hunt we fire a few shots to check zero, shoot it (hopefully) and hang it back on the rack next to our new game mount when we get home.

## Buckshot is the shotgun round that people fear the most.

In interior (not mixed interior/exterior) home defense situations, buckshot and slugs are totally out of the question, unless perhaps you are using them in a .410 shotgun. In a shooting we had at my Sheriff's Office several years ago, the offender, a man of average stature, was shot in the area of the navel square on with a Remington® 870 12 gauge pump loaded with Remington Reduced Recoil 8-pellet (yes, eight pellets – it eliminates the one stray pellet normally encountered in 00 buck shot patterns) 00 Buckshot load at a distance of about seven yards.

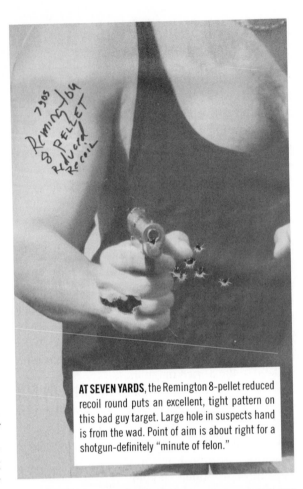

**AT SEVEN YARDS**, the Remington 8-pellet reduced recoil round puts an excellent, tight pattern on this bad guy target. Large hole in suspects hand is from the wad. Point of aim is about right for a shotgun-definitely "minute of felon."

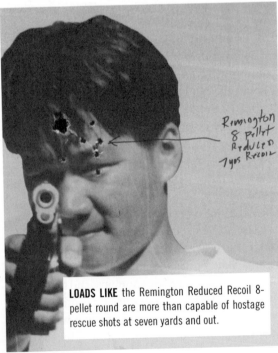

**LOADS LIKE** the Remington Reduced Recoil 8-pellet round are more than capable of hostage rescue shots at seven yards and out.

This load, by the way is excellent, one of the very best law enforcement loads, and one of the tightest patterning loads I have ever shot in any shotgun. It increases the safe usage of 12 gauge buckshot well out to 30 yards, and is great for head-shots at seven to 10 yards, or a little further out in improved cylinder choke barrels.

Anyway all eight pellets blew through the suspect's intestines and impacted in the dirt on the other side of him. He stopped his threatening actions but did not die. This means that if you hit an offender square on (facing you) with 00 buck-shot, even with a lower velocity reduced recoil load, the pellets can and do punch right out the back, endangering others. Remember, the load is called "buckshot" because it was originally used for killing large animals, like buck deer, and in places like India sometimes tiger. It is powerful stuff. Legendary in terms of its killing and stop-ping power, buckshot is the shotgun round that people fear the most.

Most criminals are too dense to realize that they face an equal amount of damage, maybe even more, due to shredding effect of all those little pel-lets from a close range load of AA Trap and Skeet as they do from the 00. However, don't be misled. These loads can and will punch right through dry-wall at close range. Remember, they only spread one inch per yard, and at close range it is a lot like getting hit with a single, solid projectile.

If you have overpenetration concerns, you may want to closely examine whether a shotgun is the best weapon to choose. A lower powered handgun, which can still punch through a wall, but is only putting a single projectile at a time through it (as-suming you are missing your intended target), may work out better for you, especially in an apartment where there are neighbors close at hand. Even then, you should limit your handgun ammo selection to pre-fragmented rounds like the Glaser Safety Slug or Magsafe.

For general home and property defense, where over-penetration is not a major concern, buckshot of various types and sizes is probably the best choice, not only for two-legged predators, but for large four-legged predators at close range as well. Those trap and skeet loads run out of steam pretty fast in terms of effectiveness over distance. The law enforcement community dumped the use of #4 buckshot as a duty load and went back to 00 buck when we began finding out that #4 wasn't giving the desired penetration. Rifled slugs are mostly to be avoided unless you need the longer range and penetration a rifled slug affords, or if you live soemwhere like Alaska, where your four legged predator problem involves large animals like bear, rather than the coyote of the Midwest. Yep, for Alaskan defense, 3- to 3-1/2-inch magnum rifled slugs, and a six to nine round magazine capacity sounds like an ideal combination.

## TACTICAL CONSIDERATIONS FOR THE HOME DEFENSE SHOTGUN

Having a tactical shotgun does not make you "tactical," nor, more importantly, does it make you invincible. Possession of a firearm does not automatically imbue you with some sort of force-field or protective shield a' la "Star Trek." In other words, just because you have a concealed carry permit or are a law enforcement officer, you

**Shot Sizes**

| Pellet Diameter | F | T | BBB | BB | 1 | 2 | 3 | 4 | 5 | 6 | 7 | 7½ | 8 | 8½ | 9 |
|---|---|---|---|---|---|---|---|---|---|---|---|---|---|---|---|
| Inches | .22 | .20 | .19 | .18 | .16 | .15 | .14 | .13 | .12 | .11 | .10 | .095 | .09 | .085 | .08 |
| mm | 5.59 | 5.08 | 4.83 | 4.57 | 4.06 | 3.81 | 3.56 | 3.30 | 3.05 | 2.79 | 2.54 | 2.41 | 2.29 | 2.16 | 2.03 |

**Buckshot Sizes**

| Pellet Diameter | No. 000 | No. 00 | No. 0 | No. 1 | No. 2 | No. 3 | No. 4 |
|---|---|---|---|---|---|---|---|
| Inches | .36 | .33 | .32 | .30 | .27 | .25 | .24 |
| mm | 9.14 | 8.38 | 8.13 | 7.62 | 6.86 | 6.35 | 6.10 |

can't just go into dangerous areas or situations with total abandon. Don't let it give you a false sense of security. The only thing that possession of a weapon does is give you an opportunity to defend yourself should you find yourself in a bad situation. Especially as a civilian or off-duty cop, you should scrupulously avoid trouble to begin

## Having a tactical shotgun does not make you invincible.

with, whether armed or not.

When I travel off-duty, I am always armed with a handgun, cellphone, personally owned X-26 Taser®, Northend Woodcrafter's® Cocobolo Straight Baton (beautiful intermediate force option – www.northendwoodcrafters.com), sometimes pepper spray, some sort of tactical light, a cutting/rescue tool, and, in the trunk of my car, something bigger, like a Mossberg 590 Tactical Shotgun and/or an AR15, plus my SWAT gear. You cops out there in particular, please take note: You need to have more with you than just a firearm or tactical blade for off-duty/plainclothes defense. You need to have intermediate force options. Off-duty encounters or personal defense situations will not always involve deadly force. You may have to intervene in a domestic, deal with an obnoxious drunk, or assist an on-duty officer with an arrest.

Even with all this gear and layered levels of defense, I take great caution as to where I am driving, (especially in unfamiliar areas-a GPS is critical here) and am alert to everything around me should I find myself in a less than desirable area.

You can be hurt or killed if your adversary or adversaries are armed with firearms or other deadly weapons. Also, that tactical shotgun can be taken from you and used against you if you are careless or lack the appropriate determination to kill your opponent. Yes, you have to be prepared to kill your opponent. You have chosen one of the most powerful civilian-legal handheld weapons to defend hearth, home and family. Hitting someone with eight to whatever number of individual pellets traveling at about 1200 feet per second and weighing around an ounce in total, rather than a

single small projectile such as whatever caliber round you are using in a handgun, multiplies the odds that irreparable damage will be done to that human body, which can result in death.

## "LESS-LETHAL" ROUNDS?

Even if you buy some of the new rubber pellet or bean bag "less-lethal" 12 gauge rounds, similar to law enforcement less-lethal rounds that are available to civilians, you can still kill or maim someone at close range, especially if you hit them in the head or throat. We now use the term "less-lethal" to describe intermediate weapons in law enforcement rather than "non-lethal" for precisely this reason. People can die due to any type of force being applied to them, so nothing is considered non-lethal in terms of force application.

That said, there will be times in property defense where a less-lethal option is desirable. Once inside your home, the dynamics change in terms of the use of lethal force. Generally, if you are not also in fear of your life, you cannot use deadly force to defend property.

What about situations involving marauding teenagers or overly aggressive dogs, threatening but not deadly? A large canister of fog delivery pepper spray is great. Note that, in this case, you are using a dedicated less-lethal device (spray canister), not a lethal device modified for less-lethal use (shotgun loaded with less-lethal loads). In home defense situations, when you employ a firearm, it should be loaded with potentially lethal ammunition (live standard rounds), not less-lethal ammunition.

At 2 a.m. when you hear your front door come crashing in, you are in fear for your life. Shocked, startled awake and scared, your mind and heart tell you that you are facing the threat of death. Anyone that breaks into an occupied structure is a serious offender, who for whatever reason is taking a big risk of doing so, and obviously feels they have the upper hand. We are after all, still living in a nation (at least at the time of this writing) with an extremely high rate of per capita firearms ownership. The chances are good that, if you break into an occupied residence, someone inside is going to have a gun, which they will

**THE SHOTGUN CANNOT DEFEND** the home itself. It takes a determined and skilled user to do that, such as this woman defending her home with a Wilson Combat/Scattergun Technologies Border Patrol.

end up pointing in your direction. That means that the burglar is likely prepared to meet your deadly force with some form of force of his own. He is probably not entering your house with pepper spray, a Taser® or less-lethal rounds loaded in his gun.

You are going to need to assume that the person who entered your home is there to kill you or cause you serious physical harm (including rape or abduction). Even if that is not their immediate objective, it may be the end result. You have to be prepared to kill the intruder first to stop them from killing you or your family members.

If you can't stomach the use of deadly force to preserve your own life, then maybe you can be prepared to use it in order to save your family. But if you feel you couldn't take a life to save even your own family (not likely for readers of this book-but good advice for others who are pondering this problem) then you shouldn't be using a lethal force weapon to defend to begin with. Instead consider using a civilian C3

Taser® or pepper spray.

I used to, when conducting police academy firearms training, take the standard, politically correct tack that when you shoot someone you are "shooting to stop" or "neutralize" an assailant or fleeing dangerous felon.

After instructing using this terminology over many years, I ended up listening to experts like Colonel David Grossman (whose book "On Combat" should be mandatory reading if you are planning on using a firearm for personal defense), and had a personal epiphany. I came to the conclusion that using the politically sensitive terms like "neutralize," especially when it comes to "active shooters," sanitizes what we might have to do to end the threat: take a human life.

Training in the politically correct mindset leaves the person using the firearm for defense psychologically unprepared for what they might have to do. Yes, we want to stop the assailant, but the only sure way to stop them is by imparting enough physical damage to the human

**THE ULTIMATE** in layered defense, all by Wilson Combat. These three weapons cover all home or escape and evade defense needs. The ULC .45 handles all the interpersonal confrontations at contact distances. The not-so-Standard Model shotgun is great for all the conflicts within the 50 yard "whites of their eyes" distances, while the new 6.8 SPC Recon with Nightforce 2.5 x 10 Illuminated Reticle Scope can take it out to 600 yards.

# A burglar is probably not entering your house with pepper spray, a Taser® or less-lethal rounds loaded in his gun.

structure that they can no longer function.

Generally, this means that death can result immediately from that damage you inflicted. It must be considered that the person you use your tactical shotgun against may very well die as a result of that use, and factually, not technically, that is what you are setting about to do when you level that shotgun against an intruder. There is a reason it is referred to as "deadly" force. As a civilian considering the use of force in self-defense or home protection, you must consider this issue before you even purchase the shotgun. Purchasing a tactical shotgun, and the use of deadly force, is not to be taken lightly.

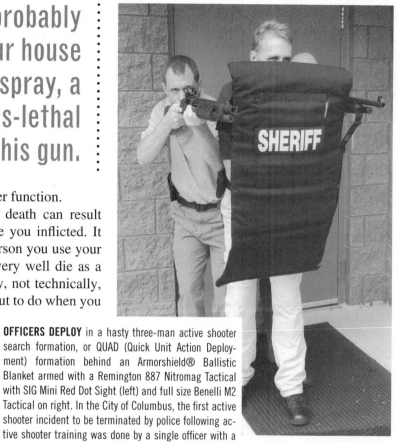

OFFICERS DEPLOY in a hasty three-man active shooter search formation, or QUAD (Quick Unit Action Deployment) formation behind an Armorshield® Ballistic Blanket armed with a Remington 887 Nitromag Tactical with SIG Mini Red Dot Sight (left) and full size Benelli M2 Tactical on right. In the City of Columbus, the first active shooter incident to be terminated by police following active shooter training was done by a single officer with a load of buckshot from a Remington 870 to the head of the suspect, thus ending the incident.

## STORING THE SHOTGUN

In almost all home defense situations, for those who can handle it, I recommend the 12 gauge pump shotgun over a double barrel or semi-auto. Examples of excellent pump gun selections are those from Wilson Combat/Scattergun Technologies, Ithaca, Mossberg, Benelli, and of course Remington. The pump is the fastest and simplest to get into action, as long as it is stored in the proper condition, and trained with that way.

The home defense pump shotgun should be stored with slide forward, action closed, internal hammer down, safety off, chamber empty, with a fully loaded magazine, or as we call it, "Cruiser Ready." This way, all you have to do to fire a

round is work the pump action to chamber the round and pull the trigger. No loading, no safety to flick off, just that awesome sound of the shotgun being racked and the shell entering the chamber. That sound may be enough to send your would-be adversary beating a hasty retreat.

A pump shotgun stored this way beats a double barrel that you have to load when you need it, or store loaded with the action open. Its also beats a semi-auto, which can also be stored in a similar way, but whose operation is a bit more complicated.

To store the weapon safely, install a Lifejacket® or similar locking system that covers the entire action area and allows key or digital entry to your gun. Never use a trigger guard lock which impinges on the inside of the trigger guard, such as the models from Masterlock™, on a loaded weapon, even if you keep the chamber empty. It

**LIFEJACKET IN PLACE** on a well worn Remington 870 at a deer camp. Weapon can be secured, but is still portable.

**LIFEJACKET SECURITY SYSTEMS** are excellent for secure yet quick access. Relatively inexpensive and key operated, they can be bolted inside a vehicle or locations within the home or locked in place as stand-alone locks allowing the guns to be moved from place to place. Here is a lifejacket locked in place over an HK autoloading shotgun. Note that the action is locked to the rear.

**LIFEJACKET FOR AUTOLOADING SHOTGUN** is shown in the open position. Note the interior padding, and how the life-jacket surrounds and encloses the entire action. The Life-jacket is also available for handguns and rifles.

Never use a trigger guard lock which impinges on the inside of the trigger guard on a loaded weapon.

is too easy to make a mistake and definitely not recommended by the manufacturer.

The lock can be left unlocked at night for easy access. Select from the many ready access systems, so unauthorized persons, children, daylight burglars who operate when you're not there, and the curious don't have access to your gun.

Conceal the location of the gun so it cannot be readily observed by others, even friends, who may be inside your house. I remember as a kid that my father told my brother and I, "Never, I repeat never, tell anyone anything about the guns we own." Although those instructions were mostly given to us due to fear of government gun registration schemes (that was before the BATFE and Federal Form 4468) which were being talked about in the violent 1960s, keeping our firearm ownership information quiet prevented word from spreading through an initially innocent starting point to someone who is a burglar.

Another piece of advice from my father is for those of you with kids at home. To help prevent a terrible tragedy, yet keep your firearm available for defensive use, remove any curiosity about the shotgun or any defensive firearm by allowing your kids to see the gun unloaded whenever they reasonably want to. My dad's willingness to let us see and handle the unloaded family firearms was coupled with the admonition that he would kill us (my brother and I) if we ever touched one of the guns without his permission and oversight. This system worked perfectly, especially after he taught us to shoot at ages 8 (me) and 6 (my brother). I got to see the guns all I wanted, learned to handle them carefully, and never, ever looked at them on my own. Our curiosity was satisfied, and the great mystery (which draws children to secretive things like moths to a flame) about firearms was gone.

If you don't think this will work, keep the shotgun unloaded with the shells stored in another location. In case of emergency, you would "combat load" the pump or autoloading shotgun by dropping a live cartridge into the chamber first, closing the action, then if you have time, loading the remaining rounds in the magazine tube. If you choose to keep your home defense gun in this condition, then the double barrel is probably the fasted to get into action when loading with loose shells, and thus a better choice for you. There is a lot less manipulation involved with a double to get those two shells online fast.

## DEFENSIVE RESPONSE: BASIC GUIDELINES

Now that an intruder has made entry, what do you do? Let's look at the defensive response in terms of some simple rules or guidelines.

### Stop, look, listen

Unless a family member is in the process of being attacked, this old adage reminds us to assess the situation before making our next move. We may have been startled awake, or otherwise disturbed, and are plenty scared. We need to allow for a short 5-10 count to allow our heart rate to drop down just a bit so we can assess the situation with a clear and calmer head as we obtain the shotgun, which ideally should be close at hand.

Next we look to visually clear our immediate area. Is the threat upon us? Do we need additional lighting? Is our weapon ready?

Then we listen. What was it that awakened us in the first place? Was it the intruder prowling about, or was the dog barking alerting us to an intruder? Was the stimulus real? Was it our imagination? Was it one of our kids or relatives coming in late? Or, was it indeed an intruder? In some cases, it might be our significant other who alerted us and we didn't hear anything. Once we can make an initial assessment and are armed, we can proceed.

Note that getting armed should ideally happen after we have calmed down and are fully awake. This can prevent accidents and tragedies.

### Stay put or search?

One thing I teach police cadets, and that I want to make readily apparent here, is that personal stuff isn't worth dying over (or for that matter, killing someone over). Nearly all your personal stuff, your property, can be replaced. That's what insurance is for. Remember, the presence of a gun does not make you invincible. Do you really want to give up your existence over the loss of a big screen TV which you see walking out the door in the hands of others?

If there is no one else in your home that you have to defend-STAY PUT! Get you and your significant other, if there is one, behind your bed and cover the bedroom doorway (assuming that you are in a night time defense situation). If the intruder makes it to the bedroom doorway looking for you, make sure you identify your target as foe, not friend, before you fire.

Know where your other family members are or should be, and then issue a verbal challenge from your room. Shouting "Get out of my house, I have a gun" works very nicely, along with dialing 911 and putting the phone on the speaker and handing it to your significant other.

Here's a tip of personal importance to me: Please don't mis-identify uniformed responding officers (such as me), as a foe. Stay on the line with 911 and do not, I repeat do not, put your gun down until you know that there are officers in the house. I say "put down" because we would rather not be greeted by someone with a gun in their hand during a high stress situation. However, there is a widley told story about a homeowner (female) who was raped and murdered after she put her handgun away at the behest of a very misguided 911 dispatcher.

If you have other family members in the house that need to be protected and who are in a different location than you, you need to begin room clearing or go straight for the threat, which leads to the next basic guideline.

### Move slowly

Move slowly during room clearing, unless a family member is being assaulted, of course. If there is an assault in progress and you know where the threat is, head straight to it and take it out, which is the same response that officers use in dealing with an active shooter. If you don't know where they are, or if you are unsure that there is someone inside, then you need to search and clear. In "SWATland," we call this a slow or methodical search.

The searcher needs to move with the utmost caution, because clearing rooms or areas of a human threat is the most dangerous activity a SWAT team performs. Note that I said this is the most dangerous activity a SWAT team per-

forms, and here you are doing a team activity all by yourself.

One of the basic principles of any building clearing/room clearing situation is that we never want to advance past an un-cleared room or area. Your home invasion situation could be a two or more person operation, and the noise you are advancing toward is only one of the suspects. If you rush to get to the suspect making the most noise and you bypass an un-cleared room, you may now find yourself confronting not only a threat in front of you but then suddenly and simultaneously confronted by that overlooked threat from behind, which could cost you and your family members their lives.

You can see that building clearing, even in your own home, is tricky stuff, and why I recommend that if you can, stay in your fortified bedroom. But you may not always have that choice if isolated family members are in danger. Therefore move slowly, with minimal noise, because you don't want the intruder taking a hostage. There are some additional simple rules for room/building clearing that you should adhere to.

1. You are on your home turf. Your intruder isn't. Not only does this give you the advantages of knowing where everything is, but it also allows you the ability to practice the room clearing in your home as many times as it takes. Take advantage of this and practice, practice, practice with that UNLOADED shotgun.

2. Move slowly. Yes, I already said that but I'm saying it again. Adrenalin triggers "fight or flight." You have to control those urges until the actual fight ensues.

3. Don't rack that pump until you are ready to shoot (unless your objective is to chase the badguy out by scaring the heck out of them with that magic sound). It can be racked and fired in a split second.

Before you move from one doorway area to the next, visually clear the area you are moving into while staying as far back from the doorway as you can. Don't allow the shotgun barrel to lead you and thus advertise and give away your position. You will have to round most corners at a low-ready position, gun tucked in at the shoulder and barrel pointed down at about a 45 degree angle. When you enter the next open area, such as the interior of a room, you can come back up to high ready (as in "I'm highly ready to shoot you now"), scanning the area through your sights.

The Mossberg 590 pump, with its M4 Carbine collapsible stock and pistol grip, works great for this purpose with the stock collapsed all the way down, yet it does allow you to fire accurately and comfortably from a shouldered position. The Knoxx recoil reduction system as sold by BLACKHAWK! has an M4 stock available as a replacement that not only provides the full range of adjustment, but reduces felt recoil. Models fit Remington, Mossberg and Winchester shotgun, and are available also in a non-recoil reducing variant which costs $60-$70 less.

4. Practice firing your gun with one hand only. Yes, the shotgun can be fired with one hand whether the stock is a pistol grip type or standard. If you have an average amount of hand and arm strength you can do this with a reasonable degree of accuracy at seven yards or a little more. It's a skill you need to develop. You may be opening a door with one hand, fending off an attacker, or injured in one arm by opposing gunfire and forced to fire (after, of course, chambering a round of ammo). It is an important skill to cultivate. If you use a double gun for defense, you can get a second shot off with no problem by another pull of the trigger; a semi-auto may jam. Just make that first shot count.

5. Examine your fields of fire in advance, and practice your maneuvers with an UNLOADED gun. You have to account for the fact that even if your shot hits the desired intruder target, it can penetrate the human body and continue into your child's room on the other side of the wall. Scope out your home with an eye towards safe directions of fire and safest backstops.

6. Use light and your knowledge of your home to your advantage. Don't go turning on all your lights as you search. Use your weapons light, if you so equip your shotgun, sparingly. You can lead and give away your position by over-illuminating in advance of your movement with excessively enthusiastic light or laser use. Use your dark adaptive vision as much as possible, then use the brightest weapons light you can find to take out your opponents night vision, and then them. You own the night in your house.

7. Be prepared to give verbal commands and challenges when you confront the intruder because ultimately you want to chase the suspect out of your home, not kill them.

8. Chase the suspect out of your home if they will give you the opportunity. You want their response to be something like one I saw a number of years ago in an American Rifleman Armed Citizen column. In that particular situation, when confronted by armed homeowner who asked the intruder "what do you want"?, the miscreant replied "I want to be someplace else" and hastily "beat feet" from the scene. If they are willing to "be someplace else" don't attempt to capture them, let them go.

You are in your own house, surrounded by your own family whose safety you can't guarantee. There are a lot of things that can go wrong in a capture. A majority of law enforcement officers killed in the line of duty are killed while making arrests. Momentarily covering the intruder as you hear the sirens coming at gunpoint is one thing. Covering them for a long period of time while help is coming from a long way off is another. Once you call 911, how soon do you think help will arrive? It will seem like a very high stress eternity. Further, suspects come in all varieties. Is the suspect you are covering a hardened escaped convict, or a scared and stupid teen? Were they there to steal, rape or murder?

Get the suspect out of your house immediately. Order them out when you confront them. Get the threat away from you and your loved ones. The police, in an organized and heavily armed fashion, with K9 units and helicopters with FLIR gear, can find and confront them later with overwhelming numbers on their side. Try and give the police the most detailed description of the suspect possible, direction of travel, and vehicle type if any. If you can do all that, and escape unharmed along with your family, you've accomplished your mission of defending hearth and home.

**UNION COUNTY** K9 officer Darrel Breneman firing department-issue Remington 870 with aftermarket pistol grip stock.

# CHAPTER TWO

# THE LAW ENFORCEMENT
## SHOTGUN

Dedicated law enforcement shotguns have always been "tactical" – they were designed for or modified for combat use. As mentioned earlier in this work, the Remington 870 has always been the gold standard by which all other police shotguns were judged, at least throughout my 30-year law enforcement career. Mossberg and Ithaca were the other two companies who were most competitive with the Remington police empire, but in my native Ohio I never remember seeing an agency equipped with either, just the odd representative model here and there. But there were others still. When I started with one municipal police department, our "arsenal" (properly termed "armory") contained two Winchester Model 12 military pump shotguns as well as one old Winchester Model 97 Pump. None of these guns were actually out on the street anymore even though they were operational, having long since been eclipsed by blue steel Remington 870 pump shotguns. While these old stalwarts were cool to play with, they were later traded in, along with a couple of M1 Carbines, for the purchase of new duty pistols.

While double barrel shotguns of various makes and models were popular with frontier law enforcement agencies for short range usage, they weren't much use at long range on the Great Plains. They were sawed off by their owners or users from their original hunting length to a more handy barrel length. But it was the Winchester Model 97 pump gun (as in 1897) that was the first shotgun to see widespread military and police service as a tactical shotgun. The Military 97 was nothing more than the sporting/hunting Model 97, designed by John M. Browning, modified for combat use.

> # In the days before the Thompson Submachine Gun, the Model 97 and the Model 1911 Colt .45 were the only game in town for clearing trenches.

The trench model, also lovingly referred to as the "trench broom," was issued to our "dough-boys" in the First World War, and was capable of mounting the Model 1917 Bayonet. It was equipped with a perforated metal heat shield over the short 18-inch barrel. In 12 gauge with a 2-3/4-inch chamber (3-inch magnums weren't around then), the 97 proved handy and very quick to fire with its pump action, decimating any German soldier who stood in its path. One only had to be careful with its straight style stock wrist which was developed before "ergonomic" was a word. When cycled, the bolt comes back as the action is opened and extends out of the rear of the receiver, unlike modern pump guns whose action is contained within the receiver. When the bolt extends out the rear, there is very little comfort gap between the bottom of it and the top of the stock wrist. If you aren't careful with your grip and hand position and actually wrap your thumb all the way around the stock, you will get "train tracks" across your thumb and the back of your hand – sort of like an "M1 thumb" type of injury.

The bolt bite of the 97 was still a small price to pay for the short maneuverable barrel and rapid firing speed of the 97 in close quarters when compared to the 24-inch long barrels and slower firing rate of the main bolt action battle rifles such as the Springfield, Enfield, Mauser and other bolt guns of the time. In the days before the Thompson Submachine Gun, the Model 97 and the Model 1911 Colt .45 were the only game in town for clearing trenches – that is, actually moving inside an enemy trench – or defending your own trench from invaders.

After the war, these Model 97s became surplus and were sold to law enforcement agencies, where they rapidly found their way into police vehicles all over the U.S., sans bayonet. There is a great picture in the Columbus Ohio Police Academy building of a group of four uniformed Columbus police officers in the 1920s (during Prohibition) riding in an open top car. In the photo, there was the driver with both hands on the wheel, the front passenger who was truly "riding shotgun" with his Model 97 pumpgun carried muzzle up, the rear seat driver's side passenger who was armed with a M1927 Thompson Submachine gun also carried muzzle up, and what is my actually favorite display of weaponry, the officer in the passenger side rear seat. He was armed with a, get this, Model 1918 Browning BAR. Imagine an officer on patrol these days carrying a fully-automatic, twenty pound .30-06 caliber weapon firing full metal jacket 150 grain bullets at a velocity of about 2800 fps in a densely populated urban area. Times have indeed changed.

The Model 97 soldiered on throughout WWII, Korea, Vietnam and even into the Gulf War. Perhaps more than anyplace else, it was at its best in jungle combat. It can probably still be found out-of-service in small police department armories across the U.S. The 97 was a seminal design that brought us to where we are today with our current crop of law enforcement shotguns. Police shotguns, with the exception of some very exotic models, are, like the old 97, nothing more than "combatized" guns which were originally designed for hunting. Nonetheless, they work very

**STORM DOG TRACKING** demonstration 'Y' formation with K9 unit. The lead tracker on the right protects the K9 and his handler with a Remington 870 pump shotgun.

well in their assigned roles.

The 97 gave us the term "riot gun," which is no longer in common use as it pertains to the tactical shotgun, which is also indicative of just how much times have changed. Back when this term was in vogue, you could actually shoot large masses of lethal buckshot at rioting crowds. If you did this from a goodly distance away, the receivers of said buckshot might not die, but they could be blinded or severely injured. Such usage wouldn't go over so well these days, which is why we now use 37mm grenade launchers loaded with wooden baton rounds or rubber pellets, which can still cause the same injury problems, albeit at a closer range than lead ball rounds, and which are designed from the get-go to be less-lethal in nature.

With that brief introduction, let's look at the modern tactical shotgun and its current use in law enforcement.

## SHOTGUNS AS PATROL WEAPONS

First, we have to realize that the police shotgun, as a regular patrol weapon, is being supplemented and in some cases supplanted by the patrol rifle, generally a variant of the AR-15 platform in 5.56mm caliber. The AR-15 admittedly has some advantages over the mighty 12 gauge pumpgun for patrol use: more rounds on board, longer range, less recoil (which makes for more accurate fire and a more enjoyable time on the range), and a manual of arms that is consistent with the operation of the semi-automatic pistol, thus simplifying training. We have hundreds of military veterans coming back from Iraq and Afghanistan who are more than a little familiar with the M4 carbine or M16A2, which drastically reduces the training curve for these folks when they join police departments. While there is a lot to be said for the AR-15 weapons system, there is also a lot to be said for the police shotgun.

There is no doubt that the 12 gauge pump, exemplified by Remington and Mossberg as the two most commonly encountered brands in everyday law enforcement service, is highly reliable in operation and withstands a lot of abuse with little attention to maintenance. The standard AR-15 needs to be kept reasonably clean and well lubricated. Try to run one for any length of time dry and, unless you have one of the new specially coated and treated bolt carriers, you won't run them for long without jamming.

The old adage says, if you want to test a new piece of equipment to see how durable it is, give it to a cop. A police shotgun sits in a cruiser, day after day, in extreme temperatures and humidity, at least in the Midwest, often mounted barrel up (or they used to be in pre-airbag days), which lets any lubricant run out. Yet, you end up with a dry action that still works. Reliability is a major factor in selecting law enforcement weapon systems, and the pump shotgun has it in spades.

Along with reliability comes durability. Shotguns have to be the most abused of all police weapons, but it is damn hard to break one. They are often tossed into the trunk with stuff thrown on top of them and just left there. They are rarely cleaned and lubed or paid attention to unless it's time for qualification. With these facts in mind, serious thought needs to be given to what type of law enforcement shotgun is issued to the masses for daily patrol use.

In order to keep department-issued shotguns operational as long as possible, an issuing agency needs to keep them basic. No fancy optical sights, especially battery-operated ones. Stick with mechanical front and rear sights of some configuration – Remington rifle type, Ghost Rings, Three Dots or Fiber Optics – just as long as it isn't a bead and doesn't need batteries. The same goes for weapon lights on the shotgun. While Surefire makes an excellent flashlight replacement forend for pump shotguns, it would require maintenance and battery changes to keep them going. While many officers would take care of the guns and battery-operated accessories, more would not, so that when you needed that light the most, it wouldn't be working.

One of the big complaints in the past about the shotgun, especially when compared to the rifle, is its magazine capacity of only four rounds. Coupled with a slower loading system than other weapons (there is no detachable box magazine), one can feel at a disadvantage. These days, in the age of the active shooter, maximum magazine capacity is a must, and that means that an extended magazine tube of six to nine rounds is in order for the patrol shotgun. While this higher capacity makes the gun a little more ungainly and muzzle heavy, it does give you between two and five rounds of additional insurance.

## RURAL AREAS AND ANIMALS

There is also the raw power factor of a 12 gauge shotgun. In rural areas where there were large and sometimes angry animals, the 12 gauge pump, loaded with rifled slugs rather than buckshot, would be my patrol car weapon of choice. Alaska, Maine, Minnesota, Tennessee and North Carolina are a few of the regions that come to mind. In Alaska, Minnesota and Maine, moose can be a problem. Large and temperamental, moose have taken their toll on humans more than a few times. Legendary African big game hunter Robert Ruark said "bring enough gun," and for something like this, I would heed his advice.

For smaller angry animals, charges of 00 buckshot work well when the attacking animal is something like a charging pit bull. For an animal moving at speed, there's a better chance of hitting it with a spread of shot rather than single rifle or pistol bullets, unless you're talking about a full-auto-capable AR-15. 00 buck is also great for finishing dispatching sick or injured animals, such as rabid raccoons or deer struck by cars.

Speaking of animals, I have worked in the past with a nearby K9 training company called

Two days before I arrived at an American Society of Law Enforcement Trainers Conference in Anchorage, Alaska, in January 1995 (yes, January, that is not a misprint) a college professor was stomped to death by a large and angry moose that had climbed onto his front porch. This occurred in town, within the Anchorage city limits, which is where I saw the most moose during the trip. This professor unwisely tried to "shoo" the moose from his porch. The moose wasn't particularly impressed by the professor. A moose, which can be seven feet tall at the shoulder and 1500 plus pounds, probably wouldn't have been too impressed by a 5.56mm bullet, or a bunch of them, unless they took the form of multiple headshots. A 3-inch magnum rifled slug or two is probably the best medicine to resolve situations like these.

Storm Dog Training (www.stormdogtraining.com) located in Sunbury, Ohio. One of their specialties is man-tracking operations, using techniques licensed from the Scott-Donelan Tracking School (www.trackingoperations.com) which is named after and run by world renowned Rhodesian man-tracker David Scott-Donelan. Having attended the Level I tracking course offered by Storm Dog, I learned a great deal about working with K9 officers, and how they should operate for safety. One of the key features is the use of a "Y" Tactical Tracking formation wherein there are two key trackers at the point of the Y, with the K9 handler behind in the fork of the Y, and then team leader and communications personnel/rear guard behind the K9. The idea is to provide safety for the K9 and handler.

Traditional methods of tracking have the K9/handler out in front leading on the track-which is in essence leading with a less-lethal force option (the dog) against the suspect you are searching for who may be planning on using a lethal force option. Here the point men at the tip of the Y are also tracking and looking for sign for the dog to follow on. When the searches are in deeply wooded area, the point man weapon of choice is the 12 gauge shotgun loaded with rifled slugs. David Scott-Donelan recommended this combination to the point men over an AR-15 because of the greater brush-bucking capability of a rifled slug weighing in at one ounce versus a 55 grain 5.56mm bullet (437 grains to the ounce). So at least one of the point men in such an area search needs to carry a 12 gauge, unless tracking in open fields or urban areas where a rifle would be the best choice.

## AMMO FOR PATROL

Each patrol shotgun should be equipped with both buckshot and rifled slugs for use in suburban/urban situations where the greater penetration of rifled slugs is not always called for and the lower penetration of 00 buckshot is more desirable. 00 buck can be turned or stopped by even the lowest-rated soft body armor. At closer ranges, for certain applications, 00 buck is excellent. Situations such as raids and working warrants or doing felony takedowns all work best with buck

over slugs. If more range is needed, then the versatility factor of the shotgun comes into play and rifled slug rounds can be selected for use.

For urban/suburban use, if you are working with an extended magazine tube as recommended, I would load up the magazine tube with 00 buckshot, one less than full capacity. (For a seven round tube, carry six rounds.) Then, if you find yourself in a situation where you need that longer range and penetration of a rifled slug, all you do is put a rifled slug in the magazine tube, rack the action, and you are ready with a long range shot. You can even put another slug in the tube after charging on top of the remaining buckshot rounds so the second round up the spout would also be a rifled slug.

By loading your shotgun this way, you can get rifled slugs into action with a minimum of manipulation under stress. You don't even have to work the action to get started, nor do you have to clear any rounds out first. If you only have a magazine tube with four rounds capacity, then don't download it. Just get good at taking a couple of live rounds out, then filling in with rifle slugs. Your rifled slugs can be carried on the side of the receiver in a "side saddle" carrier type arrangement, so you are not fumbling around in a glove box or gear bag looking for your slugs; they are always right there on the gun.

> **If you are an officer going into an active shooter situation and your primary weapon system is the shotgun, then the rifled slug is an absolute must.**

It is unfortunate that two weeks prior to the infamous 1997 Los Angeles bank robbery shootout, the former L.A.P.D. police chief had ordered the removal of all rifled slug ammunition from L.A.P.D. patrol cars, as rifled slugs were determined to be too harsh for use against bad guys.

**MOVING WHILE SHOOTING** (not moving and shooting) is an important part of qualification. Deputy Rich Crabtree demonstrates the lateral movement portion of the qualification course.

**THE BENELLI M1** Tactical with a 14-inch barrel makes a fine SWAT gun. Note the maneuverability of the weapon when exiting a Lenco Bearcat SWAT vehicle.

When the robbery went down, featuring two heavily-armored perpetrators armed with converted full auto AK-47 and SKS rifles in 7.62x39 calibers, the officers long-range response consisted of 9mm Luger rounds fired from Beretta and Smith and Wesson pistols, and 12 gauge shotguns firing 00 buck. While the L.A.P.D. was not totally helpless and could somewhat contain the threat, they were essentially unable to take the threat out with the means they had at hand.

For the record, in this shootout the shotguns did not fail the officers. Rifled slugs combined with rifle sights and a cool head should prevail in most police engagements out to a range of 75 yards, and could have ended the L.A. situation much sooner and without SWAT.

This was actually one of the very first "active shooter" (before we used that term) incidents, since it ended up being much more than a bank robbery. If you are an officer going into an active shooter situation and your primary weapon system is the shotgun, then the rifled slug is an absolute must for engaging a threat like this. However, if you have a choice of an AR-15 rifle in an active shooter incident or a shotgun – especially if the shooter is in a large building with long hallways or large open areas, or an outdoor situation – then the rifle is absolutely the weapon of choice.

If the incident is in a small building with close confines, then the shotgun will work very well with its close-range stopping power. In those rural areas where the big angry animals dwell, a shotgun loaded with rifled slugs, with spare rifled slugs in a side saddle receiver-mounted carrier is a good choice. Buckshot could be kept in the cruiser for special circumstances.

For training and duty issue, reduced recoil rounds are recommended, especially 8-pellet Remington Reduced Recoil in both Buckshot and Slug rounds, which I have worked with extensively. Although I was skeptical when they first came out, they truly are easier on the shoulder when firing than standard loads, and the eight pellets do pattern extremely tight. This lowered recoil produces, in general, greater accuracy, since the shooter isn't being beaten to death by the weapon when they shoot for training or qualification.

**THIS SWAT BENELLI M**1 is equipped with a magazine tube mounted Surefire light with remote pressure switch. Note sling and elastic spare shell holder on stock.

After training and qualifying with standard loads, some officers dread the recoil of the shotgun so much that they won't take it out of the cruiser when they should. Range officers should be working with trainees and the shotgun to find out what works best for them. Reduced recoil loads are great, not only for small statured officers, but for officers of any size or gender, as it makes the whole shotgun experience less unpleasant.

Reduced recoil loads feel much like firing something like Winchester AA Trap and Skeet loads in terms of felt recoil. The only downside is that they may not have enough "oomph" to function in some semi-automatic shotguns, especially in recoil operated semi-autos such as Benelli's fine M2 Tactical. I haven't had any issues with the Mossberg 930 Special purpose semi-auto in cycling reduced recoil rounds or even light field loads. But the 930 is a gas operated shotgun, not recoil operated. For pumps, on the other hand, Reduced Recoil loads are the only way to fly. All the big three ammo makers – Remington, Winchester and Federal – offer reduced recoil law enforcement loads in both 9-pellet and 8-pellet configurations. Go with the 8-pellet for the tightest patterns.

## LESS-LETHAL OPTIONS

Day-to-day police operations require the use of the shotgun for everything from perimeter control to felony traffic stop takedowns to use as a less-lethal cartridge launcher with " beanbag" rounds (the most common type of less-lethal ammo). Even as the shotgun is being replaced by the rifle in many patrol cars across the U.S., this is one area where it can't be replaced by the rifle: as a dedicated less-lethal weapon launcher.

Many shotguns in police inventories are being converted to less-lethal use with wooden stocks being traded out for orange or yellow polymer replacement stocks. Some are being spray-painted with those colors to avoid being accidently loaded with standard lethal rounds when a less-lethal shot was intended. No new weapons system is needed to deliver a less-lethal punch, just a changeover of the rounds of ammo and the stock. In economic times like these, this is a very cost efficient method of upgrading force response options for any agency.

**OFFICER CHAD WILLIAMS** demonstrates proper form with the Mossberg 930. Note the 930's tall AR front sight, adjustable Ghost Ring rear, eight-round magazine tube, large bolt handle and top picatinny rail available for optics.

**PLAINCLOTHES OFFICERS** confront crazed sword wielding suspect. Officer in foreground is equipped with Mossberg/Taser X12 Less-lethal "shotgun" launcher, officer in background has the lethal cover with Mossberg 930 semi-auto. Officers are initially in a bad position. Note the X26 Taser on the picatinny rail on the shotguns forend.

**OFFICERS HAVE NOW MOVED** to solid cover behind trees, ready to deploy Taser XREP or lethal buckshot. Suspect is given multiple orders to drop the sword.

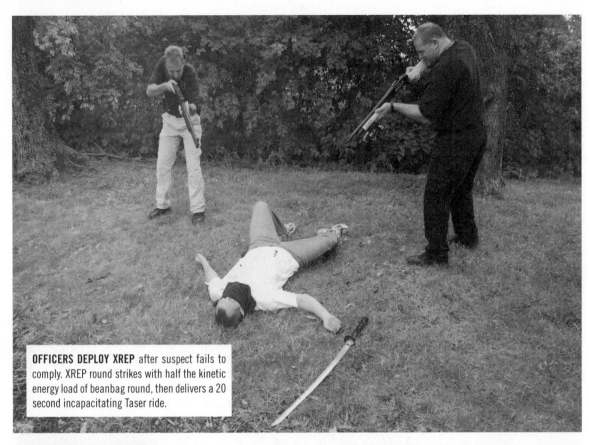

**OFFICERS DEPLOY XREP** after suspect fails to comply. XREP round strikes with half the kinetic energy load of beanbag round, then delivers a 20 second incapacitating Taser ride.

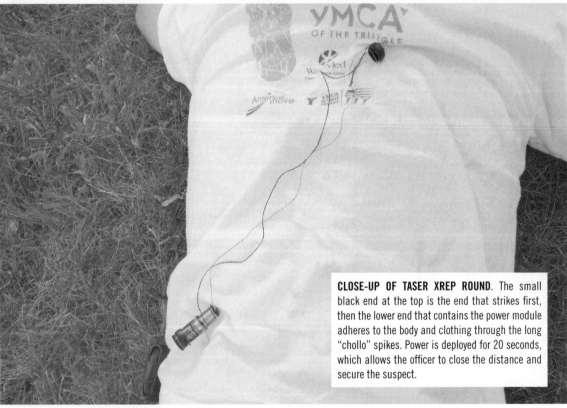

**CLOSE-UP OF TASER XREP ROUND.** The small black end at the top is the end that strikes first, then the lower end that contains the power module adheres to the body and clothing through the long "chollo" spikes. Power is deployed for 20 seconds, which allows the officer to close the distance and secure the suspect.

**CLOSE-UP OF DOWNED SUSPECT** and deployed XREP round, which is in two segments connected by wire.

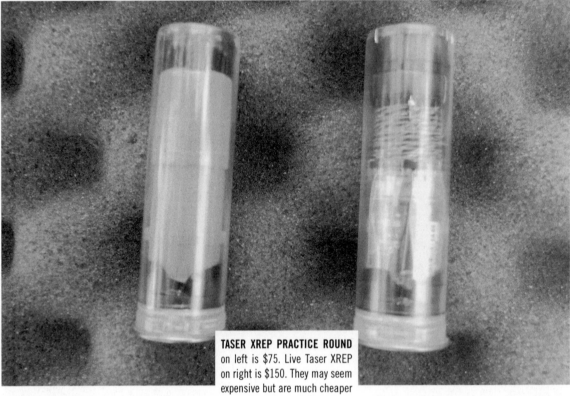

**TASER XREP PRACTICE ROUND** on left is $75. Live Taser XREP on right is $150. They may seem expensive but are much cheaper than a lawsuit out of even a justified lethal shooting. Taser XREP rounds and the Mossberg X12 are not available to civilians.

There isn't an agency out there that can't afford to take one shotgun from their inventory and dedicate it to less-lethal use. Please do not make the mistake of just unloading live rounds from a standard in-service patrol shotgun and loading it with beanbags when in a less-lethal crisis. Something very bad will eventually happen with this system.

Another less-lethal shotgun option is the new X12 LLS Taser "Shotgun," produced by Mossberg in cooperation with Taser®. With its bright yellow polymer stocks, the X12 is a highly modified Model 500 series shotgun (well, it's really not a shotgun anymore; it is a less-lethal launching system) and will fire only the Taser® XREP® Electronic Control Device Cartridge. No other lethal or less-lethal round will chamber in it. You can, however, fire the XREP out of a standard 12 gauge shotgun and have it work properly, but this launcher is the safest, most accurate firing system for it.

For this particular shotgun, Mossberg moved the safety from their traditional ambidextrous position at the rear of the receiver above the stock and placed it as a crossbolt pushbutton ahead of the triggerguard in Remington fashion (except that Remington's is at the rear of the triggerguard). This was done to make it more similar in function to the Remington, as the 870 is the gun used by the majority of law enforcement agencies in the U.S. The midst of a critical situation is not the time for weapons system retraining and refamiliarization. The X12 is also equipped with a small section of railed forend to which is attached an adaptor on which to hook a standard X26 Taser for close range control. The X26 could then be fired if need be by the forend control hand of the operator.

The XREP cartridge itself is an amazing piece of technology. It has an accurate/effective range of 50 feet (technically 100, but in firing the XREP practice cartridges I found the practice rounds work best at no further than 50 feet). Since a live XREP cartridge costs around $150, you won't get to fire many of those in practice. At those distances, the XREP strikes with approximately half the kinetic energy of a standard 12 gauge beanbag round. This is the initiation of the major "ouch" effect that is to follow.

OFFICER CHAD WILLIAMS FIRES PRACTICE XREP round downrange. The only sound they make is a small pop, quieter than an X26 Taser, with zero recoil. The Mossberg/Taser X12 Launcher (it really isn't a shotgun anymore) features Ghost Ring sights, forend rail section for light and optics mounting, and an attachment point for an X26 Taser if a close-in shot is needed.

What is really amazing about the XREP is that, unlike the standard cartridge being fired from the M26, X26 or C3 Taser handheld units, there are no wires trailing back to the firing unit to conduct power. Instead, the XREP cartridge itself contains all the power, circuitry and connections needed to activate and power the Taser effect.

As a certified Taser Instructor, I could describe the action upon impact, but instead I will quote from the Taser website (www.taser.com): "In the XREP® series, the nose assembly of the projectile contains four forward facing barbed electrodes. On impact, the forward facing barbed electrodes attach to the body of the target. The energy from the impact breaks a series of fracture pins that release the main chassis of the XREP projectile which remains connected to the nose by a nonconductive tether. The XREP projectile autonomously generates NMI" (Neuro-Muscular Incapacitation – the electrical impulse) "for 20 continuous seconds" (as opposed to the five-second standard X26 Taser "ride"). "As the chassis falls away, six Cholla electrodes automatically deploy to deliver the NMI effect over a greater body mass."

Again, the NMI effect was preceded by the impact of the XREP round itself.

I've taken the five-second Taser ride in instructor school. I'm here to tell you that I cannot imagine experiencing a full 20 seconds of time under power, preceded by the "thunk" of the XREP round itself.

The XREP cartridge fired out of the X12 gives the operator plenty of standoff distance when confronting dangerous suspects. This way, they may be taken into custody without having to kill them. The 20 seconds of ride time allows responding officers plenty of time to close the distance to the suspect and restrain them with handcuffs, even while the ride is still going on.

The XREP isn't used for the average drunk and disturbed call – that's what the X26, a baton, or good old pepper spray is for. Deploying an XREP or a beanbag round is pretty serious stuff. If someone is struck in the head or neck the round is no longer less-lethal, but is likely to become lethal. We save these things, especially $150.00 per shot things, for folks who can cause us serious physical harm.

**MOSSBERG'S TASER X12 SHOTGUN** with XREP practice and live loads, as well as an expended XREP cartridge.

**OFFICER USING THE TASER/MOSSBERG X12** shotgun deploys (in simulation) the XREP cartridge. Note that the XREP round is fin-stabilized, and the barrel of the X12 is rifled.

**TACTICAL OFFICER DEPLOYS** the Taser XREP round from the Taser/Mossberg X12 shotgun. The X12 can only fire the XREP round and no other.

**A VIEW OF THE XREP** projectile as seen after it has been fired but before it has contacted a target. The initial impact of this round alone is about half that of a standard bean bag round. This serves as a split second initial attention-getter, before the Taser charge is initiated.

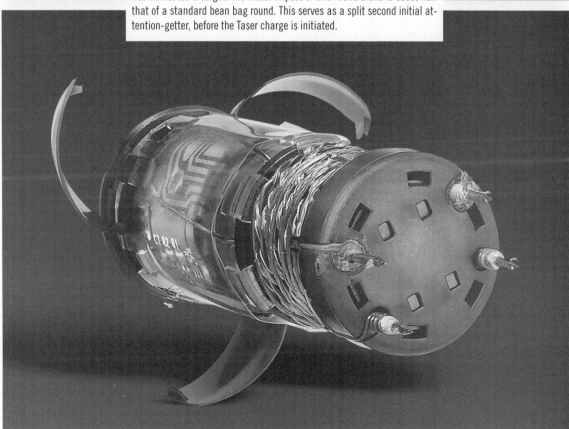

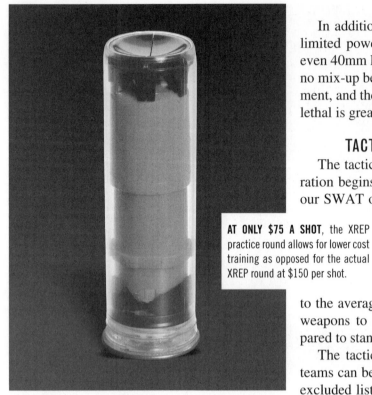

AT ONLY $75 A SHOT, the XREP practice round allows for lower cost training as opposed for the actual XREP round at $150 per shot.

Beanbags and XREPs are not general issue rounds for everyone on the street. They are generally reserved for supervisors or road units who are also members of the SWAT team.

In addition to the 12 gauge rounds that have limited power, there is the much larger 37 and even 40mm launchers and rounds so there can be no mix-up between lethal and less-lethal deployment, and the chance of a less-lethal shot turning lethal is greatly reduced.

## TACTICAL TEAM DEPLOYMENT

The tactical shotgun's character and configuration begins to change when we deploy it with our SWAT or specialty teams. After all, SWAT stands for Special Weapons and Tactics, which also implies that more training is given to the members of SWAT with any given weapons system than is given to the average street officer. This allows SWAT weapons to become more "exotic" when compared to standard patrol weapons.

The tactical shotgun for SWAT and special teams can be equipped in ways that were on my excluded list for patrol. They can, if desired, be semi-automatic rather than restricted to pump action, have optical red-dot sights and tactical lights mounted, and be equipped with ultra-short barrels in the 14-inch range.

THIS IS HOW THE ACTUAL XREP round is packaged and sold by Taser (to Law Enforcement only).

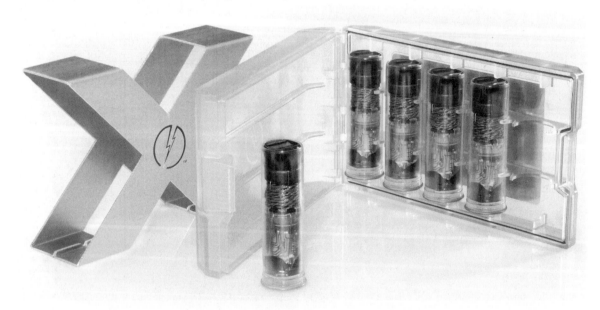

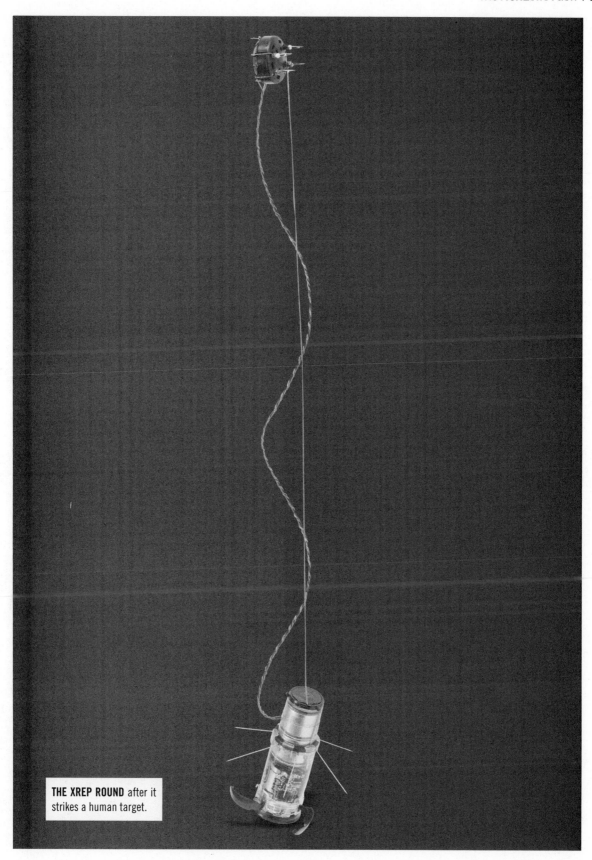

**THE XREP ROUND** after it strikes a human target.

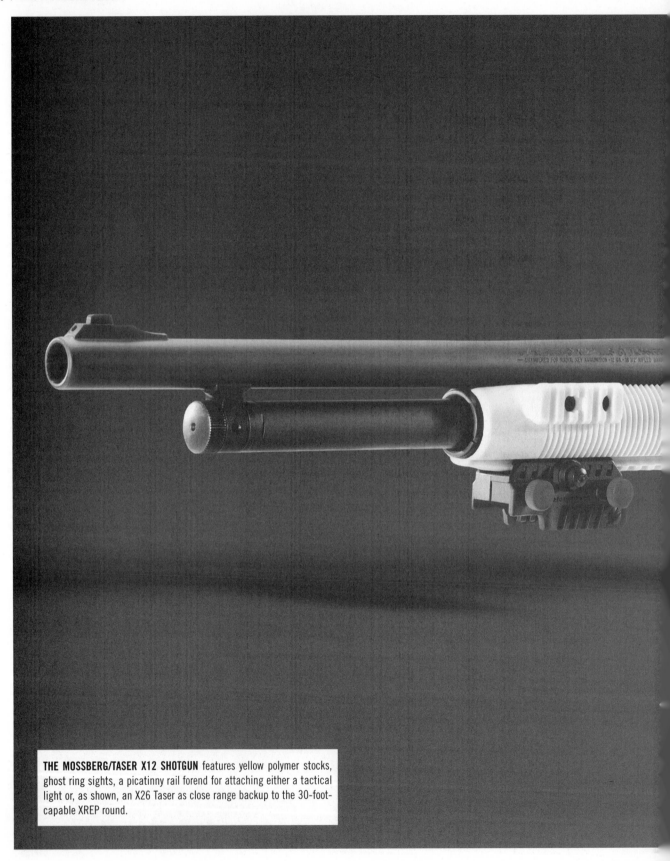

**THE MOSSBERG/TASER X12 SHOTGUN** features yellow polymer stocks, ghost ring sights, a picatinny rail forend for attaching either a tactical light or, as shown, an X26 Taser as close range backup to the 30-foot-capable XREP round.

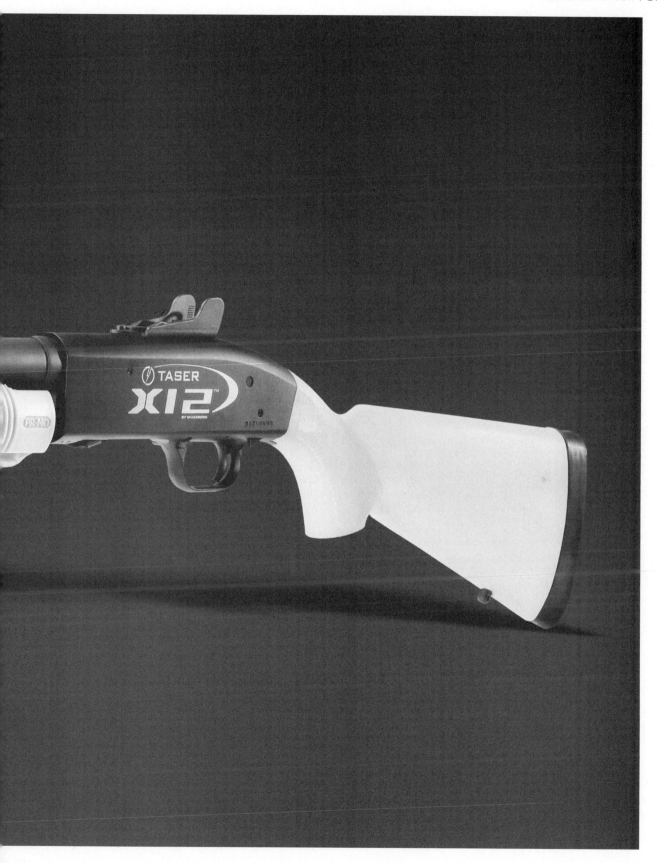

## BARREL LENGTH AND THE CRUISER

There has been a return to vertical mounts in cruiser for rifles and shotguns of late. For many years, since the introduction of airbags, long guns were exiled from their former vertical positions to either the cruiser trunk or in a behind-the-head mount on the rear of the cruiser screen (prisoner safety partition). While these mounts work, they are a pain to work with to obtain or replace the gun. Now airbag technology has improved so that apparently we can go back to vertical mounting. There is one problem, however, for those mounts in Dodge Charger cruisers, and that is the low, sleek roofline. It's difficult to get the guns out of the car in an emergency due to the standard shotgun barrel length of 18-18.5 inches, or the 20-inch barrel length of a fixed-stock M16A1.

Perhaps its time to set up patrol shotguns with the 14-inch barrel for ease of egress from the cruiser. Considering all the gear that is in the modern police car, shorter barrel shotguns may be an idea whose time has come.

The mission for SWAT tactical guns is different than their street patrol counter parts. They are precisely configured for CQB (close quarters battle) in tight confines as found during dynamic entry operations, or for even more specialized tasks such as door breaching using "shot-lock" rounds (don't use regular shotgun shells) in purpose driven shotgun configurations. What I'm referring to here is a shotgun that will only be used for one thing (like a less-lethal launcher) – a door breaching gun. As such, it is perfectly fine for the gun to be pistol grip only style, such as the Mossberg 500 Cruiser model with the Stand-Off barrel. Since you are shooting the shotgun while in contact with the door lock assembly area, it's unlikely that you'll miss. You don't need a shoulder stock, it just gets in the way. Door-breaching rounds are designed to disintegrate after they hit the lock, putting less (I didn't say "no") material on the other side of the door like a standard round would do. Therefore, there is less chance that innocents will be harmed on the other side. Once the lock is breached, the gun, which must have a shoulder sling, can be slung across the back while its bearer switches to the

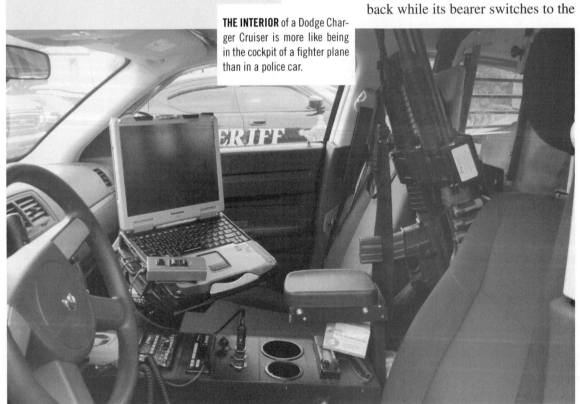

**THE INTERIOR** of a Dodge Charger Cruiser is more like being in the cockpit of a fighter plane than in a police car.

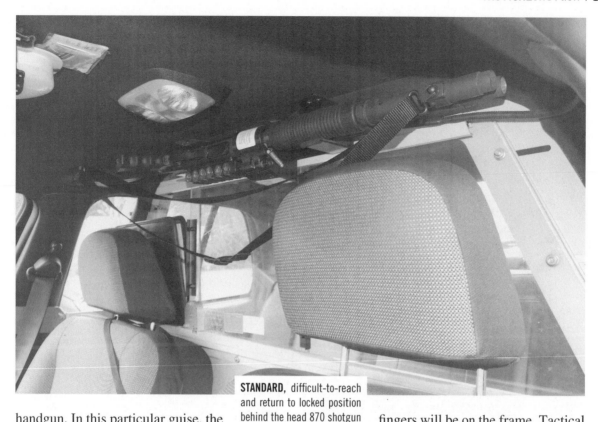

**STANDARD**, difficult-to-reach and return to locked position behind the head 870 shotgun mount in a Ford Crown Victoria Cruiser.

handgun. In this particular guise, the tactical shotgun becomes a halligan tool that goes "boom".

A semi-automatic tactical shotgun, especially with a shortened barrel, is nearly ideal in most entry situations in a contained and area limited structure. By contained I mean that there has been a perimeter set around the structure, usually a home, so that the suspect inside does not have unlimited freedom to move about. When a SWAT or specialty team does a dynamic entry, there is usually plenty of time to prepare for it. There is a mission briefing and assignments made before anything happens at the scene. In these situations, there is plenty of time to check and load your weapons properly, and make sure they are ready to rock. It's not like in an urgent street patrol situation where the officer is grabbing the shotgun as they pop out of the cruiser, bringing it immediately to bear on the threat. In the standard SWAT situation, the officer will chamber a round prior to entry, before exiting their vehicle. The safety will be in the "on" position, just like officers who are carrying their assigned AR-15s or M4 carbines, and their trigger fingers will be on the frame. Tactical officers so equipped will have up to nine rounds of 00 buck or other type shot at their disposal, with a handgun or two for backup, plus the other 10 or more guys on the entry team with whatever weapon they are carrying. How much ammo in a magazine does one need (unless you are facing that Beslan School situation with heavily armed terrorists)?

## ADVANTAGES OF THE SEMI-AUTO FOR ENTRY

The semi-auto possesses two main advantages for entry over the pump gun. First, a corded pressure switch for a weapon light can be affixed to the semi-auto's forend with less worrying about it being torn loose or tangled. On the sliding forend of a pump shotgun there is concern about that happening since the light itself is usually attached to the magazine tube and doesn't move with the forend, unless you use the Surefire forend system. Remington's 887 Nitro Mag Tactical mounts a section of Picatinny rail on the barrel clamp, but this piece also does not move with the forend, so a corded light is still in danger of being tangled or pulled free.

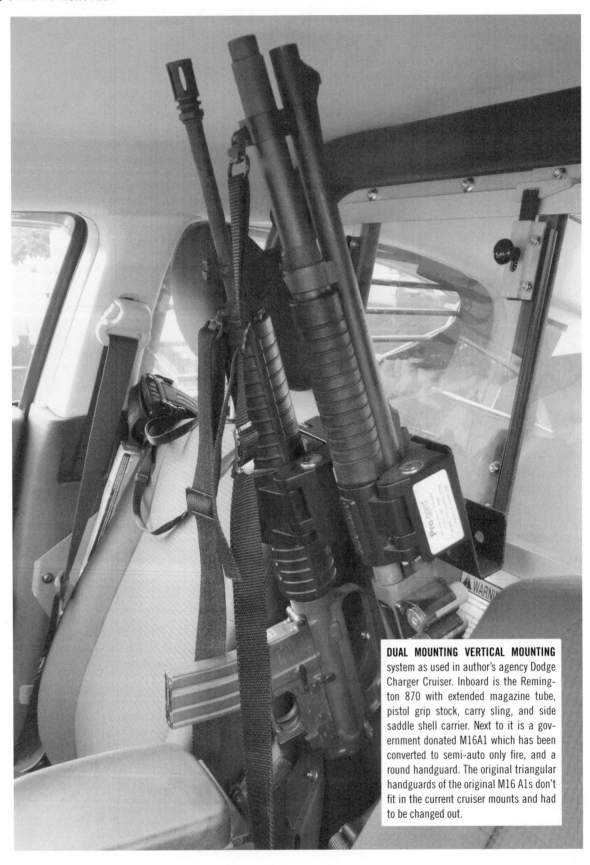

**DUAL MOUNTING VERTICAL MOUNTING** system as used in author's agency Dodge Charger Cruiser. Inboard is the Remington 870 with extended magazine tube, pistol grip stock, carry sling, and side saddle shell carrier. Next to it is a government donated M16A1 which has been converted to semi-auto only fire, and a round handguard. The original triangular handguards of the original M16 A1s don't fit in the current cruiser mounts and had to be changed out.

The second advantage is the ability to fire rapid double taps. Yes, I know the pump is fast, but a semi-auto is faster still. That's why folks who participate in sporting clays use over/under doubles or autoloaders rather than pumps – two shots can be fired "right now."

Also, in a tight hallway or room, the less movement you have to make, the better. With the semi-auto, there is no movement of your support arm required for working the action, which means you won't be bumping that arm into anything while trying to cycle the action in a critical moment. You just have to concentrate on disengaging the safety and pulling the trigger.

Definitely, a semi-auto 12 gauge is the choice for entry or even perimeter containment where the confines are close for tactical operators. Even so, in today's entry stacks, there usually is only one shotgun for every 10 or more guys. Most of the officers are carrying an M4 5.56 variant or a 9mm subgun such as an HK MP-5.

## HEAD SHOTS AND HOSTAGE RESCUE

Personally, I would rather have the 12 when things are tight, which brings me to another point. Make sure that whoever is assigned the shotgun really likes using it. You can't have the attitude of "that's his assigned weapon and by god he's gonna use it." Not everyone, not even on a tactical team, likes the shotgun or can use it well. They need to have confidence in it, and I think that too many officers, even some tactical officers, still view it as an almost "indirect fire" type weapon that really doesn't require precision. It's for body shots only, right? I'm here to tell you that's wrong, and again, it's not taking full advantage of the mighty 12's capabilities. It can be used, in the right circumstances for head shots and hostage rescue.

Here in Columbus, Ohio, on Friday, December 10, 2004, Nathan Gale entered the Al Rosa Villa nightclub with the goal of killing band leader, "Dime Bag Darryl Abbot," whom he felt was a rival. He killed him and three other patrons, and wounded two. He was in the process of killing a fifth when Officer James Niggemeyer of the Columbus Police Department, who had just been trained in active shooter intervention, entered through the rear door of the restaurant as patrons were running out screaming.

Officer Niggemeyer, who entered alone through the door while other officers were preparing to enter from the front, was armed with a Remington 870 pump shotgun loaded with 00 buckshot. He confronted Gale, who was on the stage and was holding another patron around the neck as a hostage. Without wasting time with a verbal command and costing the next victim in line their life, he ended the shooting spree with a 12 gauge headshot. The shooter was "DRT" (Dead Right There), and Officer Niggemeyer received many well deserved accolades and national recognition for his act of heroism.

Contrast this with another rescue of a hostage in the nearby City of Reynoldsburg, Ohio, in 1996. Officer Al Grundy responded with other officers to a holdup alarm at a local bank, and it was not a false alarm. It also happened that there was a news photographer in the area as this robbery went down who captured the entire situation with his 35 mm camera. The robber, whose family said had turned his life around and wanted to do missionary work, had apparently decided to obtain funding at this particular bank. In the process, he took two hostages, both female and one pregnant, using a handgun (it actually turned out to be a CO2 pellet gun) and a butcher knife (that was real).

He attempted to get them into his car and make a getaway. The non-pregnant female managed to break free from his grasp and run to safety as Officer Grundy was confronting him at the car. Officer Grundy was within a range of 10 feet or so and was armed with a Remington 870 shotgun loaded with 00 buck. Now, read this carefully first before you read any further. I am not, repeat not, questioning Officer Grundy's tactics, especially since he is a good friend of mine. He ended the situation and is an unquestionable hero. Okay, continue. Officer Grundy was worried about the buckshot from the shotgun spreading too far if/when he had to fire, and was worried about stray pellets striking the hostage. He put the shotgun down and switched to his Smith and

.CP duty pistol. As the hos-
..pted to take off, Officer Grundy
...unds of 230 gr. Speer Gold Dot JHPs
...n the back window and through the would
...hostage taker/missionary's head. He was, you
guessed it, also DRT.

The result here was that Officer Grundy won numerous awards for his action, and much gratitude, particularly from the pregnant woman's husband. She was physically unharmed. It is a rare thing to have such a clear view of an incident like this. How often is there a professional photographer around with the camera ready, who said he would testify in the officer's behalf that there was no other action possible? The point is that Officer Grundy could have safely used his 870, and did not need to transition to his handgun in order to resolve the situation. He was looking at it as an area fire weapon rather than a precision one. He is just like many other officers who, through lack of experience or training, either overestimate or underestimate the shotgun's limitations or capabilities. More work is needed with this weapons system if we hope to use it to its full potential and keep it in our first line inventory.

## SHOTGUN TRAINING TIPS FOR OFFICERS AND CIVILIANS

Shotgun training seems to get short shrift in terms of time spent and effort put forth compared to other weapons systems. This may be related to that old training philosophy that said that you really don't need to aim a shotgun to be effective, just point it in the general direction of whatever your target is and you are bound to hit something. Let me say this once and for all, particularly about the tactical shotgun: you have to aim it, and you have to practice aiming it. Even if it's only a flash sight picture (where only the front sight is located in a rough reference to the rear) you still have to aim it.

You are responsible, morally, civilly and even in some cases criminally, whether you are a civilian or police officer, for each and every pellet that you launch downrange. You have to know how far is too far away to take your shot with the shotgun, or any other weapon for that matter.

Even if the point of aim that you take is dead on but a pellet or two misses the target for whatever reason, you are responsible for those strays. You have to know the limitations of you particular shotgun and your duty or self defense load, its rate of spread, and its penetrative capabilities in order to be safe and effective with it.

> You are responsible for each and every pellet that you launch downrange.

As with any weapon, the shotgun is only a precision weapon within its usable precision range (UPR). The usable precision range is the distance that any particular person can fire a shot from any particular weapon and have it strike close enough to its intended point of aim so that nothing else is endangered other than that intended target itself. There also must be enough kinetic energy left in the projectile(s) fired at that target to be capable of causing the appropriate level of damage to it. If the target is a sheet of paper then the projectile just needs to be able to punch a hole through that paper. If the target is large and violent, then the projectile(s) must be capable of punching through to the vitals and stopping that violence. Usable Precision Range (UPR) varies from person to person and from weapons system to weapons system.

Other factors that affect the UPR are quality of the sights and use of a rest. The use of a rest or rested position greatly increases the UPR, as does the quality and magnification power of an optical sight, mainly in the case of the rifle. The shotgun is somewhat of a different story. Its UPR is generally regulated or limited by pellet spread. Even with the best buckshot loads, I would limit my shots to no further than 25 yards as there is just too much chance that the pellets are going to miss their target. Yes, most people can hit the center of a silhouette target with 00 buck at 20 yards with proper sights, but that doesn't guarantee that all the pellets will end up on the target, especially at greater distances.

The final thing that throws all this fine talk of Usable Precision Range right out the window is the phenomenon of "someone else is shooting at me." This is a huge variable and affects everyone to a different degree. Experienced combat veterans are going to be much more capable under fire than those who have never been in a gunfight. There are ways you can plan and train for it, through training known as "stress inoculation," which involves scenarios using airsoft weapons and Simunitions®. High quality paintball training might even be helpful.

A book I would recommend as critical reading to understand what happens physiologically and psychologically in combat is "On Combat" by world renowned authority in military and law enforcement combatives Colonel David Grossman. It explains the dynamics of interpersonal lethal combat before, during and after a lethal force situation whether you are a civilian, soldier or cop. I recommended it to one of my fellow deputies recently involved in a fatal shooting who was exhibiting some very natural stress signs. It has helped him a great deal. It is important to read it before you are involved in such an event, because it will help you through the engagement. Re-read it in the aftermath of any such event for reinforcement and recovery.

## PATTERN-TESTING YOUR WEAPON AND LOAD

It is critical that you become totally familiar with your tactical shotgun and chosen defensive load before you have to use it. With a shotgun of 20 or 12 gauge, many people assume you can grab most anything off the shelf that will reliably go bang, regardless of brand or even shot size, and it will get the job done. Up until recently, all the advertising for shotgun loads has been for hunting loads, birds, upland game and the like. There were really only two choices for self-defense, at least in a home defense environment: birdshot or buckshot. Now, shotgun loads specific to self-defense abound. This may be due in large part to the emergence of the .410 gauge as

a self-defense round, as well as the popularity of the tactical shotgun itself. The .410 which, with less recoil, can still deliver multiple shots on target with each pull of the trigger, although not nearly as many as a 12 or 20 gauge gun.

Having a milder-shooting, shotgun-like weapon is nothing new. Back in the 1990s Remington had a series of "Multi-Ball" loads for the handgun, particularly in .38 Special and .357 Magnum caliber. These loads would in theory increase the stopping power of a handgun, making it more like a handheld shotgun. Apparently theory wasn't borne out in fact, and the rounds disappeared into self-defense oblivion, taking us back to the drawing board with the standard type shotgun. Taurus has been able to build on this success with its wildly popular Judge™ series of .45 Colt/.410 gauge combination revolvers. The Judge series has been much more successful than were revolvers using the multi-ball loadings due to the increased power and capacity of a .410 shotshell over a .38 Special cartridge.

Specific defensive ammunition types will be covered in a later section of this book, but suffice it to say for now that once you select an ammo brand/type for your shotgun, you need to take it out and pattern-test it. Fire it at different distances – three yards, 10 yards, 15 and 20 yards – and see what type of pattern it holds. Just barely staying on a silhouette isn't enough; it has to pattern tighter than that if you are going to use it within that range, as the target may be turned sideways toward you. Ten to 12 inches of consistent spread should define the UPR with a particular load, as that is about the average thickness of a man's body when turned sideways. If a particular load doesn't fall within the parameters, try something else, especially some of the new specific home defense-type loads, such as those offered from Remington, Winchester, Hornady and others. Get a feel for the UPR distance for your weapon and load combination so that you know when you are beyond it and should switch to rifled slugs.

You can also run your own penetration tests against materials like sheetrock, 2x4s, plywood and aluminum or vinyl siding, whatever you materials you might face in a home defense situation. While you cannot guarantee against over-penetration in a home defense situation, you can prepare for it.

If you do your own testing, do not shoot at something really hard, such as concrete or cinderblock, as bouncing pellets and injury could occur.

If you are a police officer, consider using the same ammo in a home defense situation as you would out on the street. Certainly don't pick something more powerful than your duty load for this purpose. In other words, you really don't need 3-inch magnum rounds for home defense if 2-3/4-inch reduced recoil rounds are your duty loads.

If you are not happy with the patterning of your shotgun and the initial selected load, try something else. They don't all shoot the same, even the same load type in a different brand. Also, if you have a shotgun such as the Benelli M2 Tactical, which comes with interchangeable chokes (full, modified, improved cylinder), you might try switching them around to see which produces the best pattern.

However you work out your defensive load selection, avoid exotic loads (from unknown manufacturers) for self defense, such as those which contain steel flechettes (darts). While it may sound fun to say "hey Billy, guess what I got loaded up in this bad boy – steel flechette rounds – these things will rip the hide right off anything they hit," it will be far less fun to hear, "Your honor, I believe my opposing attorney's client loaded up his shotgun like a weapon of mass destruction for the express purpose of obliterating anything he shot, rather than just trying to stop the threat that may or may not have been posed by my deceased client." Stick with standard defensive shotgun loads from recognized manufacturers. They should sufficiently do the job.

### CHECKING FOR RELIABLE OPERATION

Another reason to test your weapon and load is for reliable operation. After all, your life depends on the proper functioning of this machine in combination with your skills and abilities in wielding it. If you have problems with functioning, check if the gun is properly lubed and reasonably clean. If it does appear clean and well lubed (but not over-lubed), consider switching loads. The culprit may be reduced-recoil loads; try full-power stuff. If the shotgun is brand new, run several boxes of your chosen defense load through it to make sure it is broken in. If the gun you are using was purchased used, was it put together the correctly before you bought it? Did you put it back together the correct way? Remington 870s, for instance, can be re-assembled incorrectly so that they will still function, but not reliably.

> If you are not happy with the patterning of your shotgun and the initial selected load, try something else. They don't all shoot the same, even the same load type in a different brand of gun.

If you can't get it to run, take it back to the shop or a gunsmith. If functioning is good (which means flawless), clean it and fire one more magazine of loads to check it a final time. Wipe down the exterior and load it again, leaving it in ready-to-use condition.

Quality, modern guns from the major American manufacturers should all run right out of the box, which is precisely what I found in live-fire testing the shotguns I used or purchased for this book. They all ran without cleaning or adding supplemental lubrication. The only time I added lubrication was if I checked and found that the gun, through long storage at a shop or in someone's home, was bone dry.

Be sure to check the functioning in pumps as well as double barrels. In the pump, does everything cycle smoothly, including ejection? There should be no hitches in the operation, and while pump shotguns need to be run firmly, they shouldn't need to be run forcefully. You shouldn't have any hitch or hangup points in the cycle.

**PROPER STANCE** is critical. Sgt Pat Kellon demonstrates a solid shotgun shooting position. Even for a large individual like this, stance is critical to control. Note use of Surefire forend with built-in tactical light.

Parkerized or coated defense guns will be just a little rough during initial operation, as opposed to polished blue sporting guns. While there is less finishing of the parts in the parkerized versions, they will smooth out as the weapon is manipulated. That's what keeps tactical shotguns inexpensive, not only in relation to AR-15s, but also in relation to those very same blued sporting guns: not much finishing is required.

Once you make your final selection, keep the ammo in your weapon fresh, and the ammo in your supply stock properly stored. Plastic-hulled shotshells can be stored, like other types of brass-cased ammo, for decades and still work if the conditions are good. Low humidity is especially important, as is keeping your ammo away from lubricants or cleaning solvents. Penetrating oils are especially bad.

## TRAINING AND PRACTICE

In training, the key is not practice makes perfect, rather "perfect practice makes perfect." You must practice using correct form and tactics. If you train in sloppiness and poor tactics, then sloppily or with poor tactics will be how you perform in a real situation.

## STANCE

In order to be a proper defensive/combat shooter with the rifle, pistol or shotgun, you must have a proper stance. The "Interview-Fight-Shoot" (IFS) stance simplifies training and understanding of the fighting concept for fists, pepper sprays, batons, Tasers, handguns, shotguns and CQB rifles. Commonality and simplicity of technique is critical. Fancy draw strokes, body positioning or awkward foot stances have no place in gun fighting. I don't believe in assuming an isosceles type foot stance to fire a gun when I'm already in a proper interview or fist-fighting stance. Why waste the time and confuse the issue? To assume the IFS stance:

1.    Place your feet shoulder width apart, with the strong foot approximately one step back from the weak foot. This sets a fighting platform and affords balance.

**COLUMBUS STATE POLICE ACADEMY INSTRUCTOR** demonstrates proper low ready position using Mossberg 590A1 with M4 stock.

**INSTRUCTOR** with 590A1 in proper high ready shooting stance. Note feet are shoulder width apart, knees slightly flexed, and the shotgun pulled tightly into shoulder pocket.

Knees should be slightly flexed, not locked out, and the body weight should be on the balls of the feet for easy movement. You should not be knocked over easily if someone pushes you.

2. The hands are brought up to a comfortable belt or chest high level for the interview if you are a police officer, or if someone begins to encroach on your personal space if you are a civilian. If you are out in public, and someone starts to encroach on your personal space, you should be moving into this stance automatically. In this position you appear like you are just talking with your hands, when in reality you are in a position to throw or block a punch, draw a pepper spray, Taser or handgun.

3. The IFS stance is the position the shotgun (or a rifle) will be wielded from, further reinforcing commonality of technique. Once you have assumed the proper IFS foot and body position, the shotgun is brought up to the shoulder, along with the strong side supporting arm/firing hand, creating a slight "pocket" in the shoulder for the gun butt to rest in. The face should naturally find the stock at the rear of the receiver, with the cheek resting against it. The weak hand goes forward to the forend or slide action of the weapon and the entire body is bent slightly forward at the waist, so that your position is essentially the same position as a boxer would have when throwing a punch. With your weight slightly forward in this fighting stance, you can better absorb the recoil as you fire.

## FIRING POSITIONS

Now that you have the proper standing shooting stance, learn to fire the shotgun from the kneeling and prone positions. You will also want to learn to fire it with one hand.

We need to take advantage of concealment and cover whenever possible. We can use kneeling positions from behind a bed while covering the doorway entrance to our bedroom, or while covering a hallway or other area of our property.

The prone position is somewhat of a different story. It's best to remain mobile for any close-

**SHOOTING CLAY BIRDS** is great training. Here, Police Cadets use author's 887 Nitro Mag Tactical with Aimpoint Comp 2 attached to aid in getting hits.

**CADETS** use clay bird shooting off a thrower. Gun is a Remington 870 Police Magnum with Pistol Grip Stock.

shotgun, even if it wasn't fun to shoot at first. Not only because the style of shooting is fun, but also because you will be firing only light target loads for most of these sports. Even if you change out the tactical barrel on guns that allow it, such as on the Remington and Mossberg, and use a field barrel for the sport activity, you are still way ahead of the game. Or, leave that tactical barrel on and take it deer hunting. Isn't a tactical shotgun ideal for hunting deer or bear in heavy cover?

Just remember you may need to plug the magazine to keep it legal in the game fields, and leave the laser sighting system off, as I don't know of any locales where they are legal for hunting.

The following drills are based on police shotgun qualification courses. They can give you an idea of what you should be doing in terms of training, but they are not a be all-end all. Certain aspects of these drills may not be permitted on public ranges. Be sure to check with range management prior to using these drills.

## POINT OF AIM

Training for combat shooting with a 12 gauge shotgun is different than training with a handgun due to the greater destructive force of the shotgun. With a handgun, which will punch on entry with the very largest common caliber pistol round a .45 caliber hole (compared to a .72 caliber and larger spreading hole of the 12 gauge), a point of aim that will hopefully allow that pistol round to strike vitals such as the heart, spine or lungs is a must. With the shotgun however, a mid-point of body aim should be taken, centering on the belt buckle or navel region.

A chest point of aim, like that taken with a handgun, when taken with a shotgun, tends to allow a stray pellet or two to go up over the shoulder. For right handed shooters, usually it's over the right side of the target. This is primarily because of less than solid control of the recoil of the shotgun. There may be a proper point of aim when the trigger is pulled, but because the recoil wasn't properly controlled the barrel moves well above the original point of aim by the time the

in shooting if possible. Also, shooting from the prone position with a shotgun is not comfortable, as your body can't roll with the recoil, so you get slammed pretty hard. Why practice it then? You need to be ready for a variety of situations. What if you are knocked to the ground, shot to the ground, or simply slip to the ground during a combat situation? Practice firing the shotgun from a grounded position, ideally from both your back and stomach, and with one hand only from your back.

Finally, remember this: Any shooting you can do with your tactical shotgun is additional training. Want some great practice? Take it sporting clays shooting, trap or skeet shooting or hunting. These shooting sports, especially sporting clays, are a great training tool, as they build familiarity with your gun. You get bunches of repetitions combat loading and unloading, firing, sighting, moving and just plain handling. Formal or informal competitive shooting allows you to "become one with the gun." More importantly, these activities helps you learn to enjoy shooting the shot emerges from the barrel. At this point, the shot is flying above the target area. If the shooter instead aims for the belt buckle, all the pellets will strike the torso even with less than perfect recoil control.

When you are talking eight or nine pellets of 00 buck or a one-ounce rifled slug, either of which is travelling in the 1100 to 1400 fps range, that's a pretty hard hit in the gut. Like a solid punch, it should fold the intended target in half. While the impact might not hit the heart/lung/upper spine area, there is still a lot of stuff in the lower region of the body to damage and take the fight out of the aggressor. Remember, your mission is to stop the attack. A load of 00 buck, rifled slug, specialty home defense load, or birdshot at lose range in the guts ought to do the trick.

### PUMP AND SEMI-AUTO SHOTGUN DRILLS

While these drills are designed for high capacity shotguns, double barrel shotguns can be used. For drills requiring four or more rounds, simply perform a rapid reload. Double barrels with ejectors (that flip the empty rounds clear of the weapon) rather than extractors (which lift the shells out to where they are plucked free by hand) are preferred.

These drills should be undertaken using the defensive shotgun loads that are most effective in your particular weapon and for your situation. Target used should be the old NRA B27 in whatever color format is available. The B27 uses a middle point of aim for the highest scoring. When using buckshot, base your score on the highest point level that 80% of the pellets are centered in. You many not be able to do all these drills on a some ranges. Outdoor ranges are preferred for shotgun shooting.

#### Rifled slug

Starting from a distance of 25 yards (50 feet is acceptable if that is all the distance your range allows) with the shotgun in Condition 3 and loaded with four rifled slugs (or whatever your magazine tube capacity is), assume a kneeling position. Charge the weapon and fire all four (or more) rounds into the belt buckle area of the target, trying to maintain as tight a group as possible

(which means all rounds should basically be in the same hole).

## Pump shotgun ready conditions
*(applies to all brands and models)*

| Condition | Operational status |
| --- | --- |
| 1 | Round in chamber, magazine full (less one round), slide forward, safety off |
| 2 | Round in chamber, magazine full (less one round), slide forward, safety on |
| 3 | "Cruiser ready": Slide forward, action closed, internal hammer down, safety off, chamber empty, fully loaded magazine |
| 4 | Totally empty, no rounds in magazine or chamber |

#### Combat load

Starting from a distance of seven yards (the average distance of a gunfight) with an empty shotgun in Condition 4 and using 00 buckshot or similar load, quickly open the action and drop one shell in, close the action and fire that round at the belt buckle area of the target. Open the action, combat load another round, and, moving the shotgun to Condition 2 (safety on), load the magazine tube to full capacity. Once the magazine is full, quickly fire three rounds into the target. Clear the shotgun down to Condition 4, and then reload it back to Condition 3.

Note: When dropping a shell in for a combat load, it means just that. Drop it in! Don't try and position it in the chamber opening or help it in, just drop it in and close the bolt. It will chamber just fine in a pump or semi-auto action. The actions of multi-round tactical shotguns have tolerances similar to an AK-47, which is why they operate so reliably.

#### Multiple targets

With the shotgun in Condition 3 from the previous course of fire, at a distance of seven yards, charge the weapon and fire one round as quickly as possible into the belt buckle area of each of three targets. Clear to the shotgun to Condition 4, then reload to Condition 3 with a total of two rounds.

### Shooting from behind cover

Using two targets set side by side and three to four feet apart, with the shotgun in Condition 3 and four rounds total loaded, at a distance of 10 yards, utilizing cover from behind a five-foot tall barricade, fire two rounds from the standing position at the outside target, and then two rounds from the kneeling position at the inside (innermost) target from the strong side.

Make sure you expose as little of yourself as possible – stay behind cover!

This drill may be repeated by moving the barricade and firing the same sequence off the weak shoulder to maintain best protective cover. Shooting from the strong shoulder from a weak side barricade position exposes more of your body to the enemy than is necessary.

### Shooting from prone

This one drill that will be really hard to pull off at an indoor public range. From a distance of 10 yards, loaded with three rounds 00 buckshot in Condition 3, drop SAFELY to a prone position and fire all three rounds at the midpoint area of the target.

### Low-level light

Using a tactical light attached to the shotgun, or the shotgun with no tactical light attached, from a distance of 21 feet, with four rounds loaded in Condition 3, fire two rounds into each of two targets set four to five feet apart. You can use optical or laser aiming devices in addition to or without a tactical light. If you have no optical or tritium sights, lasers or tactical lights (you will probably find that you will want one when you try this), you will need to correct and check your sight alignment off of each successive muzzle flash.

### Transition drill: Fighting your way to the shotgun

If you utilize a handgun as part of your defensive system, remember that its purpose is to buy you time to get to your primary weapon, be it your shotgun or rifle. Therefore, you need to practice transitioning from one weapon system to the other.

Also, there could be a problem with your shotgun; it may be out of ammo or disabled. In a recent shootout at my agency, one of our depu-

ties' .357 rounds struck and penetrated the side of the offender's shotgun barrel and punched a hole in it. Had the offender fired another shot, his barrel would have totally burst. It is possible that your shotgun could suffer a fate such as this, and you may need to revert back to your handgun to finish the situation.

Starting with your shotgun in Condition 3, loaded with two rounds in the magazine, and your handgun loaded with six rounds of ammunition, while facing two targets placed the same way as in the low level light course, fire the two shotgun rounds in the target on your left. Then switch the shotgun into the weak hand and, still maintaining a hold on it, draw your handgun and fire the six rounds from your handgun into the target on the right. Repeat this drill by firing the handgun first with all six rounds into the left target, transition to the shotgun while maintaining control of the handgun (you can holster it), and fire the two shotgun rounds into the target on your right.

### One-handed shooting

Starting with your shotgun in Condition 4, at a distance of three yards, combat load one round into the chamber, extend the shotgun away from your body with one hand only and, without concern over the exact sighting arrangement (this is a lot like extending your arm out and pointing your finger), fire one shot into the center of the target. Repeat until you are comfortable and confident firing one-handed.

Once confident with this drill, you can try firing one-handed while laying on your back with your feet pointing at the target. Please be careful: If you don't have the strength to lift the shotgun off the ground one-handed, don't try this drill.

# CHAPTER THREE

# PUMPS, SEMI-AUTOS, OR DOUBLES:
## WHICH IS BEST FOR YOU?

Previous sections outlined action types as they applied to use by law enforcement street patrol officers, SWAT team members and detectives. For those individuals, the shotgun is selected, approved and issued by their employing agency. This section addresses the issues related to selecting a shotgun for civilian use, as the civilian has the most options available to them and who are not restricted by departmental policy.

Gauge is the first factor to consider. While I've written nearly everything to this point in terms of the standard 12 gauge, there are other effective gauges available that might actually be a better choice if you are recoil sensitive, or the gun is going to be used by other family members who are recoil sensitive or smaller statured.

The 20 gauge cartridge is currently being overlooked in terms of self defense loads. The biggest favorite is of course the 12 gauge, but the .410 is darn near as popular thanks to the Taurus Judge and several tactical pumps that are chambered for it. But what do the differences in gauge really mean in terms of defensive use? Let's compare the three main gauges that are used for defensive or combat shooting.

aren't. Forgo them totally, there are no advantages in them. You can pick up an inexpensive pump on sale for roughly the same price.

The double barrel is a different story, and I think they have some value. The main value is that, when facing a lone attacker in particular, there is nothing more intimidating than looking down the twin bores of a side-by-side double, particularly in 12 gauge. These are the guns that

## COMPARATIVE DEFENSIVE SHOTGUN LOADS

Source: Winchester 2010 Ammunition Tables (Standard loads represented, unless otherwise noted)

| Gauge | Projectile Type | Weight in Oz./number of pellets | ....Velocity/fps |
|---|---|---|---|
| 12 | 00 Buckshot | 9 pellets | 1325 |
| 12 | Rifled Slug | 1 oz | 1600 |
| 12 | Birdshot (Heavy Target) | 1 1/8 oz | 1200 |
| 20 | #3 Buckshot (largest available) | 20 pellets | 1200 |
| 20 | Rifled Slug | 3/4 oz | 1600 |
| 20 | Birdshot (Heavy Target) | 1 oz | 1165 |
| .410 | 00 Buckshot (Remington Home Defense) | 4 pellets | 1300 |
| .410 | Rifled Slug (2-1/2 inch) | 1/5 oz | 1830 |
| .410 | Birdshot (Target) | 1/2 oz | 1200 |

As can see from some of the velocities and shot charges, there is a vast power discrepancy between the .410 and the very popular 12 gauge. A .410 rifled slug, while very fast, is very light, about the weight of a .380 ACP bullet. Due to its velocity, it is delivering 651 foot pounds of energy on the target, about the same kinetic energy as the 175 grain 10mm Winchester Silvertip bullet delivers, but with much less weight behind it. Contrast that to the 1865 foot pounds of energy of the 20 gauge rifled slug and the whopping 2488 foot pounds of the 12 gauge rifled slug. While I might be willing to consider a .410 gun to defend my apartment or common walled condominium with, or get one for someone who is EXTREMELY recoil sensitive, (I would rather they have a 20 and plenty of training) my default gauge is going to be the 12. You choose what will work best in your situation.

## THE DOUBLE BARREL

While there are single-shot shotguns available that appear to be "tactical," or parts sets available to convert one and make it appear tactical, they

made "shotgun weddings" a tradition in this great nation of ours, and they are still available, thanks in large part to the popularity of the sport of Cowboy Action shooting. As long as you go with hammerless, single-trigger models, which are a little hard to find, you have two very quick shots and simple operation.

The double is also sort of like the bullpup rifle of the shotgun world. Because of the construction of the action, which takes up next to no space in the overall length of the receiver, the barrel and receiver is shorter than the length of any pump or auto, whose receiver and action make up a fair portion of the overall length. This makes the double more maneuverable than many other types of shotguns. The only type of pump or auto that is as short or shorter are models that have an M4-type collapsible stock.

The downside of the double is trying to get decent accuracy at any distance with rifled slugs. Much time is spent by experts regulating their double barrels to shoot reasonably close to the same point, and these guns cost many thousands of dollars. If you keep your combat double barrel

loaded with shot and the range close, you'll be fine, as long as you aren't being attacked by a ninja assault force numbering more than two ninjas.

A double barrel can work very nicely for you in most home defense situations. Its intimidation affect can't be denied. Store it ready to rock, with the two rounds chambered but the action not fully closed. When needed, close the action and remove the safety. Keep your finger on frame until ready to fire.

## THE PUMP SHOTGUN

The pump is my favorite action type for shotguns, probably because it is the shotgun type that I've used (specifically the Remington 870) for 30 years of law enforcement work, and the action type that I cut my teeth on. Before that I learned to shoot using a pump action .22 rimfire rifle, my dad's Winchester Model 62, so operating a pump action just seemed to be the natural order of things. It was fast, smooth and reliable.

The pump has a lot going for it. It is highly reliable and simple in operation. It is generally very simple to field strip and maintain. There is very little to wear out. Most Remington 870s I've seen in police service or training have had many thousands of rounds through them with no parts breakage. Rust is the number one undoing of them, and that's just in terms of surface appearance.

The pump is generally very simple to modify to specialized usage. For instance, it's a simple matter to change out the barrels to switch from use as a tactical gun to a field or sporting type barrel. Fully-rifled barrels are also available which allow for some very accurate fire with sabot-type slug rounds. This gives true rifle-type accuracy for hunting in states that prohibit rifle

**THE STOEGER DOUBLE DEFENSE** in 20 gauge is, in the authors opinion, the ultimate in double barreled defense guns. With Picattiny rail on top of the barrels, at the receiver for optics mounting and below the barrels for light mounting, the lighter recoiling 20 gauge version (12 is also available) packs plenty of punch for most defense situations that can be handled with shot loads. Single trigger/hammerless operation makes the Double Defense easy to use.

calibers but allow shotguns. However, firing sabot slugs out of a smoothbore barrel doesn't work so well, as, unlike rifled slugs, they need rifling stabilization for accurate shooting.

Sabot slug rounds use smaller-than-caliber projectiles of a more aerodynamic shape than the old Foster-type rifled slugs. They are held centered in the slug and the shotgun bore with a plastic sabot or sleeve. They are designed for hunting use alone. If you have or purchase a fully rifled barrel for sabot use, just remember that it doesn't offer good performance with buckshot. If you want to also use buckshot, you will need a smoothbore short barrel of 18 to 20 inches in length.

Another plus for the pump gun is that the sound of the action being racked is intimidating, and that sound alone may be enough to stop an intruder dead in his tracks and have him turn tail without having to fire a shot, which is the desired outcome of this situation anyway.

Another big plus with the pump is that, after you fire the shot you wanted to fire, you don't need to chamber a live round right away. You can wait until you feel another round is needed; it is you who makes the decision to chamber a fresh live round, not the gun.

# When selecting a shotgun for extreme cold weather, choose a pump over an autoloader.

Also, and perhaps most important of all the factors that favor the pump gun as your weapon of choice, it is not finicky about ammo. Low brass light trap and skeet loads, mid range hunting loads, full power 2-3/4-inch magnum loads, in some cases 3-inch Magnum and even the mighty 3-1/2 magnum loads are all handled with aplomb and without adjustment by the pump. Semi-autos either won't work with all those loads or need adjustment to work with them. It doesn't matter (as long as you are using cylinder bore or improved cylinder bore chokes if you have rifled slug in the mix as well) what you load and shoot from it. It all works, usually without question and without complaint.

This willingness to always work also extends to climate extremes. If I am selecting a shotgun for cold weather use, I will definitely select the pump over the autoloader. Places like Minnesota and Alaska call for the pump. If the gun lubricant

**THIS IS THE BASIC MODEL** of the Remington 870 that is used for law enforcement training at the author's police academy. It features hardwood stocks (black synthetic stocks are also available), a comfortable fit and recoil pad, rifle sights and a smoothbore 20-inch barrel (while a rifled barrel is available, don't use it. It limits the versatility of the gun as it affects the patterning of shot loads). Finish is parkerized and the price is very reasonable. This model is available in a combo package with a field barrel, which increases its utility, and your familiarity with it. It is a good, basic home defense weapon that lends itself to easy customization by the owner.

gets thick or sludgy due to the extreme temperature, you will be relying on your arm strength to cycle the action, not recoil spring momentum or the small amount of powder gases that were siphoned off when the shot was fired.

While it may be a semi-automatic world when it comes to the handgun and, of late, the rifle world, it's not that way in the shotgun world. New models of pump guns continue to appear on the market. The pump gun is definitely here to stay.

## AUTO-LOADING SHOTGUNS

While the pump-action shotgun ranks number one for me among action types, the auto-loading shotgun has its place, and there are plenty of models and options available out there to satisfy any type of user. There are two basic operating systems currently in use.

## GAS OPERATED

The first and most common system is the gas operated system, as exemplified by guns like the Remington 1100, 11-87 and VersaMax, the Mossberg 930, and Benelli M4 Tactical. These guns work like any other gas operated semi-auto action arms. They utilize various forms of a piston operating system that bleeds off a small

**THE MOSSBERG MODEL 500** Persuader is available in a wide array of tactical models, as well as sporting versions. This model 500 variant features a "stand off" type muzzle brake for door breaching (or just cool good looks) and a standard style synthetic stock.

amount of gas from a port in the barrel that draws gas from each cartridge that is fired. This gas does the work of cycling the action that you would normally do by hand. Benelli's ARGO™ system uses a different type of dual piston operating system. The M4 Tactical has been adopted for combat use by our military due to the reliability of its ARGO™ operating system. One of the main advantages of any type of gas operating system is that it tends to reduce felt recoil by dissipating some of the energy (that would be transferred into free recoil) through the stock to operate the piston system. This, in turn, cycles the action. This additional mechanical operating movement has taken a portion of the recoil away from your shoulder.

Like all gas piston operating weapons systems, these gas operating systems tend to shoot very cleanly. No powder gas is likely to be blown back into the action or the bolt, unlike the direct

impingement gas operating system of a standard AR-15. The newer gas system also tends to be more reliable than in earlier semi-auto shotguns, since they feature various forms of automatic regulation of the gas system to compensate for the use of target, full power, and magnum loads interchangeably. This is one of the features that was the hallmark of the Remington 11-87 when it was introduced.

## RECOIL OPERATED

The other type of semi-auto shotgun action is the recoil operated action, typified by Benelli in their excellent M2 Tactical shotgun. These guns are simple in terms of operating components, and there is not much to them, no gas seals or pistons etc. The operating components are basically one unit that is easy to disassemble and clean.

Actually, cleaning is not all that necessary for recoil operated shotguns, particularly the Benelli. The action stays cleaner than the gas action of a Remington 1100. I was shocked when I first fired my M2 Tactical. After firing both buckshot and slug loads for testing, then a couple rounds of sporting clays, there was no fouling in the action, maybe just a couple of small pieces of debris. I took the gun apart, in case the fouling was hiding someplace and was just not readily visible on the surface of the bolt. Nope, no crud anywhere that I could find. The hard chrome bolt was still nice and shiny. Remarkable, I thought.

Since I had it apart I decided to clean it anyway and, after cleaning the barrel and action, I just put it back together. After that I didn't fully disassemble the M2 as long as I owned it. I just wiped down the hard chromed bolt assembly with some large patches, lubed it a little and let it go at that.

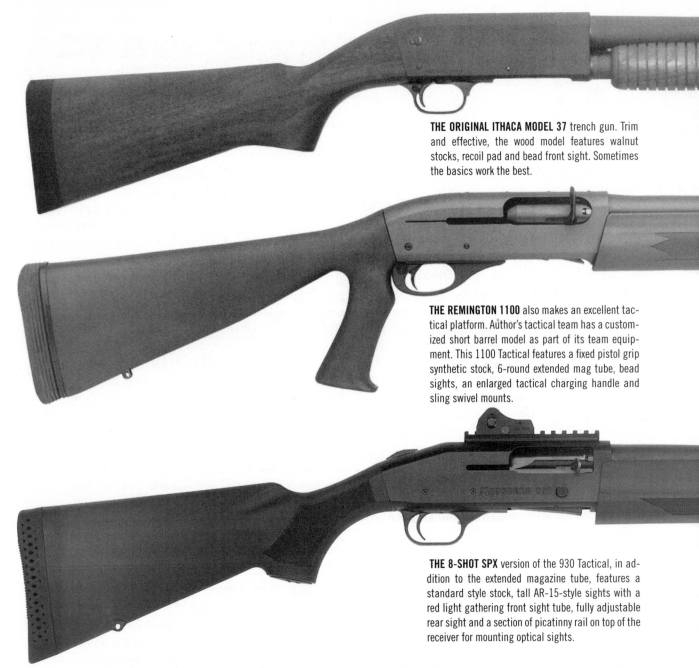

**THE ORIGINAL ITHACA MODEL 37** trench gun. Trim and effective, the wood model features walnut stocks, recoil pad and bead front sight. Sometimes the basics work the best.

**THE REMINGTON 1100** also makes an excellent tactical platform. Author's tactical team has a customized short barrel model as part of its team equipment. This 1100 Tactical features a fixed pistol grip synthetic stock, 6-round extended mag tube, bead sights, an enlarged tactical charging handle and sling swivel mounts.

**THE 8-SHOT SPX** version of the 930 Tactical, in addition to the extended magazine tube, features a standard style stock, tall AR-15-style sights with a red light gathering front sight tube, fully adjustable rear sight and a section of picatinny rail on top of the receiver for mounting optical sights.

The M2 is a finely crafted product, as are most modern Italian-made firearms in the Beretta family, which is why I love my 9mm Beretta 92. The action on that 92 guns feels like it runs on ball bearings, and I admire that type of craftsmanship. The Benelli M2 Tactical is much the same way. However, I did have two issues with it. One was slight, the other more problematic.

The first issue, the slight one, is endemic to all recoil operated shotguns, and that issue is, well, recoil. Recoil operated shotguns kick more than gas operated guns, as it is the recoil of the gun that operates to move the action. Since the M2's receiver is aluminum, it has a little less weight to soak up recoil as well. I suppose that the recoil operated shotgun should, in theory at least, have less recoil than a pump shotgun. I haven't really found that to be the case. In any case, the recoil is not a big deal, especially if you are using 2-3/4-inch 12 gauge rounds.

## ADVANTAGE OVER PUMPS

Any semi-automatic shotgun gives you one big advantage over pumps: the ability for double-tap, rapid fire shots. While I played around with my 870 pump while shooting clays for a period of time, I later switched to the M2 tactical. I could run the pump pretty good, but not like I could the auto. For serious clays competitors, there is no question; they use a semi-auto or, even faster, an over/under double barrel. A two shot limit for the double gun doesn't matter here, since in sporting clays there are only two birds thrown at any given time.

> With so many available, there is no reason to not find a tactical shotgun that's absolutely perfect for you.

Combine this capability with an extended magazine tube in a tactical shotgun and you can send a lot of lead (in California, copper) down range in a short amount of time, and in the case of a gas gun, keep reasonable control of the recoil generated by those rounds to boot.

Here's what may be the biggest advantage of a semi-auto shotgun. For those who have trouble remembering to work the action of a pump each time they want to fire it, there is no such issue with the semi-auto shotgun. Even if under stress, al that needs to be done is cycle the bolt of the semi-auto to chamber a round and cock the firing system. Then, make sure the safety is off and begin launching rounds downrange. Nothing much else to worry about.

Now it's time to get specific about makes and models of shotguns. With so many available, there is no reason to not find a tactical shotgun that's absolutely perfect for you. And if you can't find only one, buy a couple. Let's start with pump shotguns, and continue with other recent models that I have tested, handled, and evaluated.

The big factor for me, however, was the length of pull of the standard Benelli pistol grip stock. It was just too long for me. I toyed with the idea of taking it to a stock fitter and having it cut down an inch or so, but never got around to it. Recoil operated guns are also supposed to be more finicky when it comes to using low power or reduced recoil loads. My M2 always functioned very well for me with AA Trap and Skeet or with field loads and buckshot or slugs. Functioning was flawless with standard power shells of any type. I recall one or two fail-to-feeds early on with reduced recoil loads, but that issue disappeared over time.

**STOEGER'S NEW DOUBLE DEFENSE** side-by-side shotgun is a straightforward, rugged and reliable home defense shotgun. Ideal for use in tight quarters and tense situations, the Stoeger Double Defense with its traditional break-action and short, efficient design is easy to load and quick to deploy in an emergency. A double-barrel shotgun has been the defensive firearm of choice for generations, but Stoeger has added practical, up-to-date features to the "tried-and-true" double gun. The Double Defense is chambered for 2-3/4- and 3-inch shells, in either 12- or 20-gauge. The tactical-length 20-inch ported barrels feature fixed, improved cylinder chokes. The fast, single-trigger design and convenient, tang-mounted automatic safety makes the Stoeger Double Defense ideal for home security use.

# CHAPTER FOUR

# DOUBLE BARREL
## SIDE-BY-SIDE SHOTGUNS:
# MAKES AND MODELS

The selection of double barrel shotguns for tactical use is somewhat limited. Here also is one area where, if the double is your weapon of choice, you have to purchase one that was made overseas, since there are no American makers that are making side-by-side guns.

### STOEGER DOUBLE DEFENSE

Of tactical shotguns for home defense, the Stoeger (an importer, not a manufacturer) Double Defense shotgun is my top pick for several reasons. The Double Defense comes about as ready to set up tactically as you can for a double gun, with picatinny rails and Hi-Viz front sight installed, making it ready for lights and optics if you want them. The barrel is also ported to control recoil.

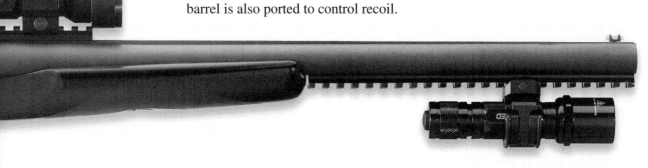

Since I wouldn't be shooting slugs out of a double, I would probably dispense with an optical sight since the Hi-Viz pipe is very "vizible" as it is, and for what you want to use this gun for it is about ideal. As I said earlier, the Double Defense is so very popular that I could not get my hands on one for testing for this book, so obviously I'm not the only one out there who thinks that the old double still has merit as a defensive weapon.

What's nice is that if you can't get your hands on a real live Double Defense, and you want a side by side double usable for home defense, there are still other options available, one right in the Stoeger lineup itself, and it's the same gun as the Double Defense, without the tactical upgrades and black paint job.

## STOEGER SINGLE TRIGGER COACH

The Brazilian-made Stoeger hammerless Single Trigger Coach Gun is my next choice, and one I actually got to test. It is listed as a specialty side-by-side on the Stoeger website, since the original Coach gun is a more historically accurate double trigger model. While the double trigger configuration may be more historically accurate for Cowboy Action Shooting where the steel targets are not attacking the shooter, double triggers are too complicated and slow for real live defensive use without a lot of practice.

The single trigger Coach Gun is available in 12 or 20 gauges with a 20-inch, un-ported barrel, in blue or nickel finishes. The nickel finish is stocked in black, and if you think a single barrel chromed 12 gauge is intimidating, imagine the effect of a side-by-side with moonlight glinting off that shiny finish.

On the standard Coach model, the barrels have fixed chokes, set up as Improved Cylinder and Modified, the first shot, right, being the Improved Cylinder-and the second shot the left Modified. This setup is designed for hunting. If I was going to build it from the ground up for defensive use, I would set it up with Improved Cylinder or Cylinder Bore chokes on both barrels. If you pay a few bucks more, you can get interchangeable screw-in chokes on the Supreme Coach Model, but for defensive use, I wouldn't bother.

The gun, which has an MSRP of $399, is nicely blued with an American Walnut stock with what can be charitably described as checkering on the grip and forend. The wood itself is actually nicely figured, and they would have been better off just skipping the checkering. I purchased mine for $349.

There is an automatic safety which needs to be disengaged after the action is opened and closed and which also cocks the internal hammers. There are extractors, not ejectors (I would prefer ejectors for rapid reloading of this gun, since it is no longer really a sporting model and you don't have to worry about capturing your spent shells in the field).

**The chamber is a three-inch, and all I've got to say is "don't" unless you upgrade to a recoil pad.**

The only sighting equipment on the solid rib is a simple and somewhat small silver bead. I would have a gunsmith install a Hi-Viz or a set of XS Express Sights in its place. Even though there is no railing, perhaps one could be installed by a competent gunsmith. If you wanted to attach a tactical light without the gunsmithing you could, very simply, put a light in the groove underneath and between both barrels and secure it with electrical tape. Take it out and shoot it and see if it holds for you. Actually it really only needs to hold in place for two shots.

The Coach Gun buttstock has no recoil pad, just a plastic buttplate. I test fired it using Remington Home Defense 2-3/4-inch loads, one shot BB, the other shot Duplex. Kids, don't try this at home without a slip-on rubber recoil pad on the thing. Better yet, get a recoil pad fitted to it. Holy smokes did that hurt-and remember, I love shooting shotguns. I have just grown

soft shooting gas guns with recoil pads. Two shots told me all
I need to know about patterning
and recoil pads, or lack thereof,
and about wanting to shoot it off
the shoulder again.

The chamber is a three-inch,
and all I've got to say is "don't"
unless you upgrade to a recoil pad. Two and
three-quarter-inch shells are plenty for this
gun.

I held dead center on the fist of the aggressor
target at seven yards average combat distance.
As expected, each barrel patterned just slightly
toward its side from the center, but both shots
struck pretty much where they were needed.

With all that being said, even if I couldn't
afford the little add-ons (except the recoil pad),
I could still pick this baby right up out of the
box and use it do defend my home and property
quite successfully. The add-ons are just niceties, not essentials. Overall I'm quite impressed
with the fit and finish of the Coach Gun and the
tightness of the action.

## SAVAGE/STEVENS 612

Another option, which I was not able to
test, is from Savage's branch product line, Stevens. Stevens doesn't have its own website, it

**THE DOUBLE DEFENSE GUN** is outfit-
ted with a green, fiber-optic front
sight and comes standard with two
Picatinny Rail accessory mounts: one
on the receiver for red-dot sights and a
second factory-installed rail under the
barrels for attaching targeting lasers
or tactical lights. All metal surfaces
are finished in matte blue and come
complete with non-reflective matte
black hardwood stock and forearm.

is merely the trade name for the
Savage line of shotguns.

The Stevens 612 Side by
Side trail gun is blued steel
wood stocked (not walnut apparently) with 20-inch barrels
in 12 or 20 gauge. The MSRP
is much higher than the Stoeger
Coach gun, at $799.95. The gun is apparently
made in Turkey. I checked on the 612 online
at Shotgun World (www.shotgunworld.com)
since I didn't actually have one to examine.
On the site, the 612 got very mixed reviews,
actually mostly bad reviews. There was one
very positive review, and it could be a matter
of some of the first guns that were imported
were not up to proper standards, with later versions being improved. If you are interested in
one, check with your local dealer or gunsmith
and see what they are saying, and examine one
for yourself. If they carry the line, ask them if
they are coming back in for repairs. But I sure
wouldn't pay $400 more for one of these over
the Stoeger in any event, as the Stoeger guns
are very well executed examples of this type
of shotgun.

# CHAPTER FIVE

# THE TACTICAL PUMP SHOTGUN:
## MAKES AND MODELS

### THE REMINGTON 870

The 870 has been the favorite of law enforcement agencies across the U.S. for many years. It's also been supported in this favored status by thousands of 870 variants that find themselves in the sporting and hunting role.

### EXPRESS MODEL

The lowest priced entry level "tactical" civilian home defense 870 is the Express Model with a 20-inch smoothbore barrel with rifle sights, parkerized finish and four round magazine capacity. No 870 is cheaper unless you find a great deal on a used blued steel 870. If you do, stay away from it if the only sighting equipment is a simple bead, unless this is absolutely all you can afford. In any event, on whatever shotgun you select, pump or otherwise, make sure the barrel is 18-20 inches in length, and remember, any barrel shorter than 18 inches on a shotgun is considered "sawed off" and illegal without a $200 federal tax stamp.

You can tell that tactical style shotguns are popular sellers by the fact that the factories are marketing the models as ready-to-go-out-of-the-box tactical shotguns, rather than leaving it up to owners to modify with aftermarket parts, as in the past. If that very basic, stripped down 870 Express isn't exciting enough for you, or doesn't have enough features, you can simply slide up the factory scale to the actual tactical line models.

## EXPRESS TACTICAL

If you are a fan of the decidedly still cool looking black gun, Remington also offers their Model 870 Express Tactical in a plain black finish, with the a six round extended magazine tube, XS Ghost ring sights, the new Remington Extended Ported Standoff-Style TAC Choke, and standard style (which I prefer on most guns) synthetic stock. To me a pistol grip on many, not all, shotguns, just takes away from the sleekness in terms of handling the weapon. If the pistol grip stock was such a great handling aid, wouldn't competition shooters use it on their shotguns? If you like pistol grip stocks, and they make you happy (and don't interfere with operational capability), go for it. The Express Tactical is also available in a Tactical Grey finish model, with a bead sight instead of Ghost Rings or rifle sights.

## EXPRESS TACTICAL A-TACS

Next up in that tactical line is the 870 Express

**THE 870 DESERT RECON** is an 870 Magnum with pistol grip and desert camouflage on the fixed stock and forend. The steel portions are finished in a flat dark earth color on the barrel and receiver and the new Remington Tactical Choke is affixed to the end of the barrel. There is a bead sight and sling swivel mounts.

Tactical A-TACS camouflage model. Featuring a six round extended magazine tube, the A-TACS camouflage pattern on all but the blued magazine tube (nice touch, making it suitable as a hunting gun as well), XS sight Ghost Ring tritium sighting system, 18-1/2-inch barrel with the Remington TAC Choke, picatinny rail on the upper receiver to allow for the mounting of electronic optics, Super Cell Recoil Pad, swing swivel studs front and rear, and a pistol grip stock. This is a nice variation of tactical that includes most features sought in a tactical gun.

Camouflage on anything is the "new black," particularly for military/SWAT usage. When viewed at night under Generation 4 night vision devices, anything colored black shows up as an iridescent sheen. That's why you see fewer tactical teams wearing all black for uniform or armor colors. Weapons colors need to change too. I like the A-TACS camo pattern in particular. It should be usable in a wide variety of situations and locales, woods, field, broken terrain, desert and urban, it seems like it should work well for all.

## TAC DESERT RECON

If you are a fan of the desert tan color style – okay, desert tan is also the new black – there is the Remington 870 TAC Desert Recon. The TAC Recon features an OD or Desert Sand-type color on the receiver and barrel, while the extended magazine tube is left black, and there

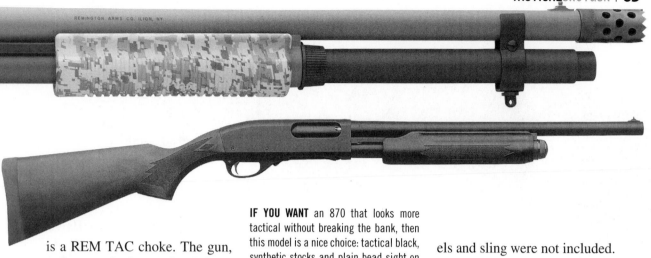

is a REM TAC choke. The gun, unfortunately has a bead front sight, and really, the term Desert "Recon" implies that this a long range type weapon, which a bead sighted shotgun clearly is not.

**IF YOU WANT** an 870 that looks more tactical without breaking the bank, then this model is a nice choice: tactical black, synthetic stocks and plain bead sight on an 18-inch barrel. It is good to go as-is for basic home and property (range limited by the bead sight) defense, and is still customizable by the owner.

## POLICE MAGNUM TACTICAL

I received a 870 Police Magnum Tactical from Remington to work with. For those of you that want a stock Tactical gun without all the additional custom shop enhancements, and thus without the increased price, this is a version to look at.

The Police Magnum tactical features a three-inch chamber, which is plenty of versatility. It has the basic black rather than greenish, parkerized finish which isn't rust proof, only slightly rust resistant, and it can be scratched off rather easily. Use due care in treating of the surface with light coats of protective oil.

There is a nice set of ghost ring sights with a white front non-tritium bead. The plain bright white front is good size and is very eye catching, even in low level light. The Police Magnum has an extended six-shot magazine and a Remington factory pistol grip stock with reasonable length of pull and good recoil pad. The really big addition in this package is the inclusion of a Surefire incandescent light forend. Nice. If I had my preference on the Remington Police Magnum, and their factory stock was short enough, I would go with a standard style, rather than a pistol grip.

Finally, there are sling swivel mounts in place on the barrel band and stock, but the actual swiv-els and sling were not included.

This package has about everything that a tactical shotgun user would want in a tactical shotgun that's not absolutely top end. There are a few things missing, such as a side saddle shell carrier for spare ammo. But here is the great thing about the Remington 870 shotgun series: There are more parts and accessories available for it than any other shotgun. It is sort of the AR-15 of the shotgun world in terms of accessories. No matter what version of the 870 you have, you can turn it into the tactical shotgun of your dreams. If you buy less common or foreign made pumps, especially those made in Turkey, there is just not much you can do with them once they come from the factory and reach our shores. If you want to have the best level of versatility, quality and service, stick with guns that are made in the U.S. for your tactical armament, and that includes shotguns by companies like Benelli and Beretta.

## SPECIAL PURPOSE MARINE MAGNUM

The Special Purpose Marine Magnum is another excellent 870 variation, designed for use in corrosive, saltwater-type environments. It would be good in any high humidity environment. The gun, while not constructed of stainless steel, is entirely coated in electroless nickel for corrosion resistance, which gives it a stainless steel appearance. The Marine Magnum comes not only with sling swivels installed, but also with a sling in the box to install on the gun.

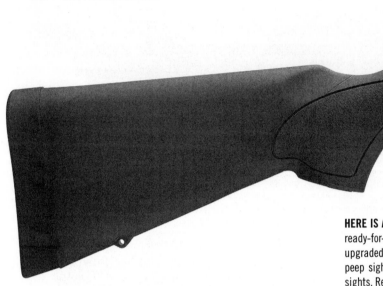

**HERE IS AN 870** that is set up with about everything you need in a ready-for-anything tactical gun. The Express Tactical starts with an upgraded, specially padded overmolded style stock, ghost ring type peep sights, a receiver mounted strip of rail for mounting optical sights, Remington's external tactical choke and sling swivel mounts. The 870 Tactical is also available without the ghost ring peep sights and receiver rail strip.

The only failing on the Marine Magnum that I can see is, as with several other Remington variants, a lack of actual sights, with only a bead perched on the end of the barrel. In open water, you will need the range of a rifled slug, and the sights to go with it. It should have rifle sights, Ghost Ring or Open, and maybe the rail for an optic mount.

Not only does the Marine Magnum make a great boat defense gun, but it would also serve well in campers, pickups, RVs or anyplace else where the standard of gun care might not be as high. Another plus, the nickel plating sure would catch your attention if it was pointed your way.

## 870 HOME DEFENSE

The Remington 870 Home Defense is another variant no longer catalogued by Remington. A plain black shotgun with synthetic stock, it's offered with an extended magazine tube and a bead sight, very basic and no frills. Even though it's not on Remington's website or in the catalogue, at the time of this writing there were still new Home Defense 870s available at my favorite gun emporium, and on sale for $299.99. Good bargain, just get a sight upgrade.

If you were only going to use the this shotgun for close range home defense, a bead sight might suffice, but there are other brands and models available in the same price range that have better sighting equipment, affording more versatility.

With the time-honored 870, options, accesso-ries, modifications and a load of different models abound. One thing is certain, you cannot go wrong with an 870 and its traditional all-steel construction. For many of us, it's like working with an old friend.

Which brings me to what is considered by many to be the ultimate upgrade of the Remington 870 platform, and that is the Wilson Combat/Scattergun Technologies Shotgun line, which also includes the "Remington Steal™" program that we will take a look at in a bit.

## WILSON COMBAT/SCATTERGUN TECHNOLOGIES

Wilson Combat, which started out with and continues to excel in custom 1911 semi-automatic pistols, took over the Scattergun Technologies company a number of years ago. Scattergun Technologies was and is famous for taking the basic Remington 870 shotgun and adding some touches to turn it into a really outstanding combat gun, ready to fulfill any mission a shotgun is capable of carrying out. Wilson Combat has added its own expertise and production methods to those originated by the Scattergun Technologies company to produce an outstanding new weapon.

Wilson Combat was kind enough to provide me with one of their "Standard Model" shotguns, which is quite the misnomer since there really

**THE BORDER PATROL** Model from Wilson Combat is in use by the Border Patrol by the thousands-hence its name. Featuring the proprietary Wilson Combat Armor-Tuff finish, the Border Patrol Model features a plain synthetic fore end, users choice of several stock types, sidesaddle spare ammo carrier on the receiver, Jumbo Head safety, Trak Lok ghost ring sights with available tritium front sight, and heavy duty sling mounts. Rock solid reliability, durability and enhanced tactical features are the reason the Border Patrol went with Wilson Combat/Scattergun Technologies.

isn't anything standard about it. It is head and shoulders above an off-the-rack basic Remington 870, which is the gun they start with.

The first thing that I really like about the Standard Model is that the metal surfaces of the entire shotgun, not just the barrel and receiver, are coated in the Wilson Combat Armor-Tuff® finish, the same finish Wilson uses on their fine line of pistols and now their line of AR-15s as well. I ordered mine in their OD green color, and the gun looks sharp. And, after having seen parkerized 870s react badly to moisture and develop surface rust, it's nice to know that the Armor-Tuff finish eliminates that issue without making the shotgun

stand out like bright electroless nickel would do. The OD color would be great for rural patrol in general and deep woodlands searches in particular. With this color finish, it would also make a fine deep woods deer or survival gun.

The barrel is 18-inch cylinder bored, which is absolutely the most versatile of any shotgun choke for defensive use (in a non-interchangeable setup). The 18-inch length allows the shotgun to be purchased by civilians without the need for a federal tax stamp. Wilson does make the Professional Model for law enforcement agencies with a 14-inch barrel with all other specifications being the same.

**THE WILSON COMBAT PROFESSIONAL** and Standard both feature a Surefire tactical light forend as part of their package.

Chamber length for both guns is three-inch. It's really not, in my way of thinking, a problem to not have a 3-1/2-inch chamber. How many of us actually fire, or want to fire, that monstrous round? I'm good with 2-3/4-inch, and in big bear country, 3-inch.

Also included on the professional model is a black synthetic standard butt stock and a 6-volt SureFire Tactical Light foregrip with an 11,000 candlepower Xenon bulb weaponlight. There is an optional shorter buttstock available along with a Knoxx SpecOps Recoil Reducing Stock or AR M4-type collapsible stock. My sample came with the standard length stock.

In addition, the Standard Model's other features include a jumbo-head safety, a multi-purpose tactical sling, a buttstock sling swivel and a rigid magazine tube front sling mount. Sights are the excellent adjustable TRAK-LOCK® Ghost Ring rear sight paired with a ramp-type front sight with a tritium self-luminous insert. The jumbo head safety is a very nice feature and makes operation of the safety much more sure. There is no need to look for the safety, feel is

enough. A sidesaddle spare ammo carrier is mounted on the left side of the receiver, and to me is much preferred over any stock mounted ammo carrying device. The TRAK-LOCK sights are very quick and more than precise enough.

## The Standard model was dead-on accurate with both slugs and shot.

I had no problem breaking clay birds off a manual thrower with the Standard Model, even when shooting the shotgun one-handed. The only problem with the standard model for me has to do with me. I found that the Surefire forend was too short for me to reach comfortably with the standard stock, due mainly to the deteriorated condition of both my shoulders. For a rather large buddy of mine with the Ohio State Highway Patrol, the fit was perfect, and he handled the

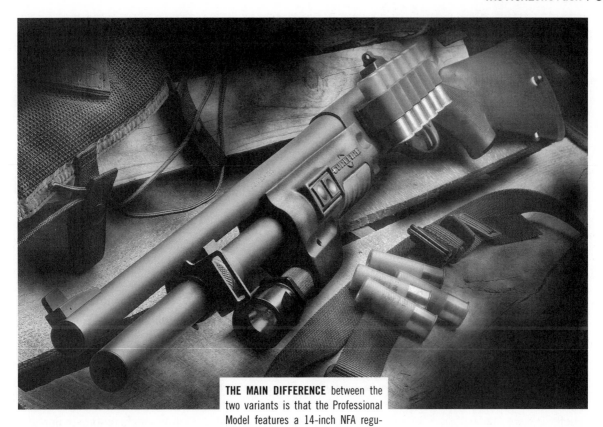

**THE MAIN DIFFERENCE** between the two variants is that the Professional Model features a 14-inch NFA regulated barrel, and the Standard (really a misnomer, it makes it sound like this is a stripped down model) features a non-regulated 18-inch barrel.

Standard model with ease. I was afraid I'd have to fight him to get it back, he liked it that much, and he's a lot bigger than me. When I handed it to him at the start of the shoot, I believe his first words were something like "come to daddy!" I would have fared much better with the short stock option, or an M4 adjustable stock pulled in fully.

Functioning of the Standard model was very slick and was dead-on accurate with both slugs and shot. Remington Reduced Recoil 8-pellet buckshot and rifled slugs were used in the testing, and were a perfect match for the Wilson Standard. These loads are the standard street issue for the State Patrol, and not practice rounds. Combined with the weight of an all steel shotgun like the Remington 870, recoil was truly negligible.

Speaking of steel, or should I say "steal," Wilson has a program called the Remington Steal program, where you send them your old and worn 870 and they convert it to a modern fighting shotgun, including adding a 3-inch chamber if necessary, in the pattern of their Border Patrol model. Using factory Remington parts, they replace worn or outdated parts that were on your gun, like old-style magazine tube followers and spring, as well as old-style shell feeds. New Remington factory synthetic stocks are installed. The cost is very reasonable as you are supplying your own shotgun. On the basic package, the metal is newly parkerized throughout, although all Armor-Tuff colors (green, black, tan, and gray) are available.

If you are looking for the absolute cadillac of fighting pump shotguns, then one of Wilson Combat's Scattergun Technologies 12 gauges is what you want.

By the way, I toured the Wilson Combat factory this past summer, spending three days at their facilities as part of a writers conference. Their production system, standards and attention to detail have got to be producing some of the finest firearms manufacturing or transformational work on the planet. With Wilson Combat, it might seem a little pricey, but you are truly get-

ting what you pay for.

## REMINGTON'S 887
## NITRO MAG TACTICAL

This is the future of not only the Remington pump action shotgun line, but for many other manufacturers as well. I ran across the Tactical model at my gun store one day while awaiting some other merchandise. It was love at first touch.

This gun shoulders like perfection, is very lightweight, is armor coated for near indestructibility, and has a great green Hi-Viz front sight pipe that fits perfectly in the u-notch rear sight trough. There is a top receiver picatinny rail for mounting optical sights, a segment of picatinny rail on the barrel band on the right side, and a sling swivel mount on the left side.

The forend, which is longer than most, gives me perfect positioning for my reach and the ability to work the action without taking my hand off of it. On normal-length stocks with a shorter standard type forend, I have to work the slide and chamber the round, then move my supporting hand towards the rear of the receiver for support while firing, then I would move my hand back up on the forend again. With the 887 Nitro Mag, my hands both stay in the same place.

I took the gun home for a closer look. The 887 Tactical was on sale for $439 with all the features I just described. When I got it out of the box I immediately noticed its smooth operating action. It worked off twin bars like the 870, but the 887 is definitely not a made-over 870. The bolt and construction of the actions is much different.

The standard straight stock is fitted with a soft recoil pad which Remington calls Super Cell. The entire gun is covered with a polymer armor that Remington calls ArmorLokt™. ArmorLokt is a great name for the coating, and it gives the 887 a decidedly brawny appearance without the weight it appears it should have (average weight is 6-7/8 pounds). ArmorLokt is unique in appearance, yet totally protects the gun.

The position of the slide release has been made totally ambidextrous by putting it in the center front of the trigger guard. It also has a larger polymer head. The safety remains in the same position as it is on the 870 and is the same

> ## If it sounds like I am enamored of the Remington 887, it is true.

size.

One thing I didn't notice right away because Remington hides it in the same chunk of packaging as the safety cable lock was the new ported, extended Remington TAC-choke (which wasn't mounted on the gun in the store display rack), which is threaded to screw in and out of the muzzle. The porting helps hide muzzle flash as well as muzzle rise, and the sharp crenelations at the end of the choke allow it to be used to "stand off"

**HERE'S ANOTHER GUN** that is not thought of as a tactical or home defense shotgun, but it certainly can serve as one. It's designed for hunting and shipped with a 22-inch turkey barrel and a 28 field barrel. The 22-inch barrel is a little long for interior movement, but the 887 Nitro Mag is an outstanding platform. Perhaps by purchasing a package like this you can more readily justify your need for a new shotgun (to your spouse) since it can also be used in a variety of hunting/shooting situations.

a door lock in order to use a "shot lock" cartridge for door breaching. Since the 887 will handle 2-3/4-inch, 3-inch, and 3-1/2-inch magnums, the TAC choke may come in handy. There is an extended tactical magazine that gives seven rounds of total magazine capacity with 2-3/4-inch shells rounding out the package. I also noted that the forend swells slightly in width near the receiver, and supports nicely in the hand.

I couldn't wait the get this baby to the range, and it just so happened that the very night I got it was our second night of police academy shotgun training, which for us includes teaching the cadets to hit clay birds off a basic thrower. I brought along an excellent Aimpoint™ Comp 2 red dot sight (which is the older, larger version of the Aimpoint sight system, but it is still absolutely an excellent sight. If you have one, there is no need to upgrade it, hang on to it).

That night, I took half of the cadets to shoot clay birds while the other half did the actual qualification course mandated by the state using buckshot and slugs. I started out shooting the 887 without the Aimpoint. This is a soft shooting pump, and the Super Cell recoil pad definitely makes a difference in felt recoil. The setup with the Hi-Viz front sight and the u-trough rear is excellent, with green being a great color choice. I had no problem breaking birds and "batting cleanup" for the birds that the

cadets missed.

Next I mounted the Aimpoint. Was I ever in for a treat! I had never fired a shotgun with a red-dot or any other optical sight on it before. There still aren't a lot of tactical shotguns (yet) with picattiny rails mounted on them for optics. They should be available on every one of them. When I fired up Aimpoint, it was dead on, even though its normal duty station is on an M4 carbine. When the birds where thrown I just put the red dot on the red bird and "blam." It worked very well. Remember with a red-dot or similar sight, there is no front and rear portion of the sighting system to hold in alignment with the target. Just put the red dot on what you want to hit and roll the trigger (not jerk, yank or squeeze it, roll it) back smoothly. The trigger on the 887 is also good, especially considering that it's a tactical gun.

I turned the gun over to one of the female cadets who was having trouble aligning the rifle sight system on the clay birds with an 870. She immediately began busting each and every bird that was thrown. As a trainer, I had no problem letting her do this for the clay bird segment of shotgun shooting as it was a training and familiarization. She used the standard 870 to qualify on the buckshot/slug state-mandated portion of the training. Breaking clay birds using the Aimpoint was a confidence builder. It lessened the trepidation about operating the shotgun.

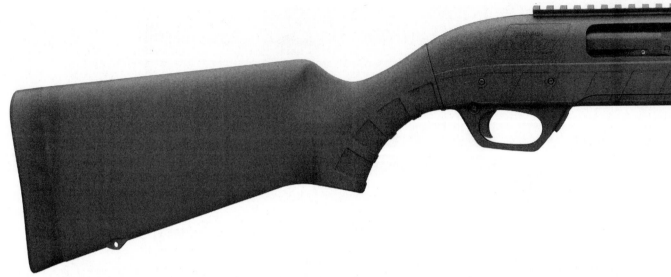

If it sounds like I am enamored of the Remington 887, it is true. Two instructors from other agencies, one large and one small, are both planning on getting testing/evaluation samples of the 887 to replace their 870s. The gun is capable of doing a bit of everything, and Remington makes it in a variety of sporting versions. Patrol work, dynamic entry, perimeter, home defense, three-gun, ranch gun in the truck – all with little or no maintenance due to the Armor-Lokt finish – makes the 887 a real winner.

### ITHACA MODEL 37: A BLAST FROM THE PAST IS "BORN AGAIN HARD"

While I have had little experience with Ithaca firearms, I am always saddened when an American company, particularly an American firearms company, goes out of business. Such was the case with the Ithaca Firearms Company, formerly of Ithaca New York, and now in my neck of the woods, in Upper Sandusky Ohio. One of the few Ithaca shotguns I ever handled was the old 20 gauge Model 37 Stakeout. At one time however, the Ithaca 37 was at the top of the heap with the Remington 870 in certain parts of the country as the primo police pump gun. Agencies like LAPD come to mind, and there are still plenty of Model 37s in police service today, not to mention all the much loved 37s at use in the gamefield.

Although some started to believe these guns were going to end up as collectors items, while Ithaca changed hands not so successfully through the mid 1990s and early 2000s, the company is now solidly in place as the Ithaca Gun Company.

If you are not familiar with the Ithaca Model 37 (first on the market in 1937, and the oldest pump design still in standard production and use on the market, and still American made), it has some unique features. Like the Remington 870, the receiver is milled from a solid billet of steel. Unlike the Remington, or any other current production pump for that matter, the ejection of shells is directly from the bottom. This bottom ejection is a nice touch if you are a left handed shooter, or if you are standing in a tight line at the range. You aren't going to get hit by ejected empty shells. There is no bolt visible on either side of the receiver, it's solid, which, in my way of thinking, helps keep the action cleaner with less chance of exterior debris being introduced into the action. The 37 was a popular military combat shotgun during several wars, and acquitted itself very well in WWII.

The Model 37 was developed, like almost every other tactical pump shotgun, as a sporting and hunting gun. While Ithaca has the Model 37 in a number of very nice traditional sporting styles, they haven't ignored the burgeoning tactical shotgun market. Their reborn Model 37, produced with CNC machining tools, which is what makes the manufacture of the receiver and other complex parts on these shores affordable and precise, is available in several different configurations of tactical.

For this review, I requested and received a Model 37 with traditional walnut stocks and an 18-1/2-inch fixed barrel with adjustable rifle sights. The chamber is three-inch, and the barrel is cylinder bore. Of all the shotguns I tested, the Model 37 was the biggest surprise. It is, without a doubt, my favorite shotgun of the entire lot. This thing is simply "old school classic."

There is a black Pachmayr™ Decelerator rubber recoil pad on the buttstock. It also features front and rear sling swivel attachment points. A modern touch on the adjustable rifle sights is that the front sight is a red Hi-Viz, while the rear has green Hi-Viz pipes on either side of the sight assembly, giving a nice, bright, three dot configuration. The slide release is on the front of the trigger guard, like the Remington 870, but on the right side, which makes it easier for a right handed shooter to use. The safety is a pushbutton crossbolt at the rear of the triggerguard. The trigger pull is a nice four to six-pound affair and very smooth. If you hold the trigger down and fast cycle the action, it will fire as fast as you can pump it, without moving your finger off and on the trigger.

The walnut "pump handle" is really like a pump handle. A small walnut cylinder, it has 15 horizontal grooves that run the circumference of the cylinder. Unlike newer designs, there is only one action bar, rather than twin action bars, on the left side of the receiver. It has been said that a single action bar is an inferior design, that it can

**THIS IS, IN THE AUTHOR'S OPINION,** the best, ready to go from the box, reasonably priced, tactical shotgun on the market. Pretty much impervious to damage due to its Armor-Lokt™ construction and equipped with all the standard and extra features that make a great tactical gun, the price of the Remington 887 is also tactically sound on your wallet. The author purchased his on sale for $439. Note the long forend which makes operation comfortable for all, the short rail strip at the barrel band, the extended magazine tube, rail strip on top of the receiver, solid rib with green Hi-Viz front sight tube and external Remington Tactical Choke.

bind and is not as smooth as the twin action bars found on other designs. I have not found this to be the case.

There is no picatinny railing, which makes this again much more of a riot or home defense gun in the most traditional of senses. There is the option of a synthetic stock or a bead front sight. You know how I feel about bead sights, and synthetic stocks are a sacrilege on a gun like this.

The standard magazine capacity is four rounds, with a seven round extended magazine tube available. For me, the seven round tube takes away from the appearance and the balance of the gun.

The features of the Model 37, when compared to the other tactical shotguns I tested or that are listed in the book, don't seem to offer enough to put it at the number one position when compared to the other guns, and I really didn't plan to declare what I felt was a number one gun. But the Model 37 really did it for me. The following reasons explain why the Model 37 is my number one choice:

1. The Model 37 is an outstanding, retro piece of firearms history. Its plain walnut stock harkens back to the "Golden Age" of policing, of police departments filled with WWII and Korean War Veterans, of prison guards in watchtowers, of TV shows like ADAM 12 and Dragnet, of battlefields and jungles in WWII, Korea and Vietnam. Even though it may not have been heavily seen in all those places, it speaks of that era.

**THE ITHACA 37** Defense Pump (trench gun) features trim dimensions, Hi-Viz adjustable sights, walnut stocks and rubber recoil pad. Out of all the guns tested, it is the author's favorite shotgun due to its retro nature.

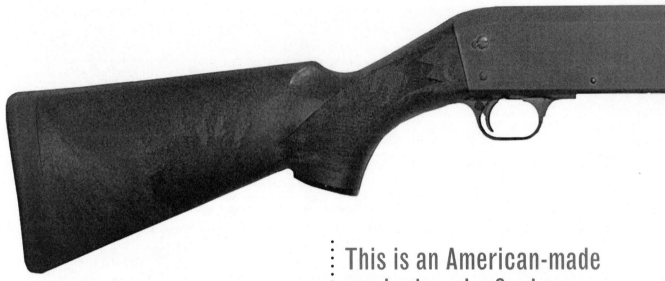

2. This is an American-made product, using modern CNC manufacturing techniques, and is a finely machined piece of firearms manufacturing, right down to the magazine tube endcap and sling swivel attachment point. It speaks of attention to detail not seen in mass produced weapons of modern manufacturing.

3. The design of the Model 37 itself is very trim in terms of handling; it's a 12 that handles like a 20. Working the action just feels "precision." When I got the gun at the gun shop, it drew a lot of interest from the sales staff. One salesman explained that his very first shotgun was a 16 gauge Model 37, so the new Model 37 evoked a lot of fond memories of his youth. Others who never handled a Model 37 were impressed by the feel of the cycling of the action. Weight with the walnut stock is seven pounds, giving it excellent swingability and pointability, which is critical in multiple target combat situations.

4. As a design that almost disappeared from modern manufacture, the 37 is sure to be the center of attention at any shooting range. With an MSRP of $539, it is a very affordable center of attention. While not truly "tactical" in appearance, it is certainly viable in home defense, even though it doesn't have a place to mount a tactical light. While a tactical light is a great advantage in many defensive situations, we have, after all, managed to get by without them for many years.

> This is an American-made product, and a finely-machined piece of firearms manufacturing, right down to the magazine tube endcap and sling swivel attachment point.

Don't let the inability to easily mount a light deter you from getting a gun that can be used for a variety of tasks. The Model 37 Defense Gun would make a fine deer gun or camp defense gun. Get a shotgun stock nylon elastic shell carrier to hold spare rounds in place. Receiver mounted holders aren't readily available for Model 37s, and, in any case, they would detract from the retro look of the gun.

These reasons for my number one pick may be somewhat esoteric. Ultimately, shooting the Model 37 bore no surprises. It functioned smoothly as expected, in fact as smooth as the gun looks. If these are the qualities that you enjoy in any of your firearms, the Model 37 just might be for you.

### MOSSBERG MODEL 590 A1 TACTICAL

Here is the pump shotgun that fits me perfectly, even better than the Remington 887 NitroMag, and the only pistol grip shotgun that I

**THE ITHACA 37**, a design that hasn't been stuck in 1937, has clearly been upgraded to compete with "newer" designs. The Defense Synthetic version features an 8-shot extended magazine tube, synthetic stocks and bead front sight. The Model 37 is characterized by having the ultimate in easy "swingability" as well as a smooth operating action that limits dirt and debris to only one entry point, through its bottom loading/ejecting port.

**SPEAKING OF UPGRADES**, the Model 37 is available with one of the best shotgun stocks available, the M4 AR-15 collapsible stock. Also featuring the 8-shot mag tube and brass bead sight, this model will easily handle body size variations between shooters, as well as those shooters wearing body armor. The slight downward angle of this M4 stock should somewhat reduce felt recoil.

like: the Mossberg 590 A1 tactical pump. This is an outstanding example of a traditional pump, based on the original and long-serving Mossberg 500 series. It was previously only available in law enforcement and military models and is part of Mossberg's extensive Special Purpose line of shotguns.

What makes this gun work so well is the use of the M4 carbine six-position buttstock complete with M16A2 pistol grip. With the M4 grip collapsed to its smallest length, it is a perfect fit. In addition to the stock configuration, the 590 A1 I tested came equipped with three-dot, non-adjustable, non-luminous front and rear sights. Very solid. The only complaint I have is that the rear notch is a tad too wide for the front, and I would prefer the ability to regulate the sights for full power or 3-inch magnum loads. The magazine capacity of this particular version is five rounds.

I had never worked with Mossbergs prior to writing this book, so I don't profess to have as much familiarity with them as I do the Remington 870, but I can tell you I really liked this gun,

and will probably purchase it to keep after this book is completed. Like I mentioned earlier, the handling of this gun is quick, and it feels more like a 20 gauge pump than a 12.

What I also noticed about it was the recoil, or lack thereof. I had it at the range the week before I had the Remington 887 out there. I also brought a Mossberg gas operated semi-automatic 930, a bigger, heavier gun with standard stock (more about that in the semi-automatic section of the book). As I got buckshot out to test both guns, Federal full power 9-pellet 00 Tactical, I expected a bigger, gas operated gun with an actual recoil pad to shoot with less perceived recoil than a smaller, lighter pump shotgun. I was surprised to find that the perceived recoil of the 590 A1 was less than that of the 930! Actually I was shocked how I got thumped by the 930 over the 590 using the same exact loads.

The stock on the 590 A1 is angled sharply downward away from the receiver, and not straight back like it would be on an AR-15 M4 due to the design of the receiver. Remember, a

**THE DEFENSE TACTICAL** can also be had with the 5-round magazine tube, excellent Hi-Viz type fully adjustable rifle sights and M4 stock. An easy-handling, quick responding combination.

sporting design had to be adapted to a military part that was originally never designed to be on a shotgun. So I'm speculating that some of the free recoil energy is being dispersed straight back into nothing, with a lesser part of it being sent downward through the stock. We've all heard that straight stocks on guns cause it to "kick more," right? That's the only way I can explain it. I hope that's plausible, but even if it's not, I'm sticking with it.

> ## Mossberg has got to be at the top of the pile when it comes to model selection and availability, and that's just for the pump guns.

Mossbergs (all except the X12 Taser Shotgun) have a sliding safety on the rear of the receiver. It took just a little bit of familiarization to be comfortable with it as compared to the push-button triggerguard safety on the 870. The main reason is that I have always worked my law enforcement shotguns out of Condition Three, and almost never actually engaged the safety during training or use in the field. I just plan on leaving the safety off during all usage. I also had been taught at an early age and in Boy Scout shooting programs that safeties, particularly crossbolt type safeties on long guns, were unreliable and should never be trusted or counted on, so I always kept an empty chamber unless actually shooting. In police work, the safety position shouldn't be a big issue. I worry more about where the slide release is than the safety, and on the Mossberg, the slide release button is on the left rear of the triggerguard, rather than the left front. The A2 pistol grip on this particular model slightly obstructs (very slightly) the release button and it took a little while to get used to it, but it was also no big problem. The entire weapon has a parkerized finish, including the sights.

The 590 A1 also worked well for smaller statured females in my academy. They found it easier to work with and/or better for them than the 870 Express magnums we use. They also felt there was less recoil than with the Remington 870.

The construction and setup of the Mossberg feels solid, and it is the only brand to have passed military spec requirements to become part of our defense inventory, so there has to be something going for it. If anything, it is priced on average about $100 less per copy than similar Remingtons, and it is a U.S.-made piece, which is remarkable for a price range that competes with Turkish-made guns.

**NOTE THE TWO GREEN** fiber optics on either side of the sight notch on the excellent rear fully adjustable Hi-Viz sight on this Ithaca Model 37. The front sight is a fiber optic contrasting red.

**NOTE THE COLLAPSIBLE M4** Carbine stock attachment at the rear of the Model 37 reciever.

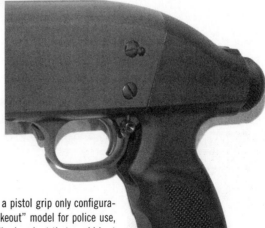

**THE DEFENSE SYNTHETIC** with 5-round magazine tube, rifle sights and M4 stock.

**THIS ITHACA MODEL 37** sports a red fiber optic front sight.

**THE ITHACA MODEL 37** is available in a pistol grip only configuration, similar to the old 20 gauge "Stakeout" model for police use, but now in 12 gauge. This is a specialized variant that would best be used for door breaching, or as an absolute emergency hideout gun. This specialization limits the utility of your tactical shotgun, regardless of brand.

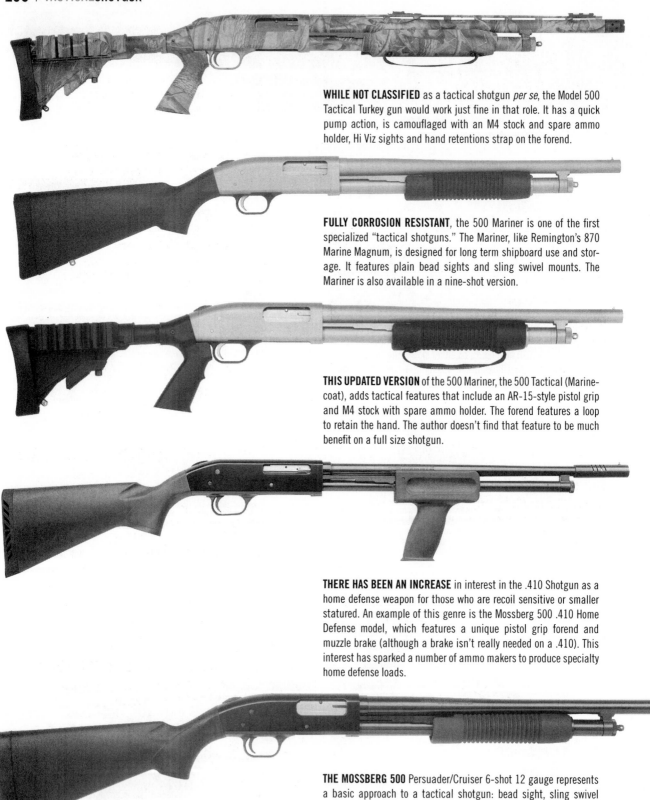

**WHILE NOT CLASSIFIED** as a tactical shotgun *per se*, the Model 500 Tactical Turkey gun would work just fine in that role. It has a quick pump action, is camouflaged with an M4 stock and spare ammo holder, Hi Viz sights and hand retentions strap on the forend.

**FULLY CORROSION RESISTANT**, the 500 Mariner is one of the first specialized "tactical shotguns." The Mariner, like Remington's 870 Marine Magnum, is designed for long term shipboard use and storage. It features plain bead sights and sling swivel mounts. The Mariner is also available in a nine-shot version.

**THIS UPDATED VERSION** of the 500 Mariner, the 500 Tactical (Marinecoat), adds tactical features that include an AR-15-style pistol grip and M4 stock with spare ammo holder. The forend features a loop to retain the hand. The author doesn't find that feature to be much benefit on a full size shotgun.

**THERE HAS BEEN AN INCREASE** in interest in the .410 Shotgun as a home defense weapon for those who are recoil sensitive or smaller statured. An example of this genre is the Mossberg 500 .410 Home Defense model, which features a unique pistol grip forend and muzzle brake (although a brake isn't really needed on a .410). This interest has sparked a number of ammo makers to produce specialty home defense loads.

**THE MOSSBERG 500** Persuader/Cruiser 6-shot 12 gauge represents a basic approach to a tactical shotgun: bead sight, sling swivel mounts, black color and six shots.

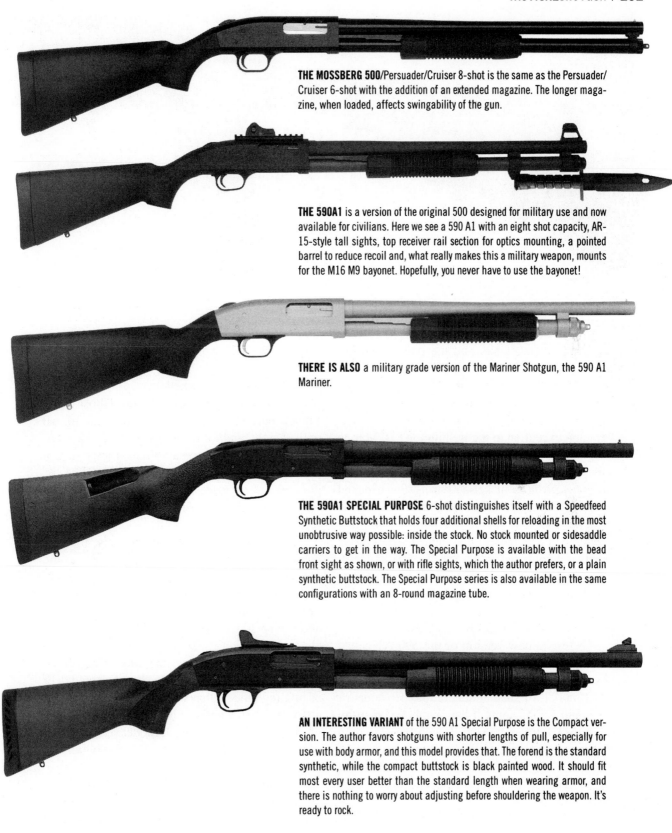

**THE MOSSBERG 500**/Persuader/Cruiser 8-shot is the same as the Persuader/Cruiser 6-shot with the addition of an extended magazine. The longer magazine, when loaded, affects swingability of the gun.

**THE 590A1** is a version of the original 500 designed for military use and now available for civilians. Here we see a 590 A1 with an eight shot capacity, AR-15-style tall sights, top receiver rail section for optics mounting, a pointed barrel to reduce recoil and, what really makes this a military weapon, mounts for the M16 M9 bayonet. Hopefully, you never have to use the bayonet!

**THERE IS ALSO** a military grade version of the Mariner Shotgun, the 590 A1 Mariner.

**THE 590A1 SPECIAL PURPOSE** 6-shot distinguishes itself with a Speedfeed Synthetic Buttstock that holds four additional shells for reloading in the most unobtrusive way possible: inside the stock. No stock mounted or sidesaddle carriers to get in the way. The Special Purpose is available with the bead front sight as shown, or with rifle sights, which the author prefers, or a plain synthetic buttstock. The Special Purpose series is also available in the same configurations with an 8-round magazine tube.

**AN INTERESTING VARIANT** of the 590 A1 Special Purpose is the Compact version. The author favors shotguns with shorter lengths of pull, especially for use with body armor, and this model provides that. The forend is the standard synthetic, while the compact buttstock is black painted wood. It should fit most every user better than the standard length when wearing armor, and there is nothing to worry about adjusting before shouldering the weapon. It's ready to rock.

I mentioned earlier some of the tactical variants that are available, and the ones I will describe don't include all models of the similar Model 500, from whence the 590 sprang. So let's take a look at a few of those.

First is the 590 A1 Mariner. Similar in concept and execution to the Remington 870 Marine Magnum, the Mariner is a five-shot 12 gauge pump with synthetic stocks and what appears to be an electroless nickel-appearing finish called Marinecoat® on all the metal surfaces of the weapon. Like the Marine Magnum, the Mariner is equipped with only a bead sight. There is also a 590 that is equipped with a Speedfeed® standard-style stock that holds a spare four rounds of ammo internally. Plain-stocked versions are available with bead sights, as well as variants with the same configuration and Ghost Ring sights.

There is a new version of the 590 A1 called The Compact. It has a distinctly shorter and overall smaller buttstock. It would appear to be a great model for smaller statured homeowners or cops, but I don't think it has as much versatility as an M4 stocked version. If you have a youth that wants to grow into their shotgun, and any of the 590 A1 Special Purpose models should make fine deer guns, then the M4-stocked variant may be an ideal solution.

There is also a new adjustable trigger model with a unique weight-saving fluted barrel, a nine-shot M4-stocked model (I think you would lose some of that "20 gauge feel" I described earlier with that extra mag-tube length, especially when you add the weight of shells).

There is a new variant with Ghost Ring Sights, ported barrel, picatinny top rail for an optical sight, and for those really close-range encounters in really desperate times, the provision for mounting an M9 (AR-15) bayonet. The list goes on and on, there are three nine-shot variants with bead sights, Ghost Ring sights, or Speed-feed stocks.

Without going into all the models, the 500 possesses at least as many tactical variants as the 590 series. There are a number of pistol-grip-only models, Model 97 Winchester trench gun style ventilated metal handguards, nine-shot models, and even a 20 gauge model with a stand off muzzle brake. I didn't take a final count of all the possible tactical variants that Mossberg offers, and that doesn't even include short barreled deer or hunting models that would qualify as tactical-adaptable, but Mossberg has got to be at the top of the pile when it comes to model selection and availability, and that's just for the pump guns.

## BENELLI NOVA AND SUPER NOVA

The design of the Benelli Nova, which I first reviewed in July of 2009, was at the time a radical departure from the standard Mossberg or Rem-

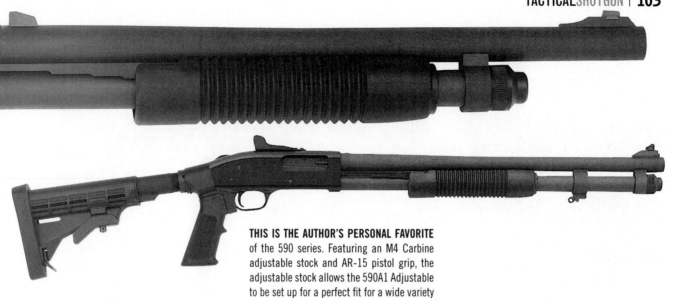

**THIS IS THE AUTHOR'S PERSONAL FAVORITE** of the 590 series. Featuring an M4 Carbine adjustable stock and AR-15 pistol grip, the adjustable stock allows the 590A1 Adjustable to be set up for a perfect fit for a wide variety of body sizes and arm lengths, with or without body armor. The author found that the downward angle of the stock helped to dissipate felt recoil, and that the 590 A1 was easier on the shoulder than the semi-automatic 930. The 590 A1 Adjustable also features fixed, 3-dot rifle sights, or fully adjustable sights as shown in the photos.

ington pump shotgun. Its style appears to be what inspired the Remington Model 887 Nitro Mag. The Nova features a parkerized 18-1/2-inch barrel with a fixed Improved Cylinder Choke. Sights are of highly visible Ghost Ring variety, with white front and white dot rear, and are fully adjustable for windage and elevation. Overall Length is 40 inches and weight is 7.2 pounds.

Construction of the receiver and stock is what made the Nova unique, in that the receiver and stock are one single piece of formed polymer. Of course working parts within this housing, such as the bolt and chamber area, are steel construction. This is what helps make the Nova cop-proof: less surface area to rust. However, the one piece construction limits the purchaser to the stock that comes with the gun. The only modification that can be realistically done is shortening the stock by cutting it down, or installing a mercury recoil reducer system. I don't feel the recoil system is really necessary in law enforcement, using reduced recoil ammunition is a simpler solution.

The stock includes a solid recoil pad, with a rounded top edge to prevent snagging as the gun is brought to the shoulder. The fore end is of the same hard polymer construction and entirely encases the twin action bars, even when the action is closed.

Safety and action release button are in the same position as the 870, so there is no transitional training needed in that area. There are mounting points for sling swivels on the lower end of the buttstock and on the ring that holds the barrel to the magazine tube. Magazine capacity is four rounds.

As far as flexibility of design goes, you will have to decide: If you are one of those folks who like to tinker with their toys, and always are trying to upgrade and perfect it from the factory, then the Nova probably isn't for you. But if you are content with your guns as they are out of the box, and this one in particular, then go for it. At the time of this writing, the Nova was on sale for $399.95.

The overall construction is rock solid and should provide years of trouble-free service. A Comfortech recoil reduction stock and a nickel plated H20 version are also available. The triggerguard style on the Super Nova is more radical than the Nova, kind of a rounded V-shape, very futuristic looking. The receiver is beefier in appearance than the Nova, and there are pistol grip versions available, one of which is a cool desert camo pattern. The Benellis function very well, are very sturdy, and have a long enough forend that they can be handled comfortably.

**AUTHOR WRINGS OUT** Benelli Nova pump gun on steel plate range using AA Trap and Skeet loads.

### BENELLI M3 TACTICAL CONVERTIBLE

This pump is, for lack of a better term, an odd duck. Reminiscent of the Franchi SPAS 12 (which was only produced from 1979 to 2000), a pump to semi-auto convertible that was more a star of Hollywood than of the street or home defender set, the M3 also has the ability to switch between both modes of operation. But I have to ask, why?

Benelli literature states that one can fire it with full power live rounds in the semi-auto mode, and then switch to pump action mode to shoot lower powered, less lethal rounds like beanbags. The practice of firing lethal and less lethal rounds out of the same weapon is now strictly frowned upon in American law enforcement. The firing process sounds like a pain to work through under stress.

According to Benelli literature, to go from pump action to semi-automatic fire you "merely rotate the selector ring 1/4 turn, push the forend forward and release the selector." Then "to switch back to pump action simply reverse the procedure by pulling back after the selector ring is rotated to lock the forend to the action bars." Sounds a bit complicated to me. While Benelli makes fine weapons that function slickly and should last forever, I can't recommend the M3. It is just too much of a complex mechanical marvel, which may be part of the reason the Franchi SPAS 12 is no longer in production.

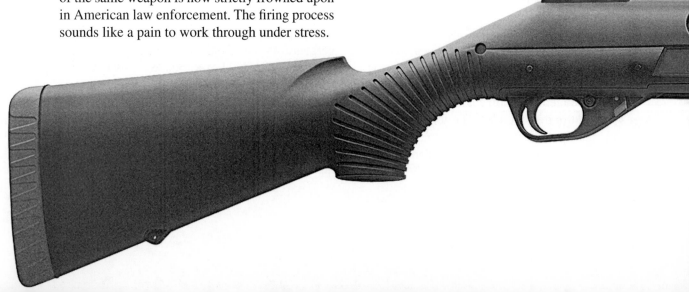

## STOEGER P350 DEFENSE PUMP

Stoeger is a part of the Benelli, Franchi, Uberti Group. The 350 Pump is their version of the excellent Benelli Nova. The 350 Defense takes 2-3/4, 3, and 3-1/2-inch shells interchangeably, and offers a light weight (6.4 pounds) due to its synthetic construction. It is available only in tactical black with a pistol grip stock and 18-1/2-inch barrel and fixed cylinder bore "choke." The style and operation of the 350 Defense is very similar to that of the Nova.

One of the hallmarks of Stoeger has been that their version of the products has been somewhat less expensive than the lead brand as many of their products are Turkish made. The only downside of the P350 is that it has a post front bead sight, but no rear sight for optimum alignment, but it still is a viable and presumably reliable option.

## NIGHTHAWK™ TACTICAL CUSTOM

Nighthawk Tactical, another fine custom maker of 1911 handguns and tactical bolt action rifles, also offers Tactical Shotguns similar in features to the Wilson Combat style shotguns. I'm not equating or even comparing quality here, I'm just saying that their combat shotgun have similar appearances and setup.

I had no Nighthawk Custom shotgun to work with for this book, but it is not like either Nighthawk or Wilson Combat is reinventing the wheel with a totally new shotgun design. They are taking existing design and refining and perfecting it for combat use. The chances of these time-proven designs being reduced to junk by a recognized custom weapon maker is pretty much nil, especially considering the reputation of both companies.

Like Wilson Combat, Nighthawk starts out their shotgun platform with the Remington 870 in the 3-inch magnum version, then adds options/treatments to it based on the customer's needs and desires. Sights are protected Ghost Ring style rear, with either red fiber-optic or a tritium front available. A top rail can be added to the receiver for mounting an optical sight. The rear sight is fully adjustable.

Nighthawk offers shotgun/scope packages and pricing utilizing either the Aimpoint™ T1 or Aimpoint M4 already mounted. The Aimpoint red dot sights are perfect for mounting on a shotgun. The plain red dot that they use is, in my opinion, the simplest CQB sight design to work with. There is no need to think about anything when you are firing on a target within the weapons UPR. Put the red dot on the target, pull the trigger and bang, (as long as you didn't mess up) the target is down. There is nothing else to consider in terms of questions of sight alignment, such as where you hold the chevron reticle, or how many dots do you hold over the target, or which of the concentric circles do you hold etc. I'm getting too old and slow to really consider those things. I want to and need to keep it simple.

As far as night sights, I only want one tritium dot, and that's on the front sight. If you are

THE BENELLI NOVA was the progenitor of a series of much-updated pump shotguns that use tough polymer in their construction. The basic Nova is smooth operating, has a good length of pull and easy-to-reach long forend. The buttstock is one piece, integral with the receiver, and thus can't be changed out. The Nova pumps are durable and reasonably priced.

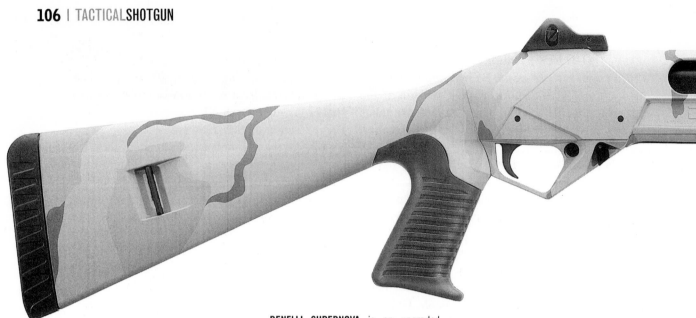

going to mount a sight – a real combat sight, and not a sight for shooting at turkeys or deer or even coyotes which don't shoot back – it seems to me that the Aimpoint is about as ideal as you can get for shotgun use. With Nighthawk, you can get the shotgun all ready to rock with the Aimpoint of your choice in place when you take delivery.

Nighthawk also has the Leupold Prismatic 1x14 sight available. There is a battery power module that illuminates the sight in red, but when that is removed or the batteries die there is still an etched glass reticle available. With that said, newer versions of the Aimpoint such as the M4 can stay powered for eight years before running out. Batteries wearing out just isn't the concern it used to be.

There are also different stock options available. The basic stock is the Hogue Rubber Overmolded standard stock. Nighthawk feels that the Hogue is the ideal starting point stock, with reduced recoil coming from their heavy rubber recoil pad. This should work for most users. Hogues are very nice, but the standard stock is just a little long for me. To remedy this issue of length of pull there are two options. The first is a shorter 12-inch version of the same stock from Hogue. The second, which I like best, is an AR-

**BENELLI SUPERNOVA** is an upgraded Nova that features even more "space age" styling, especially in the area of the triggerguard. The model shown here features the desert camo scheme (the author would prefer a more all-occasion OD green for use here in the U.S.), fixed pistol grip stocks and ghost ring sights.

style, shotgun-specific (meaning it won't work on an actual AR) five-position adjustable stock with storage tubes on both sides for CR123 lithium batteries. This stock is combined with a Hogue Overmolded pistol grip. For this stock, there is an optional hydraulic recoil buffer made by ITT Industries to compensate for recoil if the customer chooses. I don't know if that's necessary, as the relatively all-steel Remington 870 is the basis for this gun, and if you stick with 2-3/4-inch shells and an extended magazine tube with its added weight, the recoil shouldn't be a huge problem. Also, the recoil reducer adds an additional pound of weight.

The stock on this gun does not angle down to the same degree as the Mossberg 590, it is in more of a straight line, so felt recoil may be a little more than the 590. If you are not recoil sensitive, you could save your money and forego the recoil reduction system.

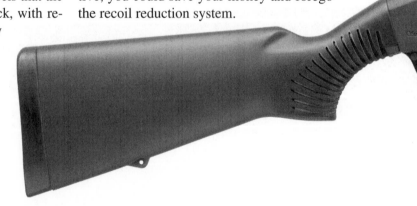

Surefire tactical light forends are available, as well a barrel clamp system that allows for the mounting of Surefire tactical lights from a picatinny rail on one side of the gun. There is a sling swivel on the other side. Nighthawk has a very nice receiver shotshell carrier machined from a solid aluminum billet that doesn't obscure the serial number of the gun. It is available in four or six-shot configurations. Even if you go with a four round magazine model, I would get the six-shot carrier. With the naturally limited magazine capacity of any shotgun, you can't carry too much ammo on the carrier.

Nighthawk uses a rounded replacement safety button called a Big Dome, which is different than standard-style enlarged safeties and it is claimed to provide better access to the safety without looking at it to find where it is.

The final option that is significant is the availability of the Vang Comp™ shooting system for the barrel. Adding the Vang Comp modification takes an additional two weeks of time to build the gun you order if you want it added. The Vang Comp System is well known in the law enforcement community. It is a patented method of re-

## If you are not recoil sensitive, you could save your money and forego the recoil reduction system.

ducing felt recoil where the forcing cone is lengthened and the barrel is back-bored. In addition, the barrel is ported to reduce recoil. The barrel modification results in better and tighter patterning of shot.

For finishes, the Standard Base Model features a ceramic-based finish called Perma Kote™ over the entire surface metal area, with color choices of Sniper Gray, OD green, Desert Tan or Black. Base price of the Nighthawk Custom Standard Model is $1350.

THE P350 DEFENSE is the Stoeger version of the Benelli Nova Pump. The model shown here has a standard style stock and bead front sight. A pistol grip stock is also available.

# CHAPTER SIX

# SEMI-AUTOMATIC
## SHOTGUNS

### BENELLI-M2 TACTICAL

I described the recoil operated Benelli M2 Tactical previously when discussing semi-auto action types. I really like this gun, and hated to part with my copy of it. It is lightweight with a five round magazine capacity. The M2 is available with a standard, Comfortech®, or Pistol Grip stock. Mine had the pistol grip, but if I had to do it over again, I would try the Comfortech design, which is supposed to reduce felt recoil by approximately 48 percent. The recoil operated action stays extremely clean, and there are less critical parts to worry about maintaining.

Sights are Ghost Ring, with a tritium version available. Gun colors are like the Model T Ford, any color you want as long as it's black. All stock configurations are set up for sling swivels. The MSRP is higher than some other autos, at $1329 for the pistol grip version, but understand you are paying for what I consider to be superior design and execution. It you want fine out-of-the-box craftsmanship on your autoloader, this is one you shouldn't overlook.

## BENELLI M4 TACTICAL

Clearly, the Benelli M4 Tactical is the Lincoln Continental of semi-automatic tactical shotguns. Weighing in at 7.8 pounds with the ARGO (Auto Gas Regulating Operation) twin piston system and 18-1/2-inch barrel, this combination makes for excellent recoil reduced shooting. It also means that all forms of shotshells should function reliably in it, which is not true of all semi-autos, gas or recoil.

The self-cleaning ARGO system and the M4 tactical were just adopted by the U.S. Marines as their combat shotgun. The sample I obtained was equipped with a pistol grip fixed stock, the

**STOEGER, WHICH IS** a part of the Benelli family, makes guns like the Model 2000 defense in Turkey, but with the same mechanicals as the Benelli guns. The 2000 defense has the same Inertia Driven recoil operating system as the Benelli M2 Tactical series. The 2000 has a fixed differently styled pistol grip stock, bead sight, 3-1/2-inch magnum chamber, and 18-1/2-inch barrel combined with high quality and a very reasonable price tag.

same type as on the Benelli M2 Tactical, and the Benelli MR1 5.56mm rifle.

Equipped with a four shot magazine and a Modified choke, the M4 excels at tight shot patterns. Like the Mossberg 930, the M4 has a strip of rail on top of the receiver for mounting optical sights, although the fully adjustable rear Ghost Ring and white dot front should suffice in most tactical situations.

There is a front sling mounting position on the magazine tube, and one built into the right side of the stock. There is a choice of plain black finishes or desert camo. The charging handle is extended, but I feel could be just a tad larger in diameter.

The Benelli M4 functioned as expected, totally flawless right out of the box. I used it for the patterning test, mixing in a round of AA Trap and Skeet, Remington Home Defense 2x4 Duplex, Remington Home Defense BB, Remington Reduced Recoil 8-Pellet 00 Buckshot, and Winchester 9-Pellet 00 Buckshot Magnum. All cycled smoothly and the recoil of even the magnum round was more than manageable and comfortable. MSRP of the black pistol grip model is $1799, Desert Camo finish is $1919.

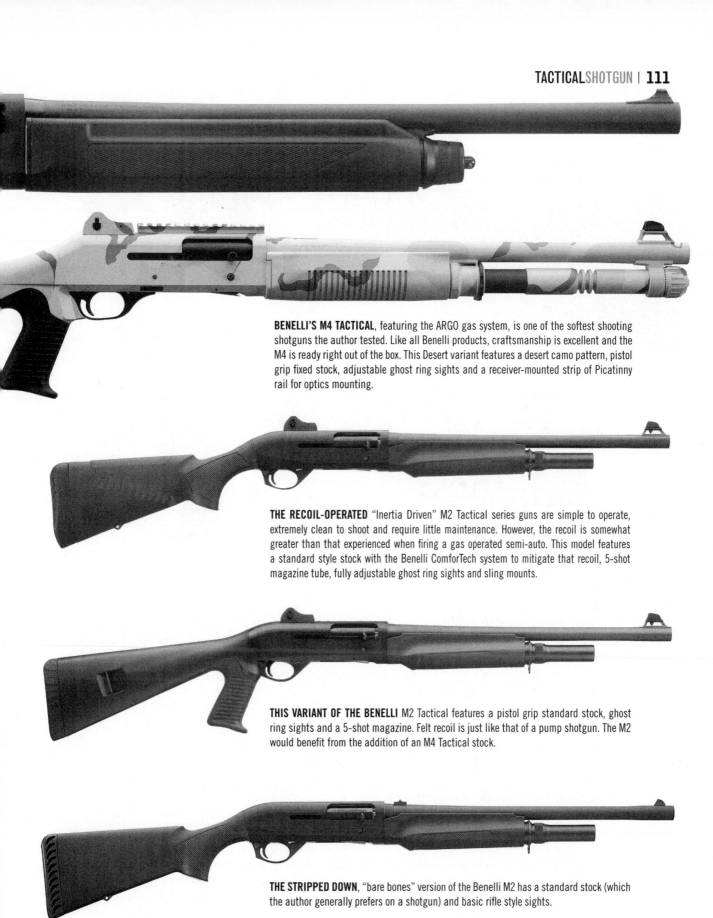

**BENELLI'S M4 TACTICAL**, featuring the ARGO gas system, is one of the softest shooting shotguns the author tested. Like all Benelli products, craftsmanship is excellent and the M4 is ready right out of the box. This Desert variant features a desert camo pattern, pistol grip fixed stock, adjustable ghost ring sights and a receiver-mounted strip of Picatinny rail for optics mounting.

**THE RECOIL-OPERATED** "Inertia Driven" M2 Tactical series guns are simple to operate, extremely clean to shoot and require little maintenance. However, the recoil is somewhat greater than that experienced when firing a gas operated semi-auto. This model features a standard style stock with the Benelli ComforTech system to mitigate that recoil, 5-shot magazine tube, fully adjustable ghost ring sights and sling mounts.

**THIS VARIANT OF THE BENELLI** M2 Tactical features a pistol grip standard stock, ghost ring sights and a 5-shot magazine. Felt recoil is just like that of a pump shotgun. The M2 would benefit from the addition of an M4 Tactical stock.

**THE STRIPPED DOWN**, "bare bones" version of the Benelli M2 has a standard stock (which the author generally prefers on a shotgun) and basic rifle style sights.

### BERETTA TX4 STORM

Beretta has one tactical-style shotgun, actually one they call a "home defense" model: the gas operated semi-automatic TX4 Storm, which shares its name with one of their pistol lines and their pistol caliber carbine.

The configuration is very much like the Mossberg 930, with the same tall front sight with a white bead, top receiver rail and removable adjustable Ghost Ring sight on that rail. It has an 18-inch barrel that is cold hammer forged and chrome lined. Magazine capacity is five shots. There is an ambidextrous safety on the trigger guard. The chokes are removable.

Since I have been whining about the length of pull throughout this book, I am happy to report that there is one very nice feature about the TX4, and that is the stock pull length can be adjusted by the use of 1/2-inch spacers.

Weight, due in part to the use of an alloy receiver (like those used on Benellis) is a mere 6.4 pounds. MSRP of the Storm is $1450.

### FN-USA SLP (SELF LOADING POLICE)

FN-USA makes some outstanding weapons, including a bunch for our military. There shotguns should be no exception. There are four variants, all gas operated. All are in basic black with barrels ranging between 18 and 22 inches in length.

One variant has a fully rifled barrel with cantilever optics mount. Another features a pistol grip stock, a three sided rail attachment on the receiver tube for lights and laser mounting, and the cantilever optics mount. The other version is setup just like the Mossberg 930 and the Beretta TX4 Storm.

**AUTHOR CONSIDERS THE BENELLI M3** Convertible to be overly complex for the average shooter, as it can switch between pump operation and semi-automatic operation, but may have some potential for tactical team operators who would work with it on a regular basis.

**THE AUTHOR FIELD TESTED** the M4 Synthetic pistol grip shotgun and found functioning was impeccable with a variety of loads, and the M4 was smooth-shooting. Author favors the adjustable stocked version.

**THE FN SLP** Mark 1 Self Loading shotguns in all their variations are ideally designed for Tactical three-gun competitions, and sport 22-inch barrels, ideal for a long sighting plane, not so ideal for clearing a tight corner.

**THE MOSSBERG 930 5-SHOT** Home Security is a basic entry level tactical shotgun: gas operated semi-automatic action to absorb recoil, black finish, bead sight, and sling swivel mounts. It's a capable self defense tool that could be improved with the addition of adjustable rifle type sights.

**DESIGNED FOR THREE-GUN** competitons, the Remington Tac4 has a 22-inch barrel, ventilated rib, bead sight and tactical charging handle, sling swivel mounts, and 8-shot magazine capacity. The chamber is 2-3/4-inch only. A little long in the barrel, but, like the 887 hunter combo, still quite usable.

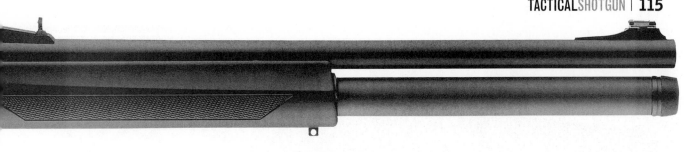

THIS SLP has a standard stock, 8-shot magazine tube, folding rear and red fiberoptic front sight.

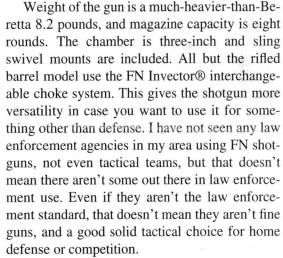

THE 5-SHOT 930 TACTICAL is essentially the same as the Home Security model with the addition of Mossberg's stand-off muzzle brake.

FOR INCREASED VERSATILITY, greater use, and familiarity, there is the 930 Field/Security Combo which gives the user the choice of the home defense or a field/sporting barrel. This is a great setup which allows for just about as much use as you can get out of a single weapon, with just a simple barrel change.

Weight of the gun is a much-heavier-than-Beretta 8.2 pounds, and magazine capacity is eight rounds. The chamber is three-inch and sling swivel mounts are included. All but the rifled barrel model use the FN Invector® interchangeable choke system. This gives the shotgun more versatility in case you want to use it for something other than defense. I have not seen any law enforcement agencies in my area using FN shotguns, not even tactical teams, but that doesn't mean there aren't some out there in law enforcement use. Even if they aren't the law enforcement standard, that doesn't mean they aren't fine guns, and a good solid tactical choice for home defense or competition.

## MOSSBERG 930

The Mossberg 930 is one of the true workhorses of the gas operated semi-auto shotguns. It is very solid and reasonably priced, they can be had in the $550 range. I received one to work with along with the Mossberg/Taser X12 for the XREP cartridge as well as the 590 A1.

**Even if they aren't the law enforcement standard, that doesn't mean they aren't fine guns, and a good solid tactical choice for home defense or competition.**

The first thing that caught my attention is the solid feel. It points comfortably and sports a tall, M16-style front sight with a red fiber optic, and an adjustable/removable rear sight mounted on a strip of picatinny rail on top of the receiver. The rear sight can be removed or moved for mounting an optical sight. It has a seven shot magazine capacity and a 7-1/2-pound weight.

I used it at the range with a variety of loads without malfunction. There is a sling swivel mount on the buttstock, but sadly none on the forend. The only thing that I could figure that was missing besides a front mount for a sling swivel was a strip of rail for a light mount. The oversize charging handle is large and easy to grasp. A semi-auto is perfect for a light mount as there is no moving forend like there is on a pump, which

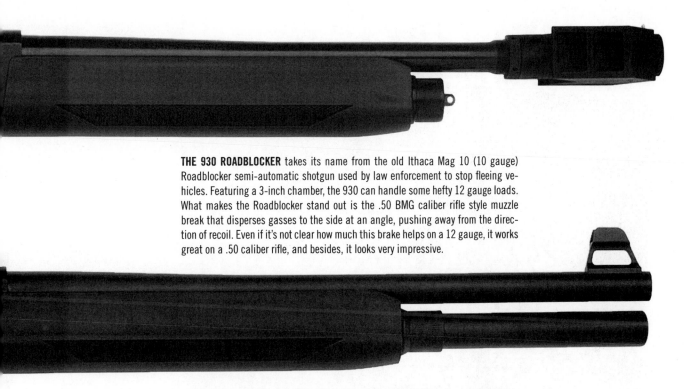

**THE 930 ROADBLOCKER** takes its name from the old Ithaca Mag 10 (10 gauge) Roadblocker semi-automatic shotgun used by law enforcement to stop fleeing vehicles. Featuring a 3-inch chamber, the 930 can handle some hefty 12 gauge loads. What makes the Roadblocker stand out is the .50 BMG caliber rifle style muzzle break that disperses gasses to the side at an angle, pushing away from the direction of recoil. Even if it's not clear how much this brake helps on a 12 gauge, it works great on a .50 caliber rifle, and besides, it looks very impressive.

**ONE OF THE NEWEST VARIANTS** of the 930 shotgun, the SPXP is fixed stock, pistol grip version of the of the SPX. All other features remain the same. The author favors a pistol grip stock for shotguns but only in the adjustable AR-15 M4 style collapsible stock. He feels there isn't enough of a tactical advantage for the pistol grip on a fixed stock versus the faster pointing standard stock.

is important if you use one with an external wire and tape switch; there is nothing to snag, which is what makes the Surefire replacement forend so nice. Mossberg should include a barrel band with a small section of rail on one side and a swivel mount that holds the barrel and extended magazine together a' la the Remington 887 Nitro Mag to allow for easy mounting of a tactical light. In any event, the 930 has got to be one of the best buys in the semi-auto tactical shotgun market.

## REMINGTON 1100 TAC 4

Designed for Three-Gun Competitions, the gas operated TAC4 features a black synthetic stock and black parkerized finish, with an eight round magazine capacity. In order to get that full round capacity and not have the tube extend beyond the barrel's muzzle, the TAC 4 utilizes a 22-inch barrel, rather than 18.5 or 20-inch, which makes it a bit unwieldy in home interior situations. It has a ventilated rib and the ever popular Hi-Viz sighting system. The receiver is old style drilled and tapped for scope mounts. It would be better if there was a section of rail mounted on the top of the receiver instead. I would probably relegate this model to what it was actually designed to do, compete in Three-Gun shoots, where I'm sure it does quite well. Even though the barrel is a bit longer that what is considered ideal these days for ultimate tactical effectiveness, it still has defensive potential, after all it is a shotgun. If you already have one of these, I wouldn't be quick to get rid of it. With practice, it will fill your mission needs quite handily.

**THE OPENING SHOT** of the "Great Chicken Ballistic Test". Note 10+ pound chicken suspended from tree. The round being tested is the Remington Ultimate Home Defense 12 gauge duplex round, a combination of #2 and #4 shot. Test gun is the Remington 870 Police Magnum with Pistol Grip.

# CHAPTER SEVEN

# AMMUNITION

One of the things that we have to get past, for the civilian user of the shotgun for home defense in particular, is the concept that any old load will do. While any load will do damage, some do it more efficiently than others.

The world and the internet are full of penetrations tests on wallboard, 2x4s, car windshields, you name it. You can go there to look at live video tests, which are really quite enlightening. Even bird shot in a 12 gauge blows through drywall at close range, where the shot is traveling through the air in one large clump. At distances of probably 15 yards or more, the fine #9 shot pellets, or 7s and 8s for that matter, won't penetrate drywall, so you can figure they will be less than effective on clothed individuals. At those distances they won't endanger people on the other side of the walls either. Up close is a different story.

**PHOTOGRAPHER CATCHES** the impact of the Remington HD Duplex round striking the chicken. Author has already moved the gun away from his shoulder (or maybe recoil took it there). Note chunks of chicken heading for the ground, chicken spray in the air, and suspension chains swinging.

Since all these tests are internet available, I wanted to do something different to demonstrate the awesome power of a shotgun at close range, as well as compare loads, and do it in a graphic way. The tests also had to be reasonably simple to do and easy to replicate.

## THE GREAT CHICKEN BALLISTIC TEST

To give an idea what kind of damage some of the most common shotgun rounds would do to muscle tissue, fresh (not frozen) chickens seemed to be a good choice. They were tightly wrapped in plastic, had a lot of moisture, and were about the size of the central portion of the average human chest cavity, at least the region of the vitals. The chicken would provide different materials for the pellets to strike and pass through: small bone, guts, muscle and water and open space, as found in the lungs.

I picked up a couple lengths of chains at the local hardware store and used a stainless steel rod as a skewer, which I ran through the top of the chicken, from side to side. Then, I ran the ends of the rod through the two chains hanging over a branch, front label facing towards me. As you can see from the photos, I was in the front yard of my "country estate" as I did this, since the flowering crab tree provided a perfect branch, and the front yard slopes up drastically to catch any pellets that would punch through the chicken. My photographer was instructed to try and capture the shot hitting the chicken. For the first shot, I tested Remington's new Ultimate Home Defense load, in the Duplex version.

## ULTIMATE HOME DEFENSE LOAD, DUPLEX VERSION

Remington's HD Ultimate Home Defense shotgun shells use tungsten-bronze hunting pellets in this premium ammunition and it is offered

**THE FIRST BALLISTIC CHICKEN** after the impact of the Remington HD Duplex round. Note plastic blown away, legs hanging down, and at a range of only about 15 feet or so, the wide spread of the pellets on the front of the bird. Pattern should be tighter at this distance.

in two loadings. The first load is 1-1/4 ounces of BB for the highest terminal energy, the pellets are heavier. The second load is the aforementioned duplex mixture of #2 and #4 pellets. The larger number two pellets should penetrate a bit deeper to help reach vitals. Remington feels that the duplex load has a reduced chance of over-penetration compared to BBs. Don't count on it though. While these rounds certainly penetrate less than the much heavier weighted .33 caliber pellets found in 00 buck, they also certainly don't bounce off drywall.

Velocity of both these loads is an impressive 1250 feet per second, and like all full power loads, these are loaded in high brass shells, in an impressive tactical black (of course) plastic hull. Very premium indeed.

As I figured that the duplex would be my favorite load for indoor use, I decided to test-fire that round first and check the chicken damage. It only seemed fitting to use a Remington shotgun to launch these Remington loads, at least for the first shot, so I selected the 870 Tactical Police Magnum as supplied to me by Remington.

I stepped off a distance of about 15 feet from the skewered and suspended 10-pound fresh chicken. I never did this before so I had no idea what would happen. I had my photographer shoot over my right shoulder, and told her I would count down from three. I combat-loaded a single HD duplex load into the 870 chamber and gave the countdown. Boom! It was way cooler than I thought it would be, and the photographer caught the impact of the duplex load as it hit the chicken.

The impact force blew the chicken pretty much wide open, tearing the plastic wrap, and causing the legs to drop out and down. There was a heavy spray of chicken juice and pieces in about a ten foot radius in the grass around the chicken. The

**LOOKING AT THE REAR** of ballistic bird #1, after the impact of the duplex load, note wide ranging penetrations and torn up packaging.

chicken, with this load, was not knocked off the chains. In photographs of both the front and back of the chicken, you can see a number of penetrations through the back, mostly the #2 shot.

The approximately three-inch wide entrance cavity (remember an average spread of one inch per yard) was very impressive, and a couple large chunks of the chicken were blown into the grass.

Remember, I am not making any special claims about this test. It is useful, I think, because the test is easily repeatable by anyone with access to a grocery store (remember to use fresh not frozen chickens), graphic in nature, and because of its repeatability, gives you a comparison of damage caused by different loads.

## WINCHESTER AA TRAP AND SKEET

The next load up for testing was the load I have been promoting for self-defense throughout much of this book: a plain old Winchester AA Trap and Skeet, the mildest load available,

loaded with the smallest size shot, (7-1/2 to 8-1/2 to 9, depending on particular shell) and the least likely to carry far through a lot of walls or other materials. I wanted to see what the ballistic chicken damage level was compared to the Remington HD Ultimate Home Defense rounds.

Using the retro Ithaca Model 37 Defense "trench gun" as the launcher, and with a brand new chicken, we reset the stage, or experiment as it were. This time, the, entrance hole was massive, with plenty of damage. There was a lot of dimpling on the back side of the chicken, indicating some penetration of the #7-1/2 shot in this particular load, but also that much of it was contained.

What was unusual was that the chicken was blown off the chains with this lighter, low brass load. Part of it, I think, is that the velocity of AA Trap and Skeet is listed as being 1300 fps, although it probably isn't that high out of 18-1/2-inch barrel. I would have no qualms using

**AUTHOR PREPARES** to fire a AA Trap and Skeet loaded with #7-1/2 shot from the Ithaca Model 37.

this simple load as an interior home defense load, based on the level of damage that it did. If I wanted to also defend exterior property, I would go for something heavier, such as the Ultimate Home Defense BB load, or something comparable from other manufacturers.

I saved the heavy hitting round for the last, and this certainly wasn't the heaviest hitting available, but one that is becoming more commonplace in law enforcement circles: the 9-pellet reduced recoil round as manufactured by Winchester at 1145 fps. I could have used a full power 00, or even a magnum, but I wanted all three loads I used to be operating within the same general envelope.

I reset my third chicken and again using the Ithaca 37 at 15 feet, I fired the 00 buck. Wow. There were chicken pieces all over. Hint to those of you wanting to try this: At 15 feet with 00 buck, even low recoil, you will need a splatter shield. The impact effect of nine 00 .33 caliber pellets, even at a lower velocity, versus the Remington Duplex load or AA Trap and Skeet was impressive to say the least. As you can see from the photos, the chicken was literally blown in half this time, and essentially upended. It would have been interesting to shoot another chicken with full power or magnum 00, but I will save that for another time. If you want to do some side by side load comparison, rifle (you might try a cheap turkey for that depending on the power), pistol or shotgun, you might give the ballistic chicken a try. It sure beats ballistic gel and water jugs. If you really want to test penetration, put a piece of sheetrock, or even cardboard behind the chicken. And remember the splatter shields.

## SPECIFIC TACTICAL DEFENSIVE LOADS: GENERAL CONSIDERATIONS

One form of "extreme duplex load" is a "buck and ball" load. Buck and ball loads date back to muzzle loading times, and were used both in the American Revolution and early parts of the American Civil War. What buck and ball consists of in traditional terms is a bore diameter main slug mixed with a number of pellets of buck or other shot. It was designed to increase the chances of hitting and taking your opponent out of the fight. A number of companies are making these types of loads, including Winchester. Winchester has the 12 gauge PDX1™. This duplex load features three pellets of Grex® buffered 00 plated buckshot posted on top of a one-ounce rifled slug. Some loads of this sort, not necessarily Winchester's, are designed to use the rifled slug as a "spreader" which will send pellets farther out to cause more damage.

For most purposes, I don't want anything causing my shotgun rounds to spread their loads farther than the standard one inch per yard. In fact, I want it to stay tighter than that, which is why I favor the Remington and Winchester Reduced Recoil 8-pel-

let buck. I want to be able to aim, and have all the shots stay where I aim at 15 yards, and I can do it with these loads. The shotgun needs to be a precision tool, otherwise it's useless. It is not an indirect area fire weapon. Test these loads for yourself, in your gun, with your choke, and make sure that they perform how you want them to. I do not recommend using anything with even a partial rifled slug in it for interior home defense.

I tested what I would consider some of the best defense loads available in a simple patterning test using orange spray paint dots on a sheet of target cardboard to compare the patterning. The loads were AA Trap and Skeet using #7-1/2 shot, Remington's Ultimate Home Defense Loads, the 2x4 Duplex and the all BB load, Remington's 8-pellet 00 buckshot Reduced Recoil, and Winchester's 2-3/4-inch 9-pellet Magnum 00. I fired these from a distance of seven yards using Benelli's M4 Tactical with Modified Choke.

**FRONTAL DAMAGE** of the AA round. The AA knocked the chicken off the chains and onto the ground, in part due to the fact that all the pellets hit the chicken in a tight pattern, no kinetic energy was lost, and damage was extensive. Surprising for a mild target load.

**THE REAR OF BALLISTIC CHICKEN** #2 shows some dimpling of the wrapping, and little penetration. AA Trap and Skeet is probably one of the safest, yet effective, shotgun loads to use inside a house.

**AUTHOR USES ITHACA MODEL 37** loaded with Winchester 9-pellet reduced recoil rounds on the final chicken at 15 feet.

**BALLISTIC CHICKEN #3** a split second after impact, on its way to the ground. There were chicken parts everywhere. 00 Buck is clearly the powerhouse load.

**WITNESS THE DEVASTATION** wrought by close range 00 Buck, when all nine pellets strike together. The ballistic chicken was ripped nearly in half.

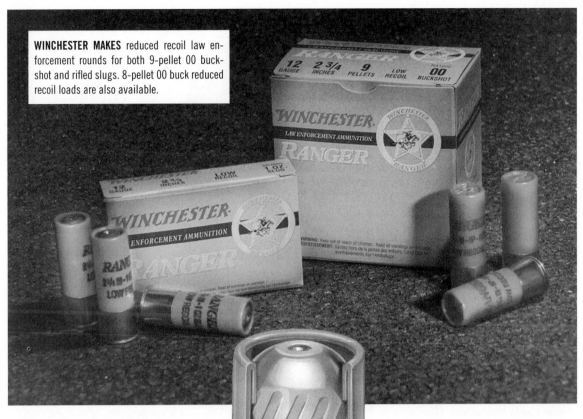

The results were interesting. The AA Trap and Skeet spread measured eight inches of spread, and the Remington Home Defense BB load measured about nine inches. The premium do-everything defense load, Remington 8-pellet reduced recoil buckshot measured an outstanding, precision-weapon 2-inch diameter. This means the expansion rate is .28 inches per shot per yard, not the rule of thumb one inch per yard. Nice! Even the Winchester Magnum 9-pellet measured only three inches, which is .42 inches per yard.

As I have experience with all the loads other than the HD rounds, there were no surprises. I have fired BB shot loads before so I knew what to expect with the Remington HD BB load. However, what happened with the HD Duplex load (#2 and #4 shot mixed together) was totally unex-

CUTAWAY VIEW of a Winchester rifled slug showing components: Standard one ounce Foster type rifled slug, protective wadding, powder charge and primer.

pected, and in my book, unacceptable. You can also see these results on the ballistic chicken tests. While the main portion of shot produced a two-inch central hole, the pellets, mostly #2s, spread some 14 inches and more out from the central hole! That's a rate of two inches per yard and if your opponent is at a distance of 20 yards your pattern will be 40 inches across! Maybe Remington meant to do this, but it's not acceptable for defensive use; hunting birds maybe yes (I don't hunt so I'm not sure if that's true or not). To defend against personal threats without endangering others in the area, this is not a good choice.

I didn't have a full choke available for the Benelli, so maybe the Duplex load would do better. Don't use it in a modified choke, and especially not in an improved cylinder choke.

Remember, the shotgun is a precision weapon, just like any defensive weapon must be, and capable of well-placed shots within its Usable Precision Range, certainly seven yards and more. Having a specialized home defense load is a good thing, but not the 2x4 Duplex, unless you use a full choke, or unless you consider the shotgun (or want to make it into) an area-indirect fire weapon.

WINCHESTER MARKETS its own line of premium defense ammo-PDX. This is a duplex load with a single slug backed up by three 00 buck pellets. Before using it, it's important to check the patterning from your particular shotgun. These loads are distinguished by their black hulls and black-coated brass base.

Stick with the HD BB, the nicely patterning AA Trap and Skeet OR for indoor/outdoor confrontations, the 8-pellet reduced recoil. And again, always check your gun for patterning and functioning with the load you intend to use.

## FEDERAL

Federal is a major ammunition supplier for both the law enforcement and sporting communities. They offer their specially designed Premium Personal Defense loads for 12 gauge shotguns in both a 9-pellet 00 buck and a heavy 34-pellet #4 buck configuration (#4 buck is approximately .24 caliber, the standard load used to be 27 pellets at that diameter). Muzzle velocities are 1145 fps.

For awhile there in the 1980s and into the 1990s, #4 buckshot was the primo shotgun load for police shotguns. It supposedly patterned better (meaning prettier and more uniform) than 00 (it had to, there were a lot more pellets) and supposedly did a "better job" of putting down opponents. Yep, sure looked good on paper, and the pattern was impressive. But it also spread faster than 00 buck at the same distance, as most round lighter weight projectiles are want to do. What we (the collective "we" of law enforcement) found was that it didn't penetrate as well or enough as 00 did. Back in those days, a popular men's fashion accessory was a goosedown vest. There were incidents where offenders were shot with #4 at ranges where the shot should have been an effective stopper and,

> For most purposes, I don't want anything causing my shotgun rounds to spread their loads farther than the standard one inch per yard.

instead of stopping, they had the poor taste to get up and take off or keep on shooting back. The down vest was turning the lighter #4 buck pellets away and preventing injury. The agencies returned to the good old tried and true 00. This is why most defensive loads today have standardized on 00. Not 000 or #1, but 00. Just the right amount of pellets doing the right amount of damage, and a lot less of them to be responsible for. Nope, 00 is the way to go for exterior (and in the right circumstances interior) defensive needs.

> ## In home defense situations, various forms of shot will almost always be the load of choice, as opposed to slug loads.

Federal Law Enforcement has a number of law enforcement-specific ammo offerings, most of which are also available as civilian offerings. One of the most notable is the Tru-Ball™ rifled slug, which temporarily in the shell base unites a plastic ball with the lead slug. The ball cushions the slug as it is forced out of the cartridge during firing and provides a very high level of accuracy, usually around two inches at 50 yards out of a smoothbore barrel, which is outstanding. Two of the civilian versions of the load whistle downrange at 1600 fps, while the law enforcement load and one of the other Tru-Ball loads are running at a more sedate, yet substantial 1300 fps.

I haven't discussed the use of rifled slugs much in terms of the tactical defense shotgun. Truthfully, they don't get used as much as they should in law enforcement. We just out of habit keep our shotguns loaded with 00. In home defense situations, various forms of shot will almost always be the load of choice, but if you wanted the utmost accuracy from a slug load, look at the Tru Ball loadings, particular the 1300 fps version.

In addition to these loads, there are the special powdered steel door breaching rounds (available

**TEST TARGET** with five shots from seven yards through Benelli M4 Tactical.

for law enforcement only) designed to destroy door locks with a minimum of dangerous projectiles being sent through the other side of the door, standard rifled slug rounds at 1610 or 1520 fps, one Tactical 8-pellet and one 9-pellet reduced recoil 00 buck load at 1145 fps, as well as a full power load at 1325 fps. I have used the Federal Tactical 9-pellet loads quite a bit and found them to be tight-patterning.

Finally there are two Premium Buckshot loads with copper plated shot for deeper penetration: one is a 9-pellet 00 load at 1325 fps and another, a whopper of a magnum load, that launches 12 00 pellets at 1290 fps. Yikes. I can't comment on tight patterning for that load – there was none available to me to test. But understand this, with that increased payload and physics being what they are, you will notice an increase in recoil, and this is where a shotgun like the Benelli M4 Tactical really comes into its own.

**NOTE THE WELL-DISPERSED** and yet tight pattern from the AA Trap and Skeet.

**IN THE SHOT PATTERN** from the Remington HD BB shot round, stray pellets outside the nine-inch circle area are strays from the HD Duplex round, which was fired above and to the right of the BB target. Author is keeping this load in his home defense gun (Remington 887 with Xiphos Tactical Light) to deal with people or smaller animal issues around his property.

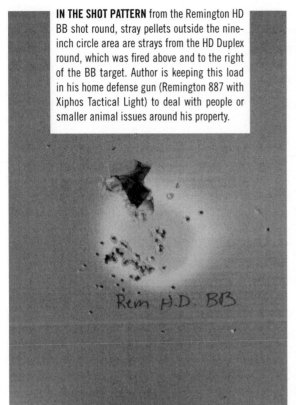

**NOTE TIGHT TWO-INCH PATTERN** fired with Remington Reduced Recoil 8-pellet load (lower left), which is the duty load for author's agency as well as the Ohio Highway Patrol. From this target, you can see why.

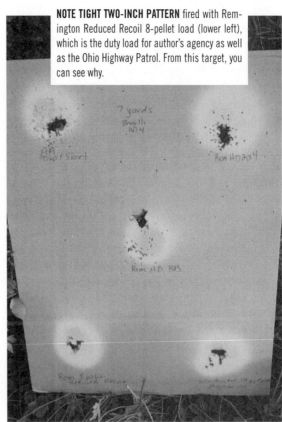

**THE PATTERN FROM THE WINCHESTER** 9-pellet reduced recoil round is typical of all 9-pellet loads. One pellet always tends to stray out, which is why 8-pellet loads are so popular.

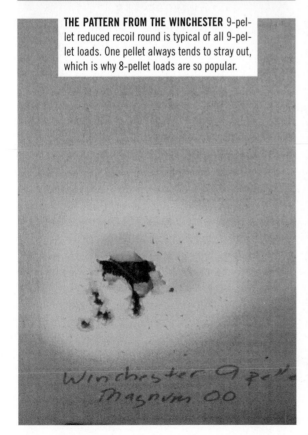

**REMINGTON HD** Duplex load. Note the wide pattern dispersion and all the stray pellets. Spread was at least 14 inches from the center. At seven yards, the author feels this is too much dispersion for tactical use.

## HORNADY

Hornady, once traditionally thought of as primarily a hunting ammunition supplier, has become the most innovative leader in self-defense ammo for cops and civilians alike. Their TAP ammunition in its various different weights is without a doubt the favorite duty load in 5.56mm of law enforcement across the U.S. In its heavyweight 69 gr. version it is a great designated marksman round. The 110 gr. .308 Tap is also a police sniper favorite where there is no heavy intervening barrier. TAP handgun rounds are also quite popular for law enforcement as is TAP FPD (for personal defense) for civilian applications.

Hornady also makes three 12 gauge 00 buck loads all at a very hot 1600 fps muzzle velocity. All three are 8-pellet loads. One is the Superperformance™ load, the other is TAP FPD and the third is the 12 gauge Critical Defense. Under the law enforcement division of Hornady, there is the 8-pellet reduced recoil 00 buckshot (anyone see a trend here?) at 1150 fps, as well as the Light Magnum 8-pellet 00 buck at 1600 fps, which mimics the civilian loads. No 9-pellet 00 loads are catalogued.

## REMINGTON

Besides the Ultimate Home Defense Loads, Remington offers the 8-pellet 00 Buck Reduced Recoil Round, first encountered as a law enforcement loading, as their RL12BK00 Express Managed Recoil Buckshot on the commercial side of the house. Velocity is 1200 fps. It should handle about any exterior situation you can expect to encounter (outside of bear country, where I would want a 3-inch magnum load).

There is also the companion Express Managed Recoil Rifled slug at 1200 fp, if you need to increase your shotgun's UPR from that of buckshot, although Remington's info claims that their 8-pellet buck is effective out to 40 yards (and after testing, I agree). The shortcomings of the Ultimate HD Duplex Defensive Load were discussed earlier.

I would also recommend trying their Hypersonic Steel Duck Load, which blasts down a hunting barrel at 1700 fps and is advertised to keep tight patterns at longer ranges. That's what I'm looking for. A lot of energy from the pellets and a very tight spread. Try that one for patterning and a chicken test. You might like what you come up with. Think outside the box. In the shotgun world, a load doesn't need to be designed for self defense to be effective as a self-defense round.

## ATK/SPEER

ATK, which owns Federal and a number of other brands, also owns Speer. Speer's Lawman line fields two law enforcement shotgun loads. They are an 8-pellet reduced recoil buckshot load at 1145 fps and a one ounce Hydra-Shok™ rifled slug load at 1300 fps. I have field tested the Speer Lawman shotgun loads and found them to be fine performers, as would be the case with about any 8-pellet reduced recoil load. Speer's specialty area is the outstanding Gold Dot™ line of handgun ammunition, and they haven't felt the need to really expand or push their shotgun line. It is out there, and it's good stuff.

## WINCHESTER

Winchester is the other big gun, next to the "Big Green" one, when it comes to shotgun ammunition. As mentioned earlier, I am not a fan of the concept of buck and ball-type loads, and feel they spread too much, but Winchester has them in 12 and .410 gauges. All I can tell you is to test them yourselves if you are interested and if your defensive situation would permit and warrant their use. I wouldn't likely permit their use as a law enforcement duty load, but our situations are much wider ranging than the average homeowner attempting to defend their property. You will have to make that decision for yourself.

Beyond the designated specialty defense load, Winchester has many other shotgun loads available, including 2-3/4-inch and 3-inch Magnum loads running out at 1450 fps, and a 3-inch magnum #4 buck load at 1210 fps. Of course there is a large selection of turkey and duck shot loads that would work, as well as the continually mentioned AA Trap and Skeet as a standard. There are also civilian low recoil 00 buck and slugs with a velocity of 1125 fps.

IF YOU WANT TO USE premium ammo as your home defense rounds, then Remington has some specialty loads for you in 12 and .410 gauge. The author found the spread of the duplex version of the HD load to be too wide, and prefers the BB shot loaded version instead. The BB load works well for interior/exterior (shorter range) home and property defense.

LIGHT, SMALL GAME LOADS like this, with a charge of #6 shot, work well for interior defense. Always test patterning for yourself through the gun you will use the load in.

THE SMALL .410 SHELL is only capable of holding a charge of four 00 buck pellets. However, they still present a formidable threat if you are standing on the wrong end. This is an ideal load for the Taurus Judge series of pistols.

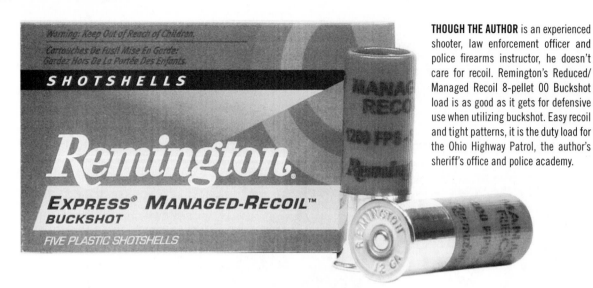

**THOUGH THE AUTHOR** is an experienced shooter, law enforcement officer and police firearms instructor, he doesn't care for recoil. Remington's Reduced/Managed Recoil 8-pellet 00 Buckshot load is as good as it gets for defensive use when utilizing buckshot. Easy recoil and tight patterns, it is the duty load for the Ohio Highway Patrol, the author's sheriff's office and police academy.

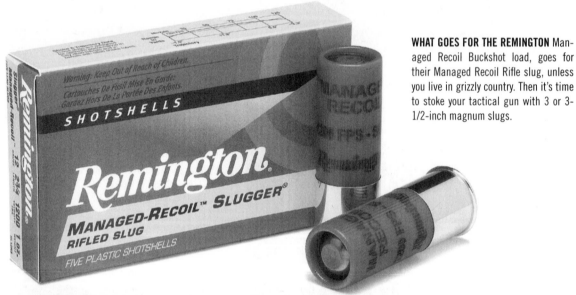

**WHAT GOES FOR THE REMINGTON** Managed Recoil Buckshot load, goes for their Managed Recoil Rifle slug, unless you live in grizzly country. Then it's time to stoke your tactical gun with 3 or 3-1/2-inch magnum slugs.

**IF THE FANCY STUFF** isn't available in your area, then loads like the basic premier buckshot may also suffice.

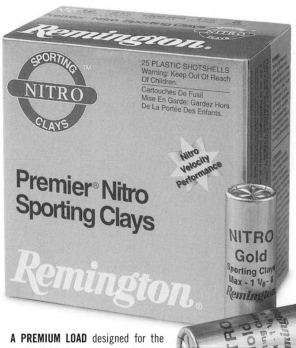

**A PREMIUM LOAD** designed for the Sporting Clays Shooter, Remington's Nitro Sporting Clays would serve well as an interior home defense load, with light recoil and small shot size. Just make sure this and any load cycles in your tactical gun.

Under the Winchester Law Enforcement line, with which I am most familiar, there are standard loads under the storied Super-X brand, as well as the newer Ranger™ line, which is specifically for cops. Winchester nicely markets their Low Recoil Ranger Slug at 1200 fps in a white hull. This is currently what we use for our duty slug round. The distinctive white color makes this load easy for our deputies to recognize in low level light conditions against the red color of the buckshot rounds. This difference reduces the potential for a mistake in load selection. Unfortunately Remington's Reduced Recoil Buck and Slug casings are both green, which means that extra time has to be taken by the deputy to look at the end of a shell before loading. It may not seem like that big a deal, but believe me, anything that can improve speed of action and reduce error is a good thing.

The Ranger line also gives a choice of, you guessed it, reduced recoil 00 rounds in 8 or 9-pellet configurations at a velocity of 1145 fps. The hulls of both loads are red.

If you are going reduced recoil, for the tightest group possible always go with 8-pellet loads. As you can see by the test patterns fired, with a 9-pellet load there is almost always a flier that extends the group. That one extra pellet isn't really going to make any difference in the terminal effect of the shot.

For those that want conventional full power loads, the Super X line is what you want to look at. There are also Supreme High Velocity Copper plated 00 buck loads in 2-3/4, 3, and 3-1/2-inch loads, all at 1450 fps, and carrying charges of 9, 12 and 15 00 pellets respectively. Available Supreme Double X Magnum Buckshot loads all run in the 1200 fps range, in 2-3/4 and 3-inch loads, with 000 and #4 buckshot. Super X buckshot loads range from 2-3/4 inch, 3-inch, and 3-1/2-inch Magnum loads, with the not-often-seen #1 buck and #3 buck as the available choices. The #4 3-1/2-inch magnum contains 54 buckshot pellets.

## SUMMARY

There are a lot of choices in shotgun ammo, and I certainly haven't covered them all here, but I recommend that you keep it simple and stick with 00 buck for most of your needs, unless overpenetration is a concern.

Here again is what is nice about a shotgun, particularly one with a 3-1/2-inch chamber: If there is ever a crisis situation in your area – whether it's a man made calamity or terrorist attack or a natural disaster – and ammo and law enforcement is in short supply, you can always find ammo. They are probably the least finicky weapon when it comes to ammo selection, and certainly a 12 gauge is a ubiquitous round.

In fact, don't feel like you just have to stock up on your chosen premium defensive loads. Purchase quantities of any reasonably available loads for what I would term "massive defense needs." For instance, I have a quantity of Hornady Tap ammo for my 5.56 ARs, but I have a much bigger stock of FMJ practice rounds. Yep, if it comes down to massive defense need times, I'm just going to have to have the poor taste to defend myself with 5.56 FMJ rounds as well as plain old bargain basement buckshot. In these situations, niceties and fancy premium ammo go out the door.

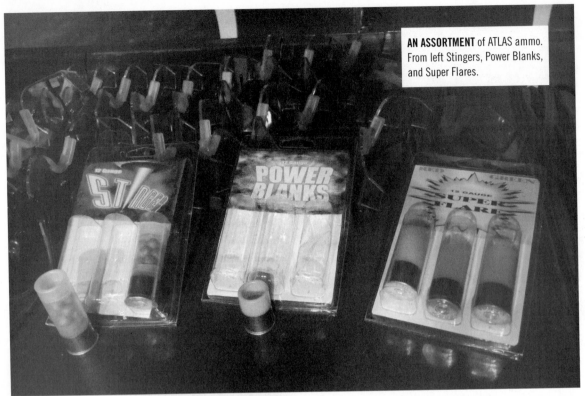

AN ASSORTMENT of ATLAS ammo. From left Stingers, Power Blanks, and Super Flares.

## SPECIALTY AMMO

The tactical shotgun, primarily because of its large diameter smoothbore barrel, lends itself to versatility not only in terms of the standard lethal loads that it can fire (various forms of bird or hunting shot, buckshot or slugs), but also in terms of the specialty loads it is capable of deploying. This gives the shotgun abilities that are unmatched by any other weapon system. Just remember that something that can do a little bit of everything can only do a little bit of everything well. The same holds true with the shotgun. While the use of rifled slugs in your smoothbore gun, for example, can give you "rifle like" accuracy at a limited range, it doesn't make the shotgun a rifle.

CPD ORDNANCE Officer fires ATLAS Ammo Mini-12 Gauge blanks. Note sparks from muzzle.

And while the 12 gauge shotgun can fire 12 gauge "bean bag" rounds, it's certainly not the same as as a bean bag round fired from a 37mm grenade launcher. That said, the 12 gauge rounds are less expensive, which leads to more departmental practice time, and they can be used in a departments existing weapons system. Again, this saves much-needed departmental funds since no specialized launcher needs to be purchased.

So, what else is our 12 gauge capable of doing? Well everything from defense to entertainment. Yes, it's okay to play with our shotguns from time to time! Let's talk fun stuff first.

I purchased a variety of shells from Atlas Ammo (www.atlasammo.com). Atlas also supplies 37mm loads for my ExD 37 grenade launcher from Bates and Dittus. For the 12 gauge testing, I ordered a small assortment of Mini-12 gauge Power Blanks, Dragons Breath, Green Super Flare rounds, and for defense use, some "Stinger" rubber pellet "00 buckshot" rounds. I tested some of the rounds with Sgt. John Groom from the Columbus Ohio Police Department SWAT Team at their academy indoor range, and some of the others at home on my seven-acre property.

## BLANKS

The results were interesting. I used my Remington 887 Nitro mag as the test mule. On the indoor range, we test fired the mini-blank rounds first. Packaged three to a plastic display pouch, like the other Atlas products, these stubbly little blanks were single loaded into the 887 chamber.

> There is something very important that you need to remember about blanks: They can be lethal.

There is something very important that you need to remember about blanks: They can be lethal, especially in a large caliber like a 12 gauge round. In October 1984, up-and-coming actor Jon-Erik Hexum was on a production set and pointed a .44 Magnum revolver loaded with blank rounds at his head, likely pretending to play Russian roulette. He pulled the trigger. The cardboard wad from the .44 magnum blank blew a .44 diameter hole through his skull, killing him instantly. Blanks should never be considered toys, especially when they are fired from a weapon that can also fire lethal ammo due to a "mixup." The one nice thing about Atlas' ammos blanks in this regard is that the rounds are half size, and cannot be mistaken for projectile rounds.

**THIS PHOTO SEQUENCE SHOWS** author firing a Super Green Flare round from his Remington 887 Nitro Mag Tactical.

## "Less lethal" for Home Defense?

I am somewhat at variance with those who advocate using less lethal shotgun rounds for home defense, even when it is backed up by live lethal rounds, due to my mindset as a cop. But others disagree. As expressed earlier in the book, you have to be very careful using less lethal rounds in a lethal round launcher. If I deploy a 37mm launcher in a situation requiring it, I know that there is no way to load a round in it that is designed to be lethal, which could happen with a 12 gauge gun.

Further, as a civilian home defender using a tactical shotgun, you must be prepared to take a bad guy's life with it.

People can be killed with less lethal rounds. All it takes is for one to strike the wrong place on the head or neck, and the less lethal round becomes lethal.

If you understand these parameters and limitations, and accept them, and are careful, you can certainly give the less lethals a try. Just be prepared that:

A. Your less lethal round might not stop a determined threat.

B. The threat might shoot at you with lethal force, which means it is no longer a fair fight in your favor ("don't bring a paintball gun to a live gunfight").

C. The threat may still die or be seriously injured by your less-lethal round.

D. You may have to resort to lethal ammo in the end anyway.

One of the best uses for civilians of any of the less lethal rounds is for animal control of various sorts, and even then you must be careful.

**AUTHOR FIRES GREEN** Super Flare round in safe direction towards hillside.

**AUTHOR FIRES** fizzled ATLAS AMMO Dragon's breath round. There should have been nearly 50 feet of flame.

Sgt. Groom and one of the CPD ordnance officers launched a couple of these rounds indoor and they were in fact, no joke. No recoil, but quite loud. Make sure you wear hearing protection when firing them.

What are they good for? Well, for fun, as a celebratory noisemaker (remember, you still cannot, by law, fire off blank rounds in most city limits just to play around). You could use them to check your weapon for function without discharging live rounds. They could be used for training to help people get over a flinch developed by shooting standard rounds, or for training hunting dogs. You could also use them to scare off wildlife, stray animals or other unwanted visitors without hurting them.

## RUBBER BUCKSHOT

Next up at the range was the Stinger rubber buckshot round. Carrying 16 rubber 00 "buckshot" pellets instead of the standard nine, the stinger rounds are designed for less lethal home and property defense.

I fired the Stinger round at a silhouette target from a distance of approximately 21 feet. Out of 16 pellets, I only counted eight hits on the target. Due to the light weight of the pellets, the dispersion is extreme; the light pellets move in multiple directions as soon as they exit the barrel. This is clearly a round that needs to be used in close. I wouldn't recommend it for chasing off the neighbor's dog, since you could fire at the dog's rear end and have pellets potentially strike it in the eye. If you want to use the Stinger round, I would suggest firing it from a choke tighter than improved cylinder or cylinder bore, and checking patterning in your weapon at various distances before deploying it. You may have better results than I did testing it with just one gun.

## SUPER FLARE

Later, back at the ranch, I gave the green Super Flare round a try. This one was excellent. It shot farther than some of the 37mm flare rounds I have tried in my launcher. It went 70 yards or more from the angle I fired it, and the flare burned brightly and for a good duration. In fact, it burned so long that I was worried I was about to set my field on fire, as it came down still burning in the relatively dry grass and trees. Fortunately, the flare didn't ignite anything. If I was going out hunting or back packing with a shotgun in a remote area, my emergency kit would contain a set of these for signaling. The Super Flares are very impressive and also are available in red, white, blue and yellow colors.

## DRAGON'S BREATH

When I was at the CPD range, the range staff begged the dayshift Sergeant to let me fire the Dragon's Breath round indoors. He wisely said no. There was combustible material from previous shotgun rounds and shredded targets laying on the floor, which he was worried the Dragon's Breath (he had seen it fired before) would ignite. In the end, I'm glad I didn't shoot it there, but for a different reason.

The Dragon's Breath loads I received were all duds. They went off,

**ITHACA 37 DEFENSE** shotgun with Ligthtfield HV STAR round. Expended flexible baton leaves muzzle at 850 fps!

but there was just a small pop and a few sparks when I fired them in my backyard. I would have been mortified to have put on such a display for fellow officers. I have no idea what the problem was, but I will find out. You can check for Dragon's Breath like this from various sources. Atlas has a large number of specialty and exotic loads on their website. Like I said previously, stay away from loads that shoot nails, balls tethered with wire, etc. They could produce liability issues in court for you later on. Trust me, 00 is plenty lethal enough on its own.

## LIGHTFIELD LESS LETHAL

Now for the more serious, purpose-driven less lethal rounds. I was sent a fine supply of loads from Lightfield Less Lethal (they also a line of specialize sabot slug shotgun rounds for hunting), a leader in 12 gauge specialty munitions for law enforcement and civilian use. One of the nice things about Lightfield is that its price point is well below that of

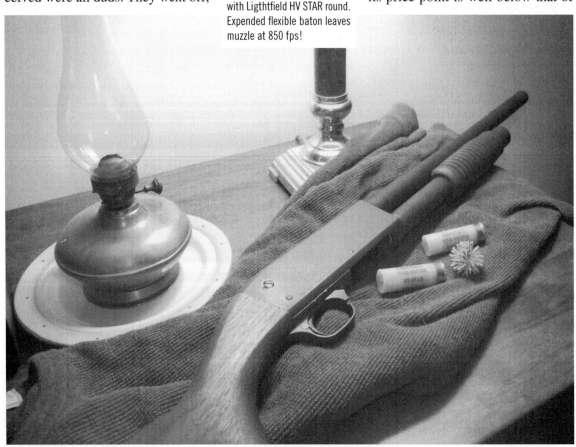

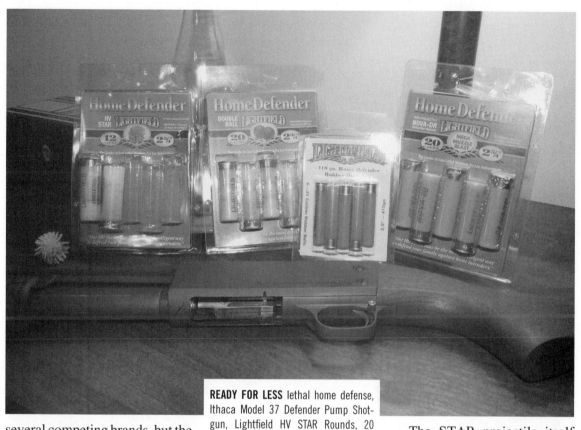

**READY FOR LESS** lethal home defense, Ithaca Model 37 Defender Pump Shotgun, Lightfield HV STAR Rounds, 20 gauge Double Ball Home Defenders, .410 gauge Multi-Ball Home Defenders and 20 Gauge NOVA Distraction Rounds.

several competing brands, but the quality seems to be very much the same, and their products perhaps more innovative.

What was nice for this project was that I was able to use one company to test rounds for both ends of the spectrum – law enforcement and civilian use. So let's start with their "Home Defender" series of less-lethal rounds, which isn't just for 12 gauge anymore. In fact, the less lethal Lightfield Rounds are available in different configurations in 20 and .410 gauges, but the widest variety is in the 12 gauge series.

Their primo round in 12 gauge is the HV STAR round. Loaded into a clear, low brass shell, the STAR Round features a 75 grain STAR projectile which travels at a velocity of 850 fps. (The Law Enforcement series also features a STAR "LITE and SUPER-STAR round, both with lower velocities than the civilian load.) I like the fact that most of the Lightfield rounds are loaded in clear cases (all the 12 gauge projectile rounds I tested), which makes it easy to see that you are working with a less lethal projectile.

The STAR projectile itself is the unique part of this round. It looks just like a miniature "Koosh Ball" with hundreds of little fingers, which served to distribute kinetic energy upon impact, but which also limit the range of the round as the fingers act like little drag chutes. This insures safety but limits the range at which this round will be effective. The Home Defender STARS projectiles are bright orange.

For animal control, I would much prefer this type of single projectile round. It's more accurate than multi-ball loads, and there is only one projectile to worry about. The folks at Lightfield, which is in New Jersey, tell me their rounds are used a lot against the black bear incursion currently underway in their state. Folks are able to drive even an animal this large off their property without permanent injury to the bear – or to themselves for that matter, since the rounds drive the bears off, rather than just making them mad. (I would still want some "real" rounds available, or some good running shoes, just in case.)

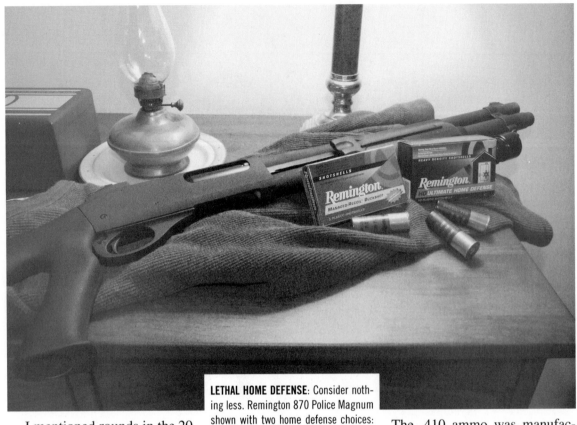

**LETHAL HOME DEFENSE**: Consider nothing less. Remington 870 Police Magnum shown with two home defense choices: 8-pellet Managed Recoil 00 Buck and Ultimate Home Defense BB shot rounds.

I mentioned rounds in the 20 and .410 gauge variety. In 20 gauge, I received their Nova DR Mega Muzzle Blast round. This is a projectile-less round loaded in a yellow case that detonates at 130db with a very bright muzzle flash and concussion. In the 12 gauge Law Enforcement version, it is the Nova Distraction Round, but more about that later. The idea is to use these rounds to drive off a home intruder without killing or injuring them (remember the previous reference to the danger of blank rounds).

The other 20 gauge load I had to examine is their double ball round. With a total weight of 68 grains, the balls exit the muzzle at 900 fps. Lightfield's packaging warns that this round can cause significant pain and severe injury, and like all other projectile rounds, is potentially lethal. They aren't NERF rounds.

The .410 rounds are loaded in 2-1/2-inch red hulls (I wish they were clear, too) and contain four .41 caliber projectiles. With a total weight of 42 grains, these rubber pellets are scooting along at 1400 fps from an 18-inch barrel. Again, ouch.

The .410 ammo was manufactured with the Taurus Judge series of .410/.45 Colt revolvers in mind. The idea is to do something like my dad did with the Model 53 .22LR Smith and Wesson kit gun he inherited from my grandfather and used for home defense. He loaded it with the old brass crimp #12 birdshot .22LR round for the first shot out the cylinder and followed that up with five .22LR hollowpoints, for use if the first shot failed to get an intruder's attention. But that was back in the 1960s. Later in the 1980s when he got a .38 revolver and crime was getting uglier, he carried a cylinder full of Winchester 158gr. +P LHP's in his Model 67.

## LIGHTFIELD LAW ENFORCEMENT

The Lightfield Law Enforcement Line is quite expansive, and each box is packaged with warnings about where to shoot a human target and where not to shoot it (large muscle mass areas vs. head or neck).

The Law Enforcement line features two versions of its Star rounds: STAR-LITE and the SU-

PER-STAR. Classified as "flexible baton" rounds (rather than something sissy like "Kooshball" or "scrunchie") the STAR-LITE features the same 75 grain STAR projectile as the Home Defender round, but with a velocity of only 500 fps, much less than the 850 fps of the Home Defender round. The baton for the LITE round is yellow rather than orange.

I received this supply of ammo the day before I was range officer at our sheriff's office. I planned to test fire some of these loads during break time against inanimate objects like our range shed, just to see how they worked. It was on this particular day that an animate target popped up in the form of one of our detectives, Jeff Stiers who was there to go through firearms requalification. Being a somewhat cool fall day, Jeff was wearing an army-type coat with

STAR-LITE round can be seen bouncing off the back of sheriff's department detective Jeff Stiers who volunteered to be shot. Note streak moving away 90 degrees from his back towards the right.

sweater and t-shirt underneath. I had just fired a STAR-LITE round at the shed, and Jeff said, in a line probably uttered before many episodes of "Jackass," that, "It couldn't hurt that bad. You can shoot me with it"! I was somewhat surprised, but not being one to pass up a chance to fully test a new police device, I said, "Okay."

We performed all the requisite safety checks and got the video camera ready. I gave him one final chance to back out and he declined. I had him turn his back toward me at a distance of about 30 feet. I then had him lower his head, and gave him a countdown. The point of aim was the middle of his back. I didn't know what to expect. I popped Jeff with it and he didn't fall down or even flinch. He turned around and reported at first that it was not too bad, that it felt like he got hit with a rock.

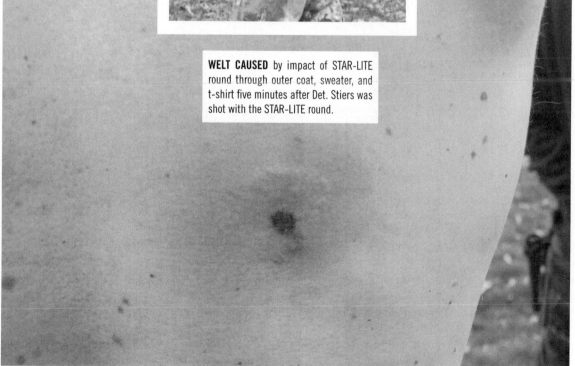

WELT CAUSED by impact of STAR-LITE round through outer coat, sweater, and t-shirt five minutes after Det. Stiers was shot with the STAR-LITE round.

**SGT. JOHN GROOM** from the Columbus Ohio Police Department SWAT team fires a Lightfield STAR-LITE round at a paper silhouette at the CPD indoor range. The white dot at the center of the target is the flexible baton projectile entering the target.

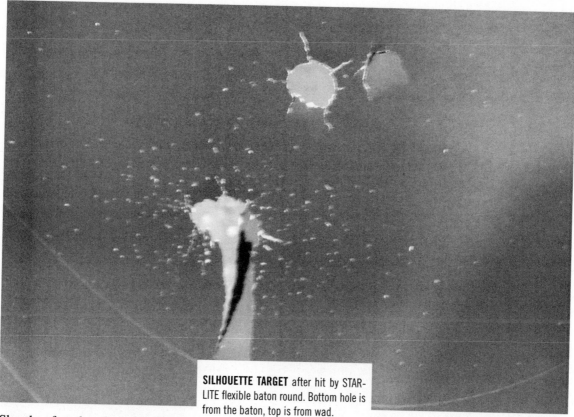

**SILHOUETTE TARGET** after hit by STAR-LITE flexible baton round. Bottom hole is from the baton, top is from wad.

Shortly after that, he said, "That hurt a lot worse than I thought!" We checked his back and found a nice welt forming. Now that's the stuff of legends. Detective Stiers felt that the STAR-LITE round would be useful and that a better area to shoot with that particular round would be the leg, thigh or knee, which might provide an actual takedown.

I imagine that the LITE round was designed for use as a distraction round against smaller statured or female suspects. The SUPER-STAR uses the same projectile, this time lime green in color, at an increased velocity of 650 fps. Why so much less velocity than the civilian rounds? Because the civilian is probably going to try and defend life with this round, so it had better be effective. In law enforcement, these rounds will be used to force a surrender or capitulation of the suspect while they are being covered by other officers who are using lethal force to protect those involved. The civilian only has one option, the officers many. My animate target was glad I didn't use the 650, or especially the 850 fps version.

Also provided by Lightfield were two samples of their harder hitting rubber slugs. Their Intermediate range rubber slug is colored black, and their extended range slug colored blue. Weighing in at 130 grains, both slugs are cylindrical with a rounded tip, with a deeply hollow base. The sides of the slugs are dimpled like a golf ball to improve aerodynamic flight. The Intermediate Range version is tooling along at 500 fps, while the Extended Range version is boosted to 600 fps.

I shot the intermediate slug at our range shed (very scientific analysis) while the crew at the range watched. The rubber slug whacked the shed with clearly much more force than the STAR round, and bounced away much farther. It also appeared to travel more accurately. Clearly, if the person you want to take down is large and very aggressive, these are the rounds you want to use. Almost twice the weight of the STAR round, these are both real attention-getters. I would still target the thighs, legs and knees if the target was in the open and I had time for that shot. Otherwise, I would go with center of mass on the body. Any test volunteers?

**SGT. JOHN GROOM** at CPD SWAT prepares to fire a NOVA DR distraction round. In second photo, notice that the concussion shook the camera. Sparks in the aftermath of the blast are visible from the muzzle.

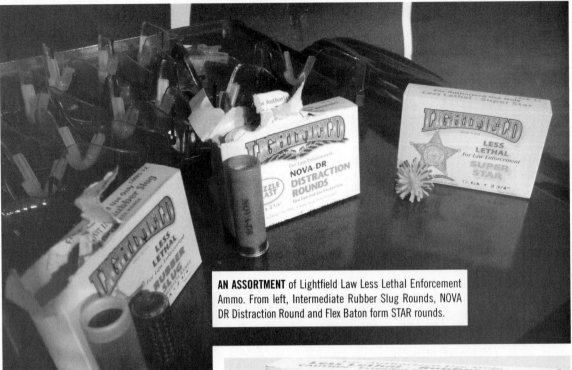

AN ASSORTMENT of Lightfield Law Less Lethal Enforcement Ammo. From left, Intermediate Rubber Slug Rounds, NOVA DR Distraction Round and Flex Baton form STAR rounds.

THE EXTENDED range rubber slug is color-coded blue and has a weight of 130 grains and muzzle velocity of 650 fps.

The final Lightfield round tested was the NOVA DR-12 gauge distraction, or in my terminology, "flashbang" round. Designed for law enforcement to be used in place of a flashbang grenade in situations where there is too much risk for an actual grenade to be used, the NOVA DR sends a large amount of concussive and flash force out of the muzzle, with no projectiles or pieces. The blast exits the muzzle at 100 DbA, compared to a DbA range of 175 for most stun grenades. I can tell you that the concussion is pretty heavy from the NOVA DR round, which I experienced while standing out of line of the muzzle and while wearing ear protectors. Although it was difficult to capture via photograph, the flash is impressive as well, and would definitely distract the unsuspecting, although not to the level of getting hit by a "bang" thrown at their feet. I think I would rather use it instead of a grenade in very tight environments, such as a transit or school bus or aircraft.

The NOVA DR has several other advantages. It won't start things on fire like a flashbang can, it is inexpensive to use at only $3.25 per round. Even if you don't actually deploy it, it would make a great low cost training substitute for flashbangs in scenario based training. It is uni-directional, and can be directed specifically at your suspect, and not others in the immediate area, and

**MID SLUG** is the Midrange Rubber Slug, color-coded black, with a weight of 130 grains and a muzzle velocity of 500 fps.

**THE STAR-LITE** impact distraction round sports a yellow "Koosh Ball" styled projectile. This lower velocity round should be used against smaller statured individuals. Muzzle velocity is 500 fps.

**THE SUPER-STAR** projectile is same projectile (other than the lime green color) as the STAR-LITE round. Muzzle velocity is increased to 650 fps.

there is no ATF paperwork or tracking required like there is with flashbangs. It gives officers an excellent option for their less lethal armory.

Lightfield also offers different law enforcement multi-ball and multi-pellet rounds, which would be most useful for crowd dispersal, firing at the ground in front of the crowds so as to skip the pellets up into the knees and legs. For unruly crowds, where people have mixed degree of involvement in the disruption, don't take body shots. Remember the female who was in the crowd a number of years ago at a "celebration" of her sporting teams victory that was getting out of hand? She was killed by a wooden baton knee knocker round to the head. I can't say it enough, rounds like this are less lethal, not non-lethal. If you keep those parameters and limitations in mind, you should have great success with specialty shotgun rounds.

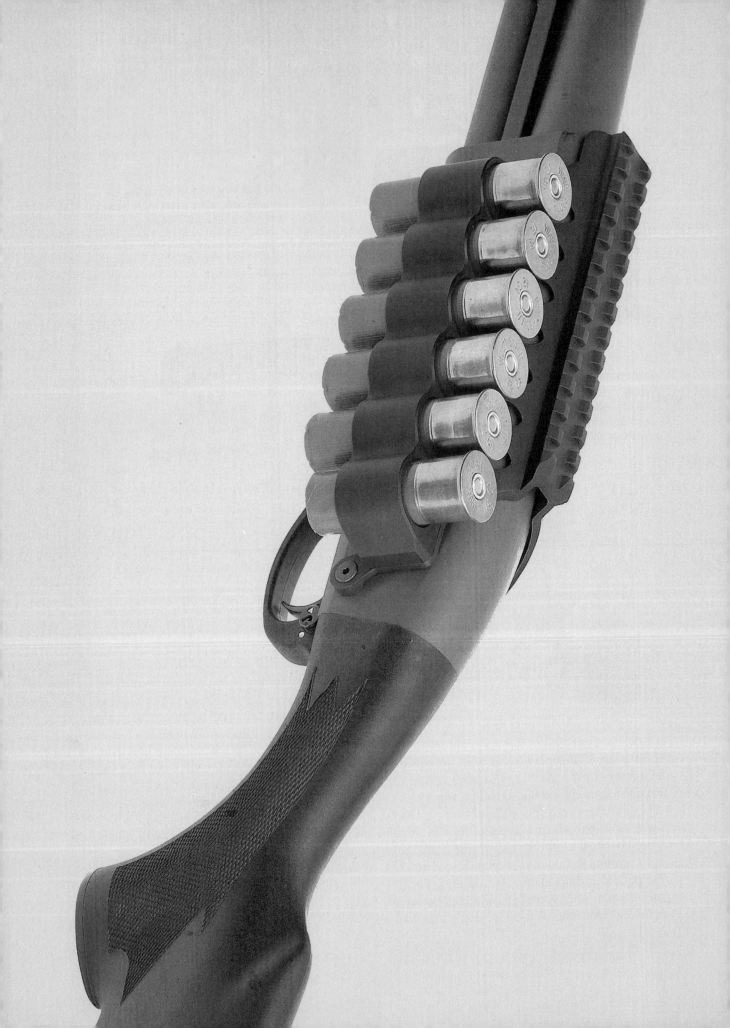

# CHAPTER EIGHT

# RECOMMENDED
## ACCESSORIES

If you want to add accessories to your tactical shotgun, I advise that you buy one that is ready to accept those accessories from the get-go, without modification. The very best, most cost-effective ready-to-go tactical shotgun is without a doubt the new Remington 887 Nitro Mag Tactical. Yes, the Model 37 Ithaca Defense gun is my personal favorite, but for about $450 you have in the 887 a gun that is all set, no modifications needed.

In review of the 887, there is a strip of picatinny rail to allow for optics mounting, and on the forend barrel band there is a strip of picatinny to mount a light. On my home defense 887, I mounted a BLACKHAWK! Xiphos 90 lumen pistol light. Works perfect for home defense purposes, and since it is a one cell lithium light and made of polymer, it adds next to no weight to the gun. Sling swivel mounts are already in place. The gun holds seven rounds of ammo. As of yet I could find no side saddle mounts, so you will have to go with an elastic type stock mount.

If you like another shotgun style better, one that isn't ready to rock, it isn't all that difficult to customize. Just remember, it's a Remington and Mossberg world out there, and to a lesser part Benelli, and most accessories that are available cater to those weapon systems because of the numbers of those guns that are sold and the wide variations within each product line.

## CARRYING SPARE AMMO

One of the problems I've encountered in the past with on-the-stock shell carriers is that some were, well, cheap. They were "one size fits all" and the elastic soon wore out to the point that these things would spin around on the stock. In all fairness, it's been hard to find a good design, but I think I have. Eagle Industries has a "Made in the USA" stock carrier that has two adjustable Velcro straps to hold it in place at the stock wrist and near the butt, along with a third strap that goes over the recoil pad itself. It holds six spare rounds of ammo in elastic loops and seems pretty secure. I am going to pick one up for the Ithaca 37 as the colors used are OD green and black, and it kind of has an old-timey military look to it. Best yet it is listed online at BTI Tactical for $18.99.

Side saddle receiver carriers are another way of carrying spare ammo. The TacStar SideSaddle® carrier is a simple polymer holder that carries six spare shells. An advantage of the polymer construction over elastic is that it will hold its shape. It is easy to mount (even I did it without screwing up the gun) and requires no modification to the weapon. It is available for the now discontinued Winchester 1200 and 1300 – 12 gauge; the Remington 870 and semi-auto 1100 – 12 gauge; the Mossberg 500 and 600 series – 12 gauge; and the Benelli M1-90 – 12 gauge.

The only thing I would say about receiver carriers is that they make the receiver area thick (an area that you might carry the gun by), and they also make it ungainly by putting weight on the left side of the receiver. Further, when in a case, the shotgun is a little slower to draw out than when the shells are mounted on a stock carrier. But try it out for yourself. The TacStars aren't expensive, retailing for $29.99. If you don't like it, they are easily removed.

## REPLACEMENT STOCKS

The replacement stock is one of the major components, particularly for the Remington 870 and Mossberg 500 series, that can be readily changed out and replaced. It's a big market area since, as I have mentioned, the length of pull for most standard stocks is too long. For most stocks, you have to be a fairly large person to have them fit well. And even for them, if you throw in heavy armor for tactical team members, the length of pull issue is exacerbated. Therefore, there a lot of aftermarket stock options available.

One of the best sources for aftermarket shotgun stocks and parts is BLACKHAWK! I have worked with BLACKHAWK! products of various sorts for quite some time – clothing, boots, tactical flashlights (both handheld and weapons mounted), slings, breaching equipment (Hammer of Thor Sledge, expandable pry bar and Mini-Break and Rake – great stuff all) and cutting tools. I can attest to their quality.

Under their long gun accessories/stocks there are 10 different styles and models available, including camo versions and an orange safety version for less lethal weapons. There are a couple of models available for shotgun breachers, which consist of basically a conversion to a pistol grip-only system. Note that they sell these pistol grip models for door breaching purposes, not for general "on the street use."

One intriguing system available as an add-on to the M4 SpecOps™ adjustable stock system is called the Power-Pak® modular cheek piece. The Power-Pak includes a raised cheek piece for use with optical sights, a shell holder that holds five 12-gauge shells ready for quick reloads, a water-tight storage compartment for earplugs and spare batteries, and a standard height cheek piece for use with low-rise sights or bead. The basic SpecOps Adjustable Stock is available for Remington® 12 gauge 870 Series pump shotguns along with the 7615, 7400, 7500, 7600, 740, 750 and 760 series rifles; all 12 and 20 gauge Mossberg® 500, 590, 835 variants, and Maverick 88 mod-

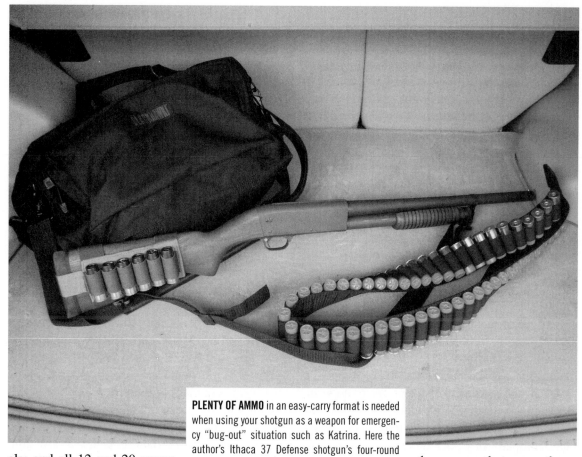

**PLENTY OF AMMO** in an easy-carry format is needed when using your shotgun as a weapon for emergency "bug-out" situation such as Katrina. Here the author's Ithaca 37 Defense shotgun's four-round mag capacity is augmented by Eagle Industries six shot buttstock ammo carrier and the simple but elegant BLACKHAWK!™ 55 round bandolier. The Eagle Industries spare ammo carrier is well designed, ambidextrous and stays in place due to strap across recoil pad. The BLACKHAWK! bandolier easily slings over the shoulder.

els; and all 12 and 20 gauge Winchester® 1300-1200 and FNH® standard Police Series pump shotguns (stock will not fit FNH® Tactical Police Shotgun).

SpecOps Stocks are not compatible with semi-automatic shotguns. The SpecOps Stock is also available with the Knoxx recoil reducing system, which reduces recoil by up to 95 percent. I have tried the recoil reducer system, and noted that it does make quite a difference in felt recoil. BLACKHAWK! also carries the standard style CompStock™ recoil reducing stock. It is not adjustable for length of pull like the SpecOps stocks, but if you are not having any issues like that then the CompStock should work out fine for you.

BLACKHAWK! also carries folding stocks for the ultimate in lightweight storage. I don't really care for folding stocks for everyday use, as they don't add a lot of tactical advantage to the weapon that wears them, and some are downright uncomfortable to shoot. You might want to put one on a gun for compact storage situations, such as in a tent, camper, boat or bush plane. At the least, it is a better option than a pistol grip-only model.

Some of the other accessories BLACK-HAWK! carries include shotgun slings (including one that holds a boatload of spare shells), cases, vertical ammo pouches for MOLLE attachment, shell bandoliers, and a combination cheek pad and stock ammo holder.

I never had a bandolier spare shotshell holder for any fighting shotgun before. Since it seems this is the age of the active shooter and potential civil unrest, being able to quickly sling 50 rounds of shotgun shells over your shoulder in case of an emergency may come in handy. There really is no more convenient way to carry shotgun ammo for quick access. A bandolier can be kept in a trunk or go-bag for long term storage, and donned when the need arises. I ordered their 55 round bandolier and found it to be a great accessory to have in a kit. Constructed of heavy duty nylon, the bandolier slings easily over the shoulder. MSPR is $30.99. Yes, you can hold more than 60 rounds of ammo in two AR mags in considerably less space. But that isn't what we are talking about now, is it? Yes, you will have to spin the bandolier around to get to all the ammo, or take it off, but if it's really hitting the fan for you then that is of little concern compared to being caught in some conflagration with only four rounds in your magazine tube and six more rounds on the stock. Plus it works for any shotgun system out there. I highly recommend it. (www.blackhawk.com)

## ADVANCED TECHNOLOGY INTERNATIONAL (ATI)

I had not heard of Advanced Technology International prior to doing research for this book, and actually prior to taking a tour of the Ithaca Gun Company in Upper Sandusky Ohio to see how the Ithaca Model 37 is manufactured these days. ATI is based out of Milwaukee, and has new ownership that seems to be committed to bringing out some of the most innovative tactical designs possible.

At Ithaca I saw two examples of adjustable stocks, and an excellent five-sided aluminum railed fore-end that had just been developed for the Model 37. Combined with these new stocks, the Ithaca 37 has been updated as a 21st Century fighting shotgun.

ATI makes a huge range of tactical products for a wide variety of long guns, including some more obscure weapons like the British Enfield and Russian Mosin-Nagant rifles. The extensive ATI line includes apparel, bipods, bolt handles, buttpads, camo stocks, cheek rests, forends, handguards, heatshields, mag clamps, mag extensions, military, law, home defense, mounts, pistol grips, rifle stocks, scope mounts, shotgun accessories, shotgun stocks, shotshell holders, sling adapters, slings, and tactical rails.

In addition to handling the new five-sided rail system, I got to work with the two of the ATI recoil reducing stocks. The first one was the Akita adjustable recoil reducing stock. Styled more like a conventional stock, rather than an M4 variant, the Akita is not only adjustable in terms of length, but also adjustable in terms of the height of the cheekpiece. But as an added bonus, the Akita also contains a recoil reduction system.

The Akita is available in tactical black or in three different patterned types. The one I saw had a new woodlike pattern, brown in color, that blended well with the blued hunting type 37s. The Akita would make a great tactical rifle stock for precision shooting. It's unfortunate that it's currently offered only for shotguns. If you wanted to have a shotgun for fighting use that had a more subdued look, and not like an overblown AR-15, or one that would double as your deer or field gun and would fit you perfectly, then the Akita system is the way to go.

Ithaca is marketing these first for their youth model with the thought that a youth can "grow into" their shotgun just by adjusting a stock, and not by Dad or Mom having to buy a new gun. I look at it in terms of it being able to fit any shooter with easy adjustment, or any shooter depending on the clothing they are wearing at the moment. It also has a matching forend available. The Akita stock, a brilliant design, retails at $159 for the stock and forend, and $129 for the stock alone.

For those of you who want a fully adjustable recoil reducing stock that is built upon the AR style, ATI offers the Six Position Side Folding Tactical Stock. Yep, since a pump shotgun has no buffer tube, ATI built the stock so that it can fold the stock to the side. Mike Farrell, president of Ithaca guns, showed me one of these models on an extended magazine model 37. This stock comes with a pistol grip and not only is adjustable for length, but adjustable for cheekrest as well. In fact, the cheekrest is removable if you don't want it on your gun. I usually work best with an M4 stock collapsed almost all the way down; on an AR my nose almost touches the charging handle. It was no different for this stock, which allowed me to get a perfect fit instantly. Since the stock folds to the left, your shotgun can still be fired with the stock folded in an emergency, or if you are on a tactical team and your shotgun is also set up as a breaching weapon. It is a work of tactical art, and is priced at $89.95. This stock is also available for AR-15s in a non-side folding variant called the Strikeforce with a removable cheekpad and recoil pad. It would be my top choice of an M4 style stock for both shotguns and ARs.

If you are happy with a fixed pistol grip type of stock for your shotgun, ATI has those too and, as expected, they are less expensive at $44.95. The fixed stock drops down from the receiver in a manner that also ought to reduce felt recoil generated to the shoulder.

If you want to jazz up the appearance of your shotgun and give it a more aggressive look, you can add a metal heatshield to your shotgun. While the actual utility of one of these may be in question (unless you compete a lot in three gun matches or plan on fending off an attack by hordes of flesh eating zombies) you probably won't need one. I don't know of any law enforcement agency that equips their guns this way since we don't fire a lot of rounds at any one time in rapid succession. Heat shields were only used by the military on fighting shotguns (trench guns starting with the Winchester 97) and only were seen in law enforcement when we inherited surplus guns from the military. With all that said, it's not always about need, or even practical value – cool counts too, right? At least this addition doesn't weigh much and won't hurt anything or affect operation, so if you like it, why not?

## BROWNELLS

If you can't find it for your shotgun at Brownells, then it probably doesn't exist. From accessories such as sighting systems and stocks, to parts kits, railed forends, choke kits, this is the place to come if the factory doesn't have it, or if your gun is out of warranty, or if you need a "one stop shop" to find everything, and I mean everything. Under the website heading of shot-gun parts, there are a whopping 415 pages listed! Under the 100 pages of the "Accessories" section, there are more shotgun items interspersed with all the other items, including things like mercury recoil suppressors, magazine extensions, and Surefire light forends.

Much of the Brownells inventory is for gunsmiths who are making more or less permanent modifications or repair to the weapons they are working on. For the tactical shotgun shooter, however, the best part of Brownells isn't on their main page, it is under the tab at the top of the page listed "Police Store.Com." This web section gives the quickest access to the types of accessories that non-gunsmith end users, such as myself, would want to modify their tactical guns with, you know, the type of modifications that don't permanently alter the gun so you can put it back to its original form or modify it to something else. Let's face it, how many of us that shoot tactical-type long guns are without a box or two of parts or accessories that once graced our weapon of choice, but are no longer in use?

What is nice about the Police Store site is that it pre-filters out all the thousands of Brownells parts and supplies that we really aren't interested in for our tactical shotgun (or any other fighting weapon for that matter) and puts it into one area. So let me tell you about a few of the important things that are available here. First, if you check under the main tab of "Firearms Accessories," you find these sub-categories:

Autoloading Pistols (40 p)
Autoloading Rifle (202 p)
Autoloading Shotguns (2 p)
Bolt Action Rifles (8 p)
Brownells Catalogs (4 p)
Magazine Accessories (14 p)
Pump Action Shotguns (24 p)
Recoil Pads & Stock Access. (6 p)
Revolvers (4 p)
Shotgun Shell Holders (6 p)
Slings & Sling Swivels (30 p)
Special Gunsmithing Tools (2 p)
Specialty Products (29 p)
Targets & Target Accessories (1 p)
Universal Shotgun Sights (6 p)

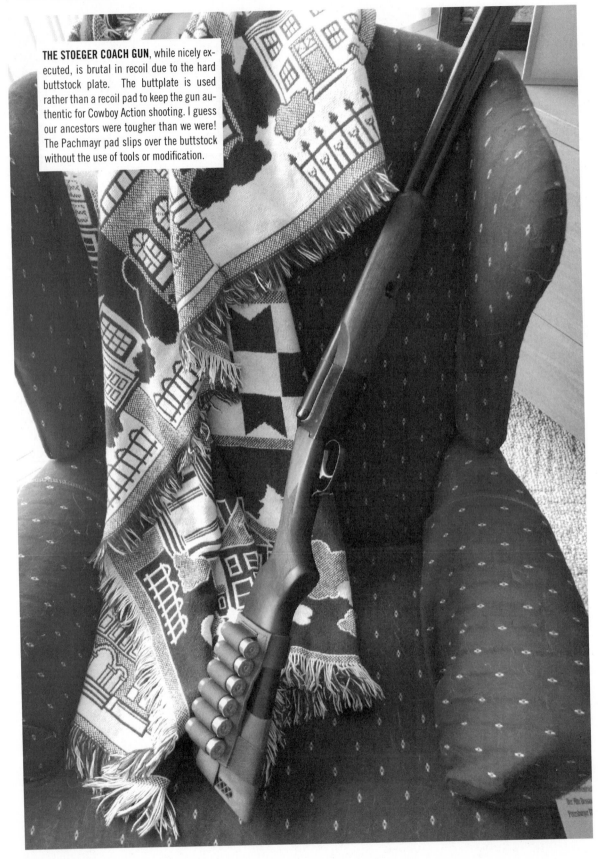

**THE STOEGER COACH GUN**, while nicely executed, is brutal in recoil due to the hard buttstock plate. The buttplate is used rather than a recoil pad to keep the gun authentic for Cowboy Action shooting. I guess our ancestors were tougher than we were! The Pachmayr pad slips over the buttstock without the use of tools or modification.

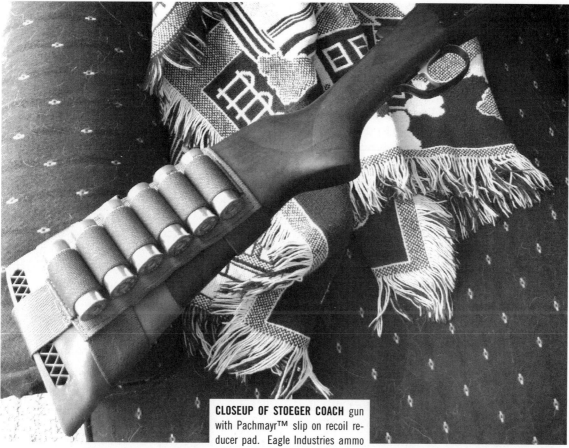

**CLOSEUP OF STOEGER COACH** gun with Pachmayr™ slip on recoil reducer pad. Eagle Industries ammo carrier slips right over the top of the Pachmayr pad.

Yes, those numbers are pages of accessories that follow for each category. As you can see, there are a lot of accessories for not only the shotgun shooter, but also for handgun and rifle shooters as well.

Under the "Pump Action Shotgun" section, I found a very important accessory for the tactical shotgun shooter, the replacement railed forend. The first one that Police Store had listed was for the Mossberg 500 series by Command Arms Accessories. The forend is of lightweight polymer construction and adds three segments of rail – short sections on the side, long section on the bottom – to allow for the mounting or tactical lights and lasers. At $54.99, this is a very affordable alternative to forend systems like the Surefire, if you already have a tactical light and mount on hand. No, its not aluminum, but really, you would have to work very hard to wear out modern polymer, and you have to keep weight down (I believe).

If you really must have aluminum for your railed forend, the Police Store site carries a Falcon Industries three-sided forend for your Remington 870 or Mossberg shotgun. It is priced at $20 more than the Command Arms forend, but that's the difference in price of materiels and machining required. Still not a bad price, though.

Here is the true beauty of a website like this: If you don't know a particular manufacturer's name but know the product type you want, you can find it in one place, without having to search individual sites for the information. Further, Brownells has a fabulous reputation, and they simply don't carry garbage. For example, if you want replacement adjustable or recoil reducing stocks for your pump shotgun and you check here, you find, by my count, 16 choices and brands all in one spot.

The Police Store sight is great, and also lists flashlights, optics, knives, training equipment and armorer's tools. You should be able to equip your weapon any way you want right from here.

One thing I couldn't find on the Police Store web page, because it's not really a tactical accessory, was a slip-on recoil pad for the Stoeger Coach gun that I tested, and found I really needed. Not wanting to take the time to modify the gun by adding a permanent recoil pad (and not having the skill to do that without butchering the job), I simply went back to the Brownells main page tab, and found the time honored Pachmayr brand slip-on pad for $14.99, got it and added it to the Stoeger. This is what is so cool: You will find what you need somewhere on the Brownells sites. Oh, if you need ammo, or anything for reloading, including shooting accessories, books and videos, hit the Sinclair International tab in the middle and you're there! They list some calibers that are less common and hard to find. Alas, no shotgun ammo, but about everything else is there. (www.brownells.com)

## BTI TACTICAL

BTI is a law enforcement product distribution company started by a Chicago area SWAT cop with the purpose of producing a one-stop shop for hardcore tactical items. BTI Tactical was where I turned to find a buttstock-mounted spare ammo carrier for the Ithaca 37 shotgun I have been working with. They had just what I was looking for – an OD green 6 shot buttstock carrier with a retro look to it. I wanted to get something which didn't spoil the trench gun look of this tactical gun, and the Eagle brand carrier they had for it is perfect.

I have not always been enamored with some of the elastic slip-on carriers for shotgun, having been subjected to them in my former police department. That administration had a penchant for trying to equip us with the cheapest equipment possible that would only marginally get the job done. One of the products given to use to carry spare ammo were these elastic, slip-over-the-stock shell carriers. They worked for awhile of course until the elastic loosened up a bit, then the carriers began to spin and flop all around the stocks.

With the Eagle Industries brand, the carrier is held in place with hook and pile straps around the stock, as well as a strap around the end of the buttstock to hold it firmly in place, regardless of the side that it is attached on. The open design allows easy access to the shells which speeds any emergency reloading needs. The price was very reasonable at only $22.00. BTI also carriers models that enclose the ammo entirely, which would be good for guns that are operated, carried, or stored in sandy or dusty environments, or in vehicles that traverse those environments. BTI also carries shotgun stocks of various types, recoil reducing, less lethal and breaching configurations, as well as slings and mounts. I would recommend BTI as a one stop tactical shop, covering almost everything that can conceivably needed. (www.btitactical.com)

## CABELAS

Cabelas also carries a huge lineup of shotgun parts and stocks. One of the ones that caught my eye was the Advanced Technology top folding stock. It caught my eye because it is modeled after the original steel Remington Top Folding stock, except this one is constructed of polymer which reduces cost and weight. One of the 870s at our department had the Remington steel folding stock. That steel stock would just beat you unmercifully, and is no longer in production ostensibly for that reason. I was concerned about what this new version of the top-folder would feel like on the receiving end. I read the reviews of the stock on the Cabelas site, and only one said anything about the recoil being rough. The rest said it was quite comfortable. It must be the difference between polymer and steel construction, because there is no recoil pad, just like on the original. The setup looks cool, and the shotgun can still be fired with the stock closed in an emergency. If compact storage is a consideration, you might want to look at this traditional style top folder.

Cabelas also carries other ATI items that work for both Remington and Mossberg guns. This includes an M4 stock and front end accessories with a heat shield and compact forend grip; perfect for the shotgun aficionado that wants to "tac" up their plain jane pump gun for a more modern, aggressive look.

Speedfeed® brand stocks are also available in pistol grip configurations that hold spare rounds of ammo internally, with easy access to the shooter. I haven't used them personally, but have never heard any bad reviews of the system. I also haven't seen them in use in law enforcement agencies in my area. They do present the shooter with a sleek option for carrying spare rounds rather than using a side saddle type carrier or a stock sling. The Speedfeed stock set also comes with a replacement forend.

For those of you who are man or woman enough to handle something like a tough-kicking double barrel, there are both Pachmayer Decelerator® and Sims Limb Saver® slip-on recoil pads.

Of course Cabelas features a huge gun store stocking about every conceivable shotgun available, as well as a huge ammo selection that can be shipped to your home. (www.cabelas.com)

## MESA TACTICAL

Mesa Tactical is one of the few companies out there that deals almost entirely with quality updates and upgrades for the tactical shotgun user. They are unique in this regard since they deal with nothing for the AR, which is a bit refreshing.

In my book, Mesa Tactical has just about solved the issue of mounting lights on shotguns, and it is nothing short of brilliant (no light pun intended there). It is another one of those "why the hell didn't I think of that" kind of things: It is a receiver rail mounting system for the Remington 870 that mounts a strip of rail right above the trigger guard, allowing you to access a tactical light with your right thumb. No more wires running across the forend! There are strips available for right or left side mounting to accommodate the individual user.

If you want more railing on your shotgun, Mesa also makes "Saddle Rails" of different lengths ( 5, 8-1/2 and 20 inch lengths are available) that fit right over the top of your 870, and provides a barrel heat shield and rail in the 20 inch length. These rails allow for light and optics mounting alike. In the plain aluminum (silver) color, it provides a cool contrast with a black tactical shotgun.

But wait, there is more! Mesa Tactical is one of the few aftermarket folks making products for guns like the FN SLP. One of their newest is their SureShell tactical shell carrier for mounting on the left side. There are also M4-type telescoping stocks and an ingenious piece for them called the High and Low Tube-Adaptors which allow for picatinny rail, SureShell carriers, optics mounting or sling mounting points right where the stock joins the receiver.

The high and low tube adaptors allow you to mount M4-type AR-15 adjustable stocks on standard stocked Remington 870 Mossberg 500 or 590 series shotguns. If you have never handled a tactical shotgun with an M4 type stock on it, you really ought to give it a try, especially with your entry or raid armor. Your existing supply of standard stocked shotguns can easily be converted without much trouble to the M4 stock system. By choosing the LE, Low Tube or High tube adaptors (which vary the relationship of the stock to the receiver), you can better accommodate the use of bead sights, rails or adjustable rifle sights.

To further enhance shotgun shooting ability, there is a recently introduced hydraulic recoil buffer system that fits in the stock where the recoil spring and buffer would go on an AR. According to Mesa Tactical, these recoil reducers drop felt recoil by approximately 70 percent. Mesa also makes mounting hardware for lights and rail in the more traditional barrel and magazine mounting style. These clamps allow for mounting lights with remote pressure pads, and they work on multiple types of shotguns. There are receiver rail mounts for Mossberg shotguns as well as Remington shotguns, as well as simple sling hooks and mounting points for 870s, Mossbergs and Benellis that mount at the trigger group pin in the receiver.

Adding Mesa Tactical products to your shotgun brings the standard pumpgun into the 21st century tactical world. (www.mesatactical.com)

## TACTICAL LINK

Tactical Link is a sharply focused company, with all of its products made in the U.S.A., and all but one (the Battery Assist Lever) having to do with slings and mounting them. I have worked with products from Tactical link for about four years now, in particular with their single point sling system for AR-15s. We have used them extensively in training at the 727 Counter Terror Training Unit at Columbus State Community College on our modified Systema airsoft ARs as well as on live fire weapons. They are rugged yet elegant, simple to work with and get the job done, and their new attachment system is second to none in terms of simplicity.

Currently, they make one set of products for shotguns, specifically the Remington 870, which all revolve around deployment of their sling system. The first is the single point sling itself, for which you also need one of their mounting systems. The sling retails at $44.94 and is available in black, coyote or olive drab. Remember that OD or coyote is the new black in the tactical world.

In order to attach the sling to the 870, you will need one of two systems that Tactical Link has available. The first is the V-870™. This unique mounting system, which according to Tactical Link is "precision machined from 7075 aluminum alloy and is the beefiest mount of its kind. Because the V-870's sling channel is uniquely reinforced with additional material, it will not bend or deform and withstands the toughest abuse. The corners of the V-870's sling channel are rounded to ensure operator comfort and sling longevity. The V-870 is compatible with our V-870 Single Point Sling as well as Knoxx Stocks".

It fits between the stock mounting point at the rear of the receiver without appreciably increasing the length of pull, positioning it at an excellent point for balance. This mount is $33.95.

The other mount is the more expensive Shot Mod™. The Shot Mod allows for use of the standard Tactical Link Single and Double Point slings, and fits in the same position as the V-870. What makes this sling excellent is the fact that the sling can be mounted on either side of the gun

with the Tactical Link quick detach swivels, and of course detached quickly in an emergency.

If you want absolutely first class slings and attachment methods for your 870 and AR, look no further than Tactical link. Hopefully they will bring out some more products for all those Mossberg fans out there too. (www.tacticallink.com)

## TACSTAR®

TacStar® has been around forever. I remember getting one of the first products from them: their universal laser, which I got for my dad's Smith and Wesson Model 67 Combat Masterpiece revolver. He really liked it, but I have to admit, I had no interest in one for duty or off-duty use at the time, even though that laser was significantly smaller than the one Arnold used in the first Terminator movie on his AMT Longslide Hardballer. That would have to wait until I got my hands on my first Crimson Trace Grip. But I digress, especially since TacStar is now under the Lyman Products banner, and no longer carries lasers sights. Those are carried by a company called NcStar, and I don't know how that all came about, but the original Universal Laser is still there.

Anyway, the current TacStar company does carry a goodly number of shotgun accessories for Remington, Mossberg, and the little seen Winchester (which dropped out of sight when the Winchester Plant closed in the U.S). These accessories include pistol grips and pistol grip forends, the well known and respected TacStar side saddle shotshell carrier, which mounts on the receiver and not the stock of the gun, tactical slings, barrel shrouds and lighting systems, and universal barrel mounts for mounting tactical lights to the barrel of the shotgun.

Not having worked with TacStar products for awhile, I decided to purchase one of their universal barrel mounts and try it on the Mossberg 930 I have been working with. I hate having cords hanging off of lights and draped and taped in various places on the gun, where they can catch or worse. When I was in Assault Weapons Instructor's school way back when, one of the officers in the class had a department issued M16 A1 which

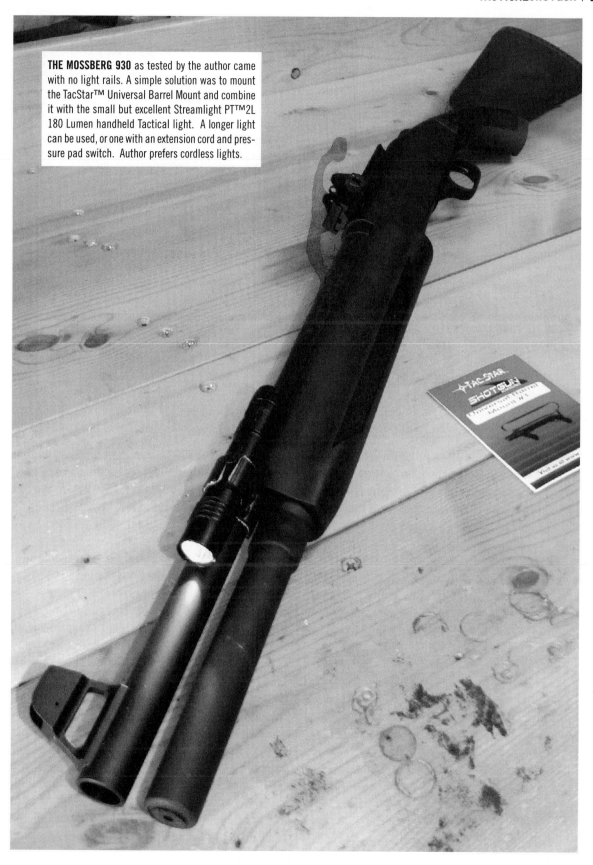

**THE MOSSBERG 930** as tested by the author came with no light rails. A simple solution was to mount the TacStar™ Universal Barrel Mount and combine it with the small but excellent Streamlight PT™2L 180 Lumen handheld Tactical light. A longer light can be used, or one with an extension cord and pressure pad switch. Author prefers cordless lights.

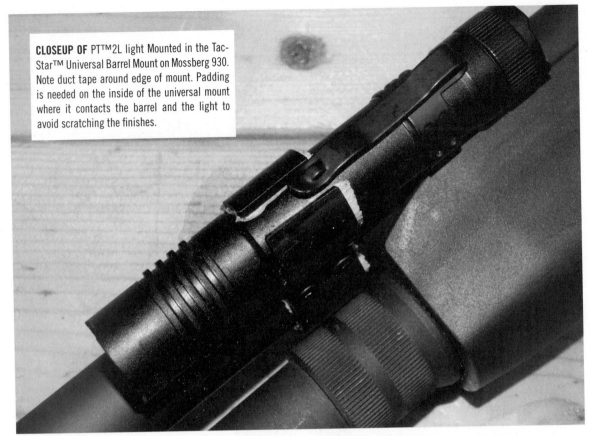

**CLOSEUP OF** PT™2L light Mounted in the Tac-Star™ Universal Barrel Mount on Mossberg 930. Note duct tape around edge of mount. Padding is needed on the inside of the universal mount where it contacts the barrel and the light to avoid scratching the finishes.

had been converted to semi-auto fire only. He had a TacStar Laser sight mounted on the gun, which is was kind of cool, but he hadn't had it long. He had run the curled cord from the laser to the forend pressure switch right across the triangular handguard cooling holes on the top. Dopey me, I thought (not having worked with an M16 much up until that point) that's cool, it keeps the cord out of the way. Well, after just a hundred rounds or so, the heat from the gas tube melted the cord, and that was the end of his laser. Live and learn right?

I had learned not to like light cords, so what I wanted to do with the 930 was to mount a tactical light that could be reached without a cord and operated by my thumb or index finger. I purchased one of the TacStar mounts from Vance's Shooters Supply in Columbus for under $20. The first thing I noticed on these all steel mounts was that there is no padding to protect your barrel or light from being scratched. So I reached for the handyman's secret weapon: duct tape. I taped a piece to the inside of both pieces of the mount, which

would protect the light and the barrel, as well as giving more gripping surface to the mount.

After experimenting a bit, I ended up mounting the outstanding Streamlight PT™2L Tactical Handheld light to the barrel. This lithium 2-cell aluminum light is compact and very bright at 180 lumens. One of the best parts is the push button switch, which requires no twisting or adjustment, but let's you move from momentary on, strobe, low power and constant on just by varying the number of times or depth that you push the switch. The other great thing about the switch is that it is slightly recessed and can't be, or isn't likely to be, activated in your pocket.

Anyway, in order to reach the switch I mounted the light to the barrel at about an 11 o'clock position (as you are looking at it from the rear of the gun) where it rests against the top of the forend on the left side. This serves to hold it in position and allows me to reach the light with my left hand thumb. The light weight of both the light and the mount don't add at all to the muzzle heft. Be careful with this mount if you

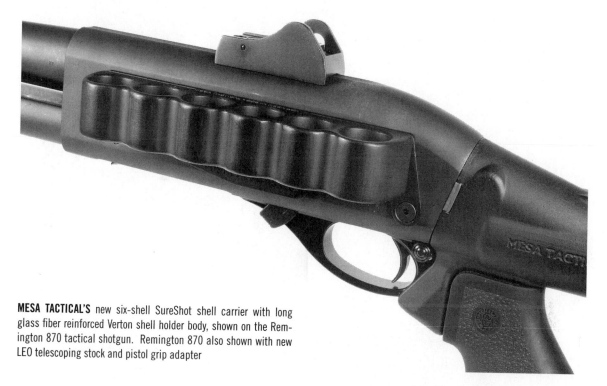

**MESA TACTICAL'S** new six-shell SureShot shell carrier with long glass fiber reinforced Verton shell holder body, shown on the Remington 870 tactical shotgun. Remington 870 also shown with new LEO telescoping stock and pistol grip adapter

try to mount it to a magazine tube, they are made of aluminum and I suppose you could dent one if you got overly aggressive tightening the allen screws (something I might tend to do, but not in this particular case). TacStar is definitely worth looking into if you want to modify your gun with quality stuff at a reasonable price.

## NCSTAR

As mentioned previously, NcStar now handles the original TacStar universal lasers, as well as a number of interesting products that you may be unaware of. Although NcStar appears to mostly favor the AR crowd, they do make a number of universal mounting systems for lights and lasers that are designed to fit any barrel.

Even if you don't find a particular mount of theirs to your liking, I would suggest looking at some of their sighting equipment, such as their ARLSRG dual red/green laser with universal barrel mounting system. This unique laser allows you to switch between a red or green laser dot simply by a short twist of the bezel. Don't know why you would want to, but you can. Interestingly the bezel of the laser has multiple serrations

which I am sure would cause injury to someone who wished to try and grab at the laser.

NcStar also carriers a number of compact red dot sights that look like they would be excellent for mounting atop the Mossberg 930 or other shotguns that have a strip of rail upon the receiver, such as the Remington 887. The red dots and a number of other optics have an appearance that is very similar to some well know brands, but which feature some different capabilities like a multi-reticle system, where the shooter can choose the reticle style that suits them best. Any of the smaller sights would work well mounted on a shotgun without compromising "pointability." (www.ncstar.com)

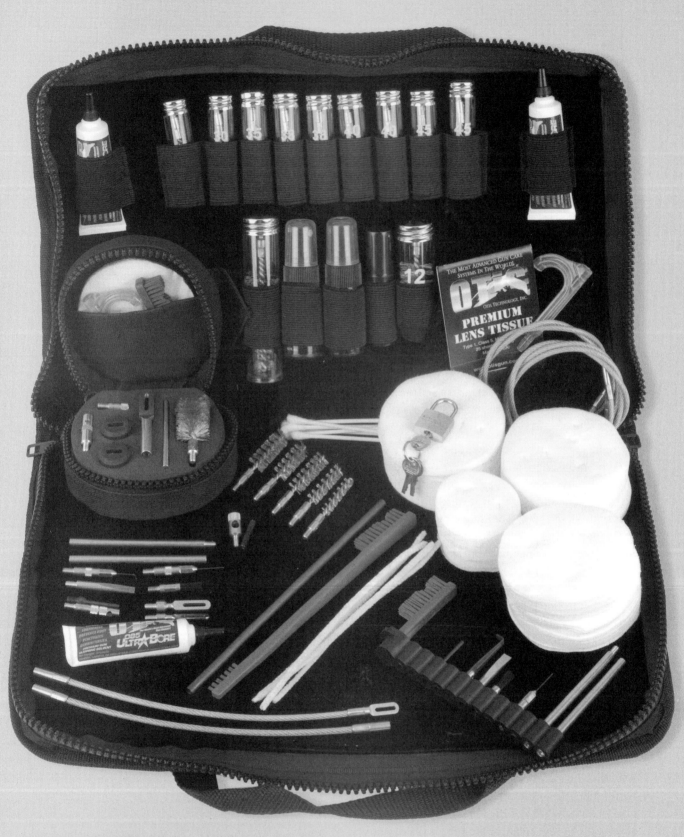

**OTIS GUN CARE PRODUCTS** come in a variety of sizes and configurations, from the Lil Pro all the way to full size kits that contain a wide variety of specific tools. OTIS products are configured to best meet the needs and missions of end users, whether they be sportsmen, military or law enforcement.

# CHAPTER NINE

# MAINTENANCE

Here is another area where the tactical shotgun outshines the AR-15 as the primo choice for defense. There is not much to maintaining and cleaning it, especially in the case of pump guns and double barrels. No carbon to scrape off of bolts and bolt carriers, no gas tubes to clean out, and a minimal degree of gunk being blown back into the action. A simple field strip, wipe down, bore swipe and wipe down of the exterior parts and you're done.

With most shotguns, you can remove the barrel for cleaning. On the Ithaca 37 Defense, you can't; it's a fixed barrel. Removing the barrel allows you to clean from the chamber end first, which is the preferred way. I don't think it makes as much difference when you are dealing with smoothbore shotgun barrels as it does with any sort of rifled barrels. If you want to clean from the chamber end out to the bore, using a cable type cleaning system allows you to clean fixed barrels in this manner. But in terms of cleaning the shotgun in general, I have found that it doesn't need to be done very often. Wipe off the exterior when the gun is exposed to inclement weather or long term storage, but otherwise, don't sweat it too much. It would take a hell of a lot of dirt down there to really affect your groups and patterning.

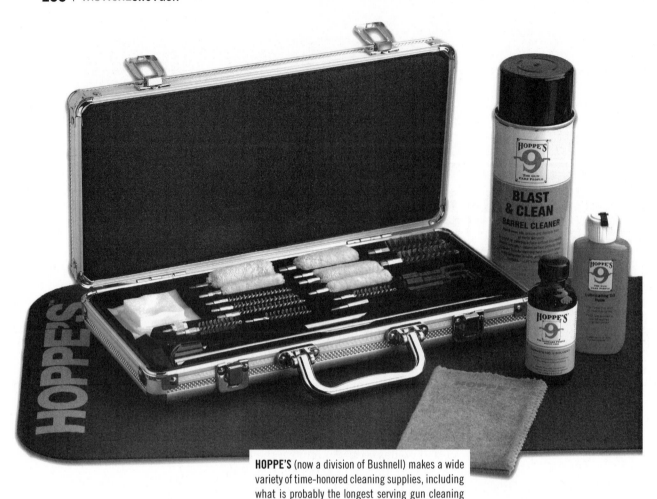

There are many products out there to accomplish this mission, with new ones introduced seemingly every day. Many of the new products are like Break Free™, they clean, lubricate and protect all from the same bottle. For the majority of cleaning needs, Break Free and products like it work great. For heavy chores, a different strategy is needed, and using different products, one for cleaning, one for lube, etc., takes care of business.

## HOPPE'S #9

It seems like Hoppe's #9 has been around since the shooting began. With its oddly cherry aroma, it conjures up great childhood memories of shooting .22s for the first time, old style gun shops that smell like gun shops, and my early days of my police academy training. Hoppe's #9 is still around and is still a great gun clean-ing product, with nostalgia being an added bonus. Use it in conjunction with other lubricants after the cleaning to preserve unprotected steel finishes and lubricate operational parts.

## BIRCHWOOD CASEY AEROSOL GUN SCRUBBER

This product is indispensable for cleaning and care of direct impingement AR-15s. It simply blasts the crud away, and it can certainly do the same on dirty shotguns (although it is hard to get them as dirty as an AR). You may not need it often for shotgun cleaning, but it is great to have on hand. Just remember to thoroughly replace lubricant on parts that need it. This product is a de-greaser; it strips away everything. Birchwood Casey is safe to use on polymer guns. Similar products used to discolor polymer frames.

**BIRCHWOOD** Casey Products make cleaning heavy fouling a breeze.

**WHEN YOU USE** use Birchwood Casey Gun Scrubber, make sure that you thoroughly re-lube your firearm, as it strips out all pre-existing lubricant. If you don't re-lube, you will be running your weapon totally dry.

### GUNSLICK ULTRA-KLENZ@

Ultra-Klenz is primarily a cleaner, although it is said to leave a light coat of lubrication and corrosion protection. Ultra-Klenz works very well, and it's lighter in terms of viscosity than some of the other products. I would use supplemental lubrication with it, especially in semi-automatic operating systems. One of the other selling points? It has a nice, fresh cedar scent which, again, will help keep the missus happy during indoor cleaning sessions. It also washes off your skin easier.

### OTIS GUN CARE PRODUCTS-OTIS 085 ULTRA BORE CLP

I have used an Otis Gun Products Tactical Cleaning system since about 1994. This compact kit contains patches, cables and jags that allow you to clean any weapon. I carry it with me in my go-bag. As I mentioned, the Otis cable kits allow you to clean a fixed barrel shotgun from the chamber to the muzzle. Their Ultra-Bore is an excellent do it all cleaner, lubricator and protector. They make a number of different kits for specific weapon systems, but the one I have seems to work fine for nearly all. Otis also makes lens cleaning kits. Their products are highly recommended and their micro cleaning kits should be in every go-bag or SWAT kit.

**RIGHT: GUNSLICK MAKES** a fine set of cleaning products, which can be purchased separately or in complete kits as shown. The odor from these Gunslick products isn't as strong as some others and may garner more "spousal support" when being used inside the home.

**BELOW: THE NEW WILSON** Combat lubricant and maintenance products are custom blended for use on 1911 pistols, AR-15 rifles and tactical shotguns.

## WILSON COMBAT

Wilson is expanding operations to include its own custom ammo line, cutting tools such as the excellent all purpose "Cop Tool", leather gear and now a line of lubricating oils. Under their Ultra Lube II label they have different purpose and viscosity levels of oil, grease and universal lubricant.

The oil is thin viscosity, and is designed to penetrate hard-to-reach areas. It is designed for cold weather use and operates well in temperature ranges of 150° to 10° F.

The grease is ideal for heavy wear areas and stays in place even under extreme conditions. It is the recommended lube for AR-15 bolt carrier assemblies and other semi-auto rifles and semi-auto shotguns. It is the lube I use on my Wilson Combat 6.8 SPC Recon. It operates best in the 150° to 45° Temperature Range.

The universal lubricant is designed for all firearms, and is the recommended lube for all Wilson Combat® Handguns. Its operational temperature range is 150° to 30°. Remember that these products are lubricants only, and not cleaners, and are set up for specific weapon systems. They are excellent formulations.

# PRODUCT
# INDEX

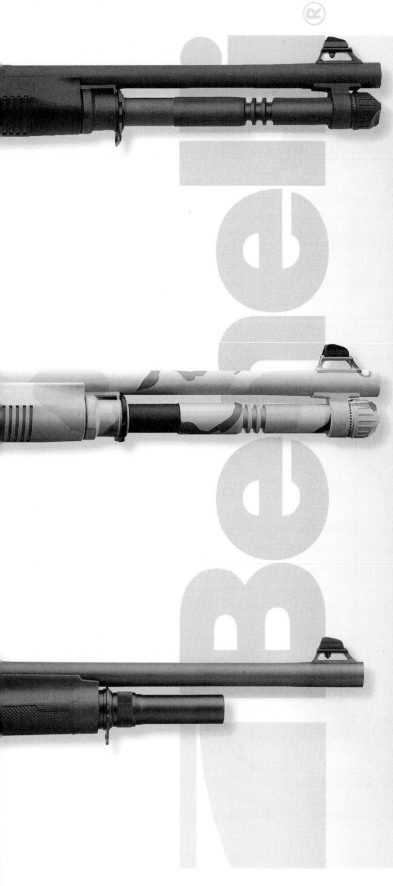

## M4 TACTICAL SYNTHETIC 12-GAUGE 2-3/4" AND 3"

**Item No.:** 11707
**Barrel length:** 18.5"
**Stock:** Pistol Grip/Synthetic
**Length:** 40.0"
**Weight:** 7.8 lbs.
**Magazine Capacity:** 4+1
**Chokes:** M
**Type of Sights:** Ghost ring; receiver is drilled and tapped for scope mount; Picatinny rail is included
**Length of Pull:** 14-3/8"
**Drop at Heel:** 2-1/4"
**Drop at Comb:** 1-1/2"

## M4 TACTICAL DESERT CAMO 12-GAUGE 2-3/4" AND 3"

**Item No.:** 11717
**Barrel length:** 18.5"
**Stock:** Pistol Grip/Desert Camo
**Length:** 40.0"
**Weight:** 7.8 lbs.
**Magazine Capacity:** 4+1
**Chokes:** M
**Type of Sights:** Ghost ring; receiver is drilled and tapped for scope mount; Picatinny rail is included
**Length of Pull:** 14-3/8"
**Drop at Heel:** 2-1/4"
**Drop at Comb:** 1-1/2"

## M2 TACTICAL 12-GAUGE 2-3/4" AND 3"

**Item no.:** 11052
**Barrel length:** 18.5"
**Stock:** Pistol Grip (also available with Tactical)
**Type of sights:** Ghost-ring
**Length:** 39.75"
**Weight:** 6.7 lbs.
**Magazine Capacity:** 5+1
**Crio® Chokes:** IC,M,F
**Length of Pull:** 14-3/8"
**Drop at Heel:** 2"
**Drop at Comb:** 1-3/8"
**Minimum Recommended Load:** 3-dram, 1-1/8oz. loads (12-ga.).

## M2 TACTICAL 12-GAUGE 2-3/4" AND 3"

**Item no.:** 11055
**Barrel length:** 18.5"
**Stock:** Tactical (also available with Pistol Grip)
**Type of sights:** Open Rifle
**Length:** 39.75"
**Weight:** 6.7 lbs.
**Magazine Capacity:** 5+1
**Crio® Chokes:** IC,M,F
**Length of Pull:** 14-3/8"
**Drop at Heel:** 2"
**Drop at Comb:** 1-3/8"
**Minimum Recommended Load:**
3-dram, 1-1/8oz. loads (12-ga.).

## M2 TACTICAL 12-GAUGE 2-3/4" AND 3"

**Item no.:** 11029
**Barrel length:** 18.5"
**Stock:** ComforTech®
**Type of sights:** Ghost-ring
(also available with Open Rifle)
**Length:** 39.75"
**Weight:** 6.7 lbs.
**Magazine Capacity:** 5+1
**Crio® Chokes:** IC,M,F
**Length of Pull:** 14-3/8"
**Drop at Heel:** 2"
**Drop at Comb:** 1-3/8"
**Minimum Recommended Load:** 3-dram,
1-1/8oz. loads (12-ga.).

## M3 CONVERTIBLE PUMP/ AUTO 12-GAUGE 2-3/4" & 3"

**Item no.:** 11606
**Barrel length:** 19.75"
**Type of sights:** Ghost-ring
**Length:** 45.6"
**Weight:** 7.2 lbs.
**Magazine Capacity:** 5+1
**Chokes:** Fixed Cyl.
**Type of Sights:** Ghost ring; receiver
is drilled and tapped for scope mount
**Length of Pull:** 14-3/8"
**Drop at Heel:** 2"
**Drop at Comb:** 1-3/8"

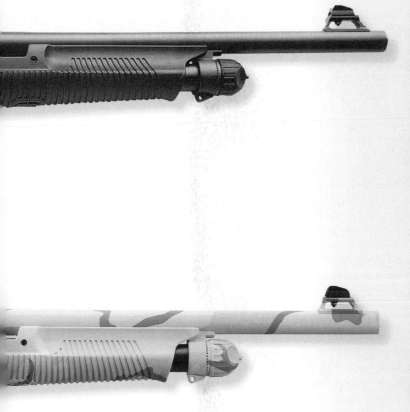

### NOVA PUMP TACTICAL 12-GAUGE 2-3/4", 3" & 3-1/2"

**Item no.:** 20050
**Barrel length:** 18.5"
**Stock:** Synthetic
**Sights:** Open Rifle or Ghost Ring
**Length:** 40.0"
**Weight:** 7.2 lbs.
**Magazine Capacity:** 4+1
**Chokes:** Fixed cyl.
**Length of Pull:** 14-1/4"
**Drop at Heel:** 2-1/4"
**Drop at Comb:** 1-1/4"

### SUPERNOVA TACTICAL 12-GAUGE 2-3/4", 3" & 3-1/2"

**Item no.:** 20161
**Barrel length:** 18.5"
**Stock:** Pistol Grip/Desert Camo
**Sights:** Ghost Ring
**Length:** 40.0"
**Weight:** 7.2 lbs.
**Magazine Capacity:** 4+1
**Chokes:** Fixed Cylinder
**Length of Pull:** 14-3/8"
**Drop at Heel:** 2-1/4"
**Drop at Comb:** 1-3/8"
Receiver is drilled and tapped
for scope mounting

## MODEL 870™ EXPRESS® TACTICAL A-TACS CAMO

**Action Type:** Pump
**Barrel Type:** Clean Barrel Rifle Sight Rem Choke
**BBL Length:** 18 1/2"
**Choke:** Rem Choke
**Gauge:** 12
**Overall Length:** 38 1/2 - 40 1/2 (Choke)
**Order #:** 81204

## MODEL 870™ EXPRESS® TACTICAL

**Action Type:** Pump
**Barrel Type:** Rem Choke
**BBL Length:** 18 1/2"
**Gauge:** 12
**Overall Length:** 38 1/2"
**Order #:** 81198

## MODEL 870™ TAC DESERT RECON

**Action Type:** Pump
**Barrel Type:** Rem Choke
**BBL Length:** 18" (or 20")
**Gauge:** 12
**Overall Length:** 38 1/2" (or 40")
**Order #:** 81420 (or 81421)

## MODEL 1100™ TAC 4
**Action Type:** Autoloading
**Barrel Type:** Rem Choke
**BBL Length:** 22"
**Gauge:** 12
**Overall Length:** 42 1/2"
**Order #:** 82801

## MODEL 887™ NITRO MAG TACTICAL
**Action Type:** Pump
**Barrel Type:** Solid Stepped Rib Rem Choke
**BBL Length:** 18 1/2"
**Choke:** Rem Choke
**Gauge:** 12 (3 1/2")
**Overall Length:** 39"
**Order #:** 82540

### 500 ROLLING THUNDER — 6 SHOT (BARREL STABILIZER)

**Item No.:** 55605
**Gauge:** 12
**Chamber:** 3"
Pistol Grip Only
**Capacity:** 6
**Barrel length:** 23"
**Sights:** Bead
**Chokes:** Cyl. Bore
**Length (in.):** 33 1/2"
**Finish:** Matte
**Stock:** Synthetic (Black)
**Weight:** 6 3/4 Lbs

### 500 TACTICAL CRUISER— 6 SHOT (STAND-OFF BARREL)

**Item No.:** 54125
**Gauge:** 12
**Chamber:** 3"
Pistol Grip Only
**Capacity:** 6
**Barrel length:** 18 1/2"
**Sights:** Bead
**Chokes:** Cyl. Bore
**Length (in.):** 31"
**Finish:** Matte
**Stock:** Synthetic (Black)
**Weight:** 5 3/4 Lbs

### 500 PERSUADER/CRUISER — 6 SHOT

**Item no.:** 50411
**Gauge:** 12
**Chamber:** 3"
Includes Pistol Grip Kit
**Capacity:** 6
**Barrel length:** 18 1/2"
**Sights:** Bead
**Chokes:** Cyl. Bore
**Length (in.):** 39 1/2"
**Length of pull:** 14 1/2"
**Finish:** Blue
**Stock:** Synthetic (Black)
**Weight:** 6 3/4 Lbs

### 500 PERSUADER/CRUISER — 6 SHOT

6 Shot Cruiser
**Item no.:** 50440
**Gauge:** 12
**Chamber:** 3"
Heat Shield, Pistol Grip Only
**Capacity:** 6
**Barrel length:** 18 1/2"
**Sights:** Bead
**Chokes:** Cyl. Bore
**Length (in.):** 28 3/4"
**Finish:** Blue
**Stock:** Synthetic (Black)
**Weight:** 5 3/4 Lbs

### 500 PERSUADER/CRUISER — 6 SHOT

6 Shot Cruiser
**Item No.:** 50450
**Gauge:** 20
**Chamber:** 3"
Pistol Grip Only
**Capacity:** 6
**Barrel length:** 18 1/2"
**Sights:** Bead
**Chokes:** Cyl. Bore
**Length (in.):** 28"
**Finish:** Blue
**Stock:** Synthetic (Black)
**Weight:** 5 1/2 Lbs

### 500 PERSUADER/CRUISER — 6 SHOT

**Item no.:** 50452
**Gauge:** 20
**Chamber:** 3"
Includes Pistol Grip Kit
**Capacity:** 6
**Barrel length:** 18 1/2"
**Sights:** Bead
**Chokes:** Cyl. Bore
**Length (in.):** 38 1/2"
**Length of pull:** 14"
**Finish:** Blue
**Stock:** Synthetic (Black)
**Weight:** 6 1/2 Lbs

### 500 PERSUADER/CRUISER — 6 SHOT

6 Shot Cruiser
**Item no.:** 50455
**Gauge:** .410
**Chamber:** 3"
Pistol Grip Only
**Capacity:** 6
**Barrel length:** 18 1/2"
**Sights:** Bead
**Chokes:** Cyl. Bore
**Length (in.):** 29 1/2"
**Finish:** Blue
**Stock:** Synthetic (Black)
**Weight:** 5 1/2 Lbs

### 500 J.I.C CRUISER

**Type:** Home Security/Special Purpose
**Item:** 51340
**Gauge:** 12
**Chamber:** 3"
**Description:** J.I.C.(Just In Case) Shotguns
**Cap.:** 6
**BBL Length:** 18 1/2"
**Sights:** Bead
**Chokes:** Cyl. Bore
**Length (In.):** 28 3/4"
**Finish:** Blue
**Stock:** Synthetic (Black)

### 500 PERSUADER/CRUISER — 8 SHOT

**Item no.:** 50577
**Gauge:** 12
**Chamber:** 3"
**Capacity:** 8
**Barrel length:** 20"
**Sights:** Bead
**Chokes:** Cyl. Bore
**Length (in.):** 41"
**Length of pull:** 14 1/2"
**Finish:** Blue
**Stock:** Synthetic (Black)
**Weight:** 7 Lbs

### 500 PERSUADER/CRUISER — 8 SHOT

**Item no.:** 50579
**Gauge:** 12
**Chamber:** 3"
Includes Pistol Grip Kit
**Capacity:** 8
**Barrel length:** 20"
**Sights:** Bead
**Chokes:** Cyl. Bore
**Length (in.):** 41"
**Length of pull:** 14 1/2"
**Finish:** Blue
**Stock:** Synthetic (Black)
**Weight:** 7 Lbs

### 500 PERSUADER/CRUISER — 8 SHOT

8 Shot Cruiser
**Item no.:** 50580
**Gauge:** 12
**Chamber:** 3"
Heat Shield, Pistol Grip Only
**Capacity:** 8
**Barrel length:** 20"
**Sights:** Bead
**Chokes:** Cyl. Bore
**Length (in.):** 30 1/4"
**Finish:** Blue
**Stock:** Synthetic (Black)
**Weight:** 6 Lbs

### 590 SPECIAL PURPOSE — 9 SHOT

**Item no.:** 50645
**Gauge:** 12
**Chamber:** 3"
Heat Shield
**Capacity:** 9
**Barrel length:** 20"
**Sights:** Bead
**Chokes:** Cyl. Bore
**Length (in.):** 41"
**Length of pull:** 14 1/2"
**Finish:** Blue
**Stock:** Synthetic (Black)
**Weight:** 7 1/4 Lbs

### 590 SPECIAL PURPOSE — 9 SHOT

**Item no.:** 50660
**Gauge:** 12
**Chamber:** 3"
Heat Shield
**Capacity:** 9
**Barrel length:** 20"
Sights: Bead
**Chokes:** Cyl. Bore
**Length (in.):** 41"
**Length of pull:** 14 1/2"
**Finish:** Matte Blue
**Stock:** Synthetic (Black)
**Weight:** 7 1/4 Lbs

### 590 SPECIAL PURPOSE — 9 SHOT

**Item no.:** 50665
**Gauge:** 12
**Chamber:** 3"
Heat Shield
**Capacity:** 9
**Barrel length:** 20"
**Sights:** Bead
**Chokes:** Cyl. Bore
**Length (in.):** 41"
**Length of pull:** 14"
**Finish:** Matte Blue
Syn. (Black), Speedfeed (Speedfeed Stock Holds 4 Extra Rounds.)
**Weight:** 7 1/4 Lbs

### 590 SPECIAL PURPOSE — 9 SHOT

**Item no.:** 50663
**Gauge:** 12
**Chamber:** 3"
Ghost Ring® Sights
**Capacity:** 9
**Barrel length:** 20"
**Sights:** Ghost Ring®
**Chokes:** Cyl. Bore
**Length (in.):** 41"
**Length of pull:** 14 1/2"
**Finish:** Matte Blue
**Stock:** Synthetic (Black)
**Weight:** 7 1/4 Lbs

### 590 SPECIAL PURPOSE — 9 SHOT

**Item no.:** 50668
**Gauge:** 12
**Chamber:** 3"
Ghost Ring® Sights
**Capacity:** 9
**Barrel length:** 20"
**Sights:** Ghost Ring®
**Chokes:** Cyl. Bore
**Length (in.):** 41"
**Length of pull:** 14"
**Finish:** Matte Blue
Syn. (Black), Speedfeed (Speedfeed Stock Holds 4 Extra Rounds.)
**Weight:** 7 1/4 Lbs

---

### 590 SPECIAL PURPOSE — 9 SHOT

**Item no.:** 51663
**Gauge:** 12
**Chamber:** 3"
Hvy Wall Bbl, Mtl Trig. Grd./safety
**Capacity:** 9
**Barrel length:** 20"
**Sights:** Ghost Ring®
**Chokes:** Cyl. Bore
**Length (in.):** 41"
**Length of pull:** 14 1/2"
**Finish:** Matte Blue
**Stock:** Synthetic (Black)
**Weight:** 7 1/4 Lbs

---

### 500 HS410 HOME SECURITY — 6 SHOT

**Item no.:** 50359
**Gauge:** .410
**Chamber:** 3"
Spreader Choke
**Capacity:** 9
**Barrel length:** 18 1/2"
**Sights:** Bead
Spreader
**Length (in.):** 37 1/4"
**Length of pull:** 13 7/8"
**Finish:** Blue
**Stock:** Synthetic (Black)
**Weight:** 5 1/2 Lbs

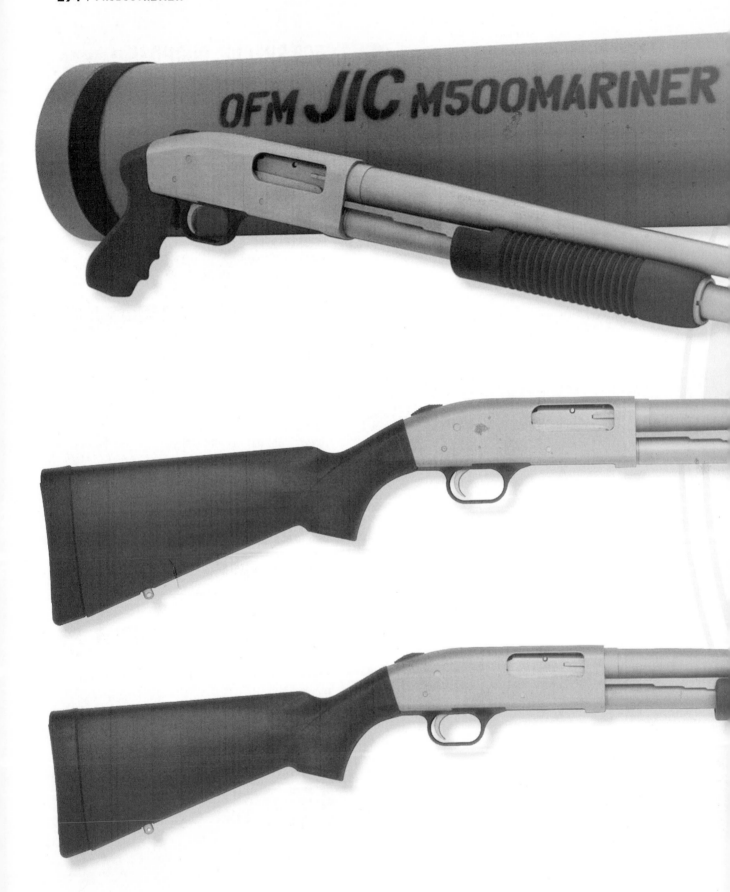

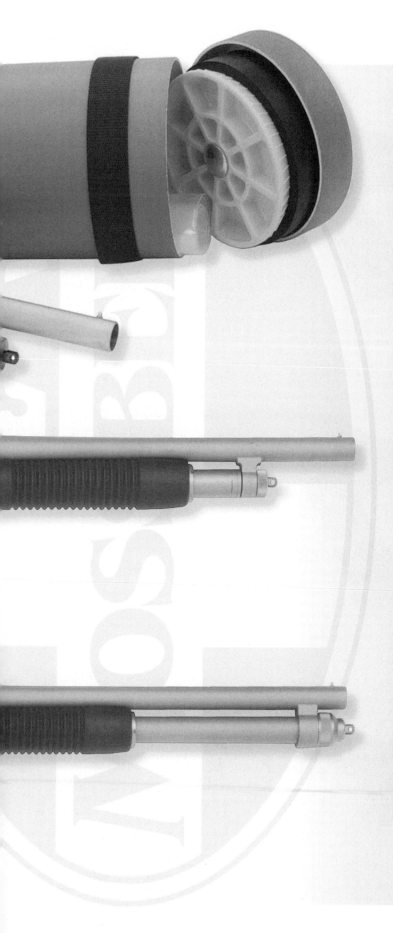

## 500 J.I.C MARINER
**Type:** Home Security/Special Purpose
**Item:** 52340
**Gauge:** 12
**Chamber:** 3"
**Description:** J.I.C.(Just In Case) Shotguns
**Cap.:** 6
**Bbl Length:** 18 1/2"
**Sights:** Bead
**Chokes:** Cyl. Bore
**Length (In.):** 28 3/4"
**Finish:** Marinecote
**Stock:** Synthetic (Black)

## 500 MARINER— 6 SHOT
**Item no.:** 50273
**Gauge:** 12
**Chamber:** 3"
Includes Pistol Grip Kit
**Capacity:** 6
**Barrel length:** 18 1/2"
**Sights:** Bead
**Chokes:** Cyl. Bore
**Length (in.):** 39 1/2"
**Length of pull:** 13 7/8"
**Finish:** Marinecote
**Stock:** Synthetic (Black)
**Weight:** 6 3/4 Lbs

## 590 MARINER— 9 SHOT
**Item no.:** 50299
**Gauge:** 12
**Chamber:** 3"
Includes Pistol Grip Kit
**Capacity:** 9
**Barrel length:** 20"
**Sights:** Bead
**Chokes:** Cyl. Bore
**Length (in.):** 41"
**Length of pull:** 13"
**Finish:** Marinecote
**Stock:** Synthetic (Black)
**Weight:** 7 Lbs

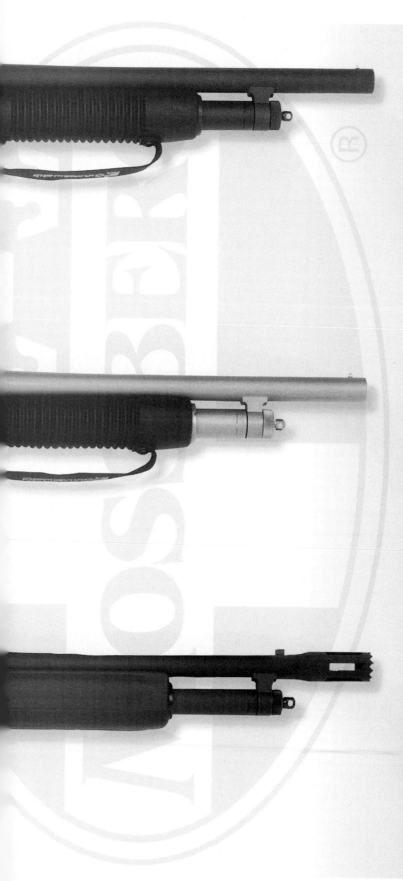

## 500 TACTICAL— 6 SHOT
**Item no.:** 50420
**Gauge:** 12
**Chamber:** 3"
Adj. Tactical Stock
**Capacity:** 6
**Barrel length:** 18 1/2"
**Sights:** Bead
**Chokes:** Cyl. Bore
**Length (in.):** 38 1/2"
**Length of pull:** 10 3/4"-14 5/8" (Overall Length Is Measured When Stock Is Set At Its Minimum Length Of Pull)
**Finish:** Matte
**Stock:** Adj. Synthetic (Black)
**Weight:** 6 3/4 Lbs

## 500 TACTICAL— 6 SHOT
**Item no.:** 50278
**Gauge:** 12
**Chamber:** 3"
Adj. Tactical Stock
**Capacity:** 6
**Barrel length:** 18 1/2"
**Sights:** Bead
**Chokes:** Cyl. Bore
**Length (in.):** 38 1/2"
**Length of pull:** 10 3/4"-14 5/8" (Overall Length Is Measured When Stock Is Set At Its Minimum Length Of Pull)
**Finish:** Marinecote
**Stock:** Adj. Synthetic (Black)
**Weight:** 6 3/4 Lbs

## 500 TACTICAL— 6 SHOT
**Item no.:** 50145
**Gauge:** 20
**Chamber:** 3"
Stand-off Barrel
**Capacity:** 6
**Barrel length:** 20"
**Sights:** Bead
**Chokes:** Cyl. Bore
**Length (in.):** 41"
**Length of pull:** 14 1/2"
**Finish:** Matte
**Stock:** Synthetic (Black)
**Weight:** 5 1/2 Lbs

## 930 TACTICAL HOME SECURITY
**Item no.:** 85330
**Gauge:** 12
**Chamber:** 3"
**Capacity:** 5
**Barrel length:** 18.5"
**Sights:** Bead
**Chokes:** Cylinder Bore
**Length (in.):** 39"
**Length of pull:** 14"
**Finish:** Matte
**Stock:** Synthetic (Black)
**Weight:** 7 1/2 Lbs

## 930 SPX HOME SECURITY
(Ext. Magazine Tube, Picatinny Rail, Lpa Ghost Ring Rear Sight & Winged Fiber Optic Front Sight)
**Item no.:** 85360
**Gauge:** 12
**Chamber:** 3"
**Capacity:** 8
**Barrel length:** 18.5"
**Sights:** Ghost Ring®
**Chokes:** Cylinder Bore
**Length (in.):** 40 1/2"
**Length of pull:** 14"
**Finish:** Matte
**Stock:** Synthetic (Black)
**Weight:** 7 3/4 Lbs

## 930 HOME SECURITY
**Item no.:** 85320
**Gauge:** 12
**Chamber:** 3"
**Capacity:** 5
**Barrel length:** 18.5"
**Sights:** Bead
**Chokes:** Cylinder Bore
**Length (in.):** 39"
**Length of pull:** 14"
**Finish:** Blue
**Stock:** Synthetic (Black)
**Weight:** 7 1/2 Lbs

### 930 FIELD/SECURITY COMBO (TWO BARREL SET)
**Item no.:** 85325
**Gauge:** 12
**Chamber:** 3"
**Capacity:** 5
**Barrel length:** 28"
Vr Ptd
**Sights:** Bead
Accu-mag Set (Accu-set: Includes Full, Modified And Improved Cylinder Choke Tubes.)
**Length (in.):** 48 1/2"
**Length of pull:** 14"
**Finish:** Blue
**Stock:** Synthetic (Black)
**Weight:** 7 1/2 Lbs

### 930 ROADBLOCKER
**Item no.:** 85335
**Gauge:** 12
**Description:** Muzzle Break
**Capacity:** 5
**Barrel length:** 18 1/2"
**Sights:** Bead
**Chokes:** Cylinder Bore
**Length (in.):** 39"
**Length of pull (in.):** 14"
**Finish:** Matte
**Stock:** Synthetic Black

### 930 SPX PISTOL GRIP - 8 SHOT
**Item no.:** 85370
**Gauge:** 12
Full Length Stock/pg/ext. Mag./picatinny Rail
**Capacity:** 8
**Barrel length:** 18 1/2"
**Sights:** Ghost Ring
**Chokes:** Cylinder Bore
**Length (in.):** 39 1/2"
**Length of pull:** 13"
**Finish:** Matte
**Stock:** Pistol Grip Synthetic Black

## 930 TACTICAL 5 SHOT

**Item no.:** 85336
**Gauge:** 12
**Chamber:** 3"
Plain, Bead Sight, Tactical Barrel With Heat Shield
**Capacity:** 5
**Barrel length:** 18.5"
**Sights:** Bead
**Chokes:** Cylinder Bore
**Length (in.):** 39"
**Finish:** Matte Blue
**Stock:** Synthetic
**Weight:** 7 3/4 Lbs

## 100 ATR SPECIAL PURPOSE – 100 ATR™ NIGHT TRAIN™

**Type:** All Purpose
**Item:** 26200
**Desc.:** Free-floating Barrel,
Top-load Magazine, Picatinny Rail
**Cap.:** 5
**BBL Lgth:** 22"
**Lgth (In.):** 42"
**LOP (In.):** 13 1/4"
**Finish:** Matte Blue
**Stock:** Synthetic (Black)
**Wt.:** 8 1/2 Lbs

## 500 J.I.C SANDSTORM

**Type:** Home Security/Special Purpose
**Item:** 53340
**Gauge:** 12
**Chamber:** 3"
**Description:** J.I.C.(Just In Case) Shotguns
**Cap.:** 6
**BBL Length:** 18 1/2"
**Sights:** BEAD
**Chokes:** Cyl. Bore
**Length (in.):** 28 3/4"
**Finish:** Desert Camo
**Stock:** Synthetic (Black)

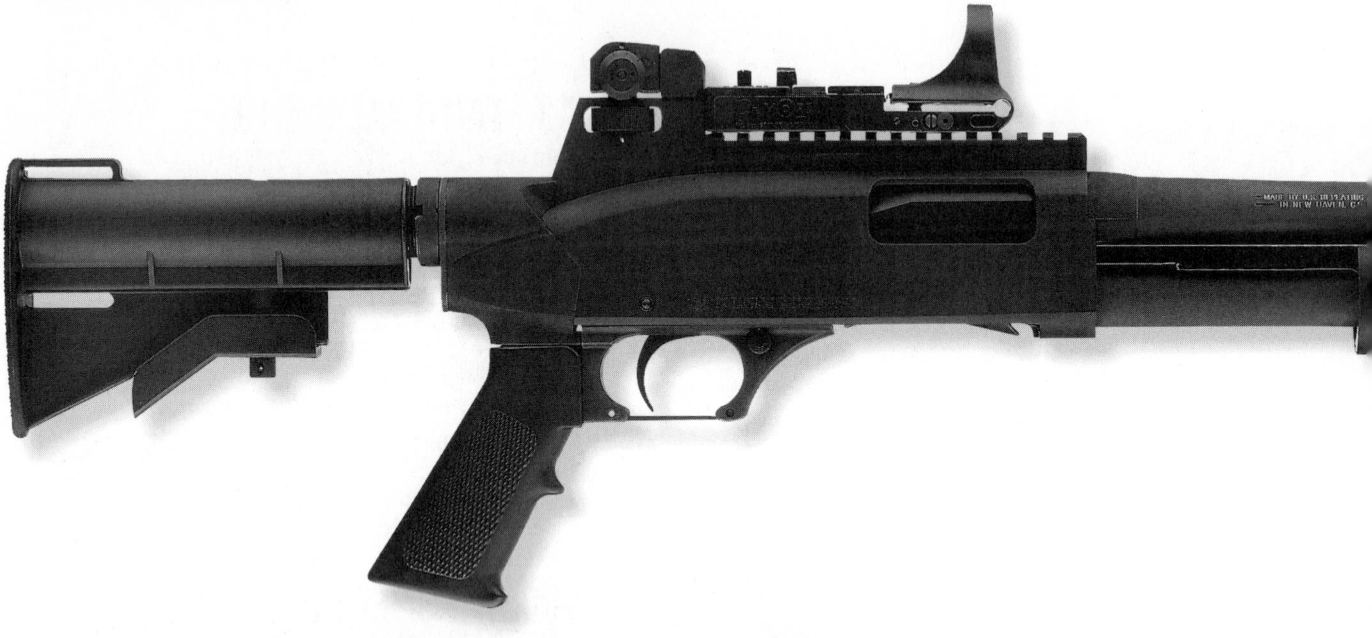

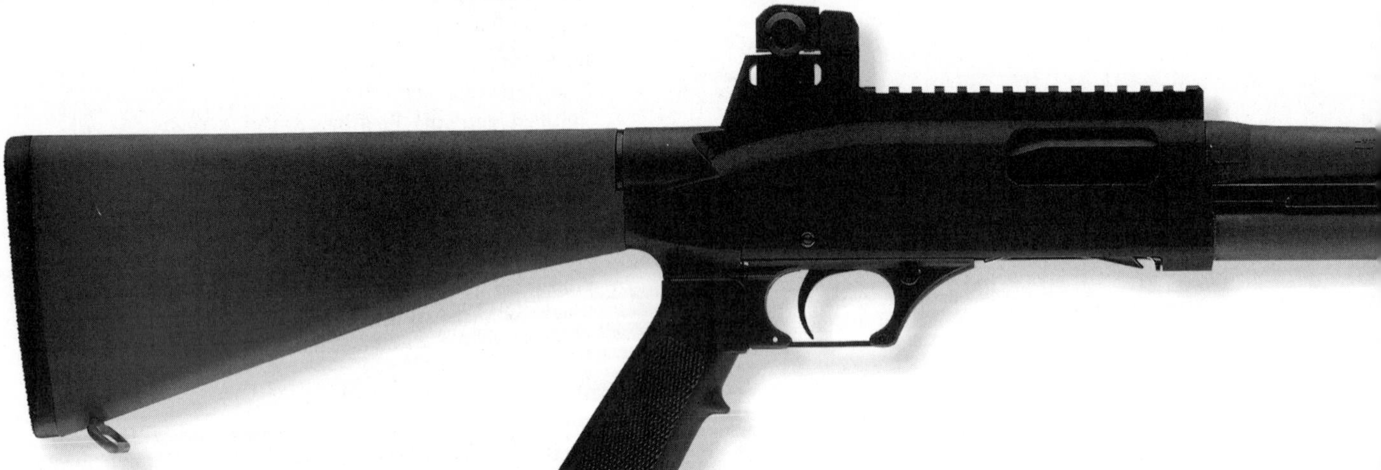

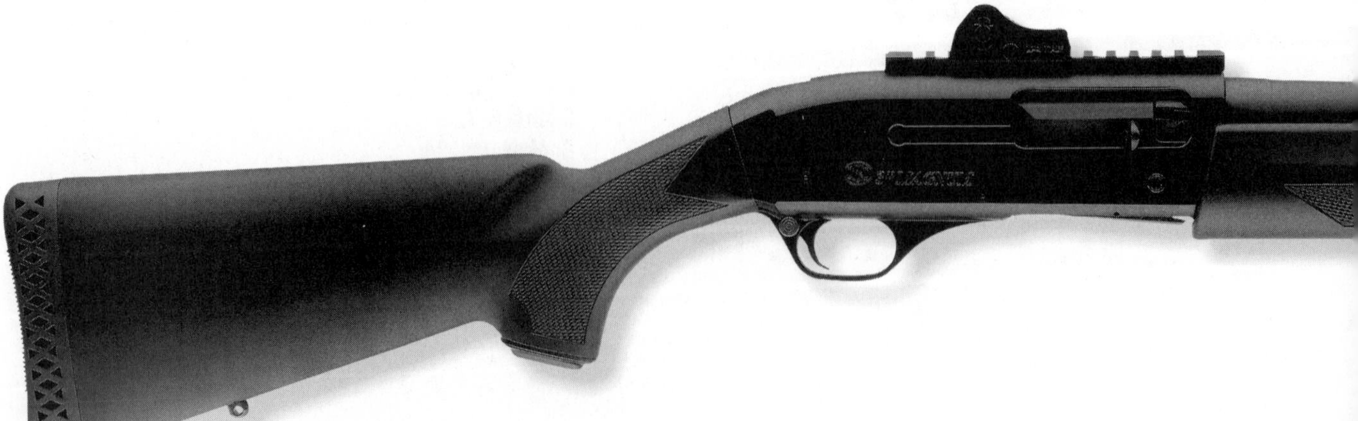

## FN TACTICAL POLICE SHOTGUN (TPS) WITH COLLAPSIBLE STOCK

**Item Number:** 17705
**Caliber / Ga.:** 12 Ga.
**Magazine Capacity:** 7 + 1 chamber
**Barrel Length:** 18"
**Overall Length:** 35"
**Weight:** 6 lbs.
**Stock / Grip:** Collapsible stock, M16 A2-style pistol grip
**Additional Description:** Interchangeable choke system, ported barrel

## FN TACTICAL POLICE SHOTGUN (TPS) WITH FIXED STOCK

**Item Number:** 17702
**Caliber / Ga.:** 12 Ga.
**Magazine Capacity:** 7 + 1 chamber
**Barrel Length:** 18"
**Overall Length:** 39 3/4"
**Weight:** 6 lbs. 8 oz.
**Stock / Grip:** Fixed A2-style buttstock
**Additional Description:** Fixed choke with back-bored barrel

## FN SELF-LOADING POLICE SHOTGUN (SLP)

**Gauge:** 12 Gauge with 3" chamber
**Operation:** Active Valve Gas System
**Barrel Length:** 18"
**Overall Length:** 38.75"
**Height:** 7.9"
**Width:** 2.4"
**Length of Pull:** 14"
**Weight:** 7.7 lbs. empty
**Ammunition Capacity:** 6+1 with 2-3/4" shells or 5+1 with 3" shells
**Choke:** Standard Invector® choke tube included

### FN SLP MARK I RIFLED BARREL SHOTGUN

**Gauge:** 12 Gauge with 3" magnum chamber
**Operation:** Active Valve Gas System
Two gas pistons come standard
**Barrel Length:** 18"
**Overall Length:** 39"
**Height:** 7.9"
**Width:** 2.4"
**Length of Pull:** 14"
**Weight:** 8.2 lbs. empty
**Ammunition Capacity:** 8+1 with 2-3/4"shells,
7+1 with 3" shells
**Choke:** N/A
Extended 8-round magazine tube
Crossbolt safety button on trigger guard
Matte black conventional synthetic stock with
checkered gripping surfaces, Steel sling studs.

### SLP TACTICAL SHOTGUNS

**Gauge:** 12 Gauge with 3" chamber
**Operation:** Active Valve Gas System
**Barrel Length:** 18"
**Overall Length:** 39"
**Length of Pull:** 14.33"
**Weight:** 7.4 lbs. empty
**Ammunition Capacity:** 6+1 with 2-3/4" shells
Standard Invector® tube included

### FN SLP MARK I SHOTGUN

**Gauge:** 12 Gauge with 3" chamber
**Operation:** Active Valve Gas system
**Barrel Length:** 22"
**Overall Length:** 43"
**Height:** 7.9"
**Width:** 2.4"
**Length of Pull:** 14"
**Weight:** 8.2 lbs. empty
**Ammunition Capacity:** 8+1 with 2-3/4"shells,
7+1 with 3" shells
**Choke:** Standard Invector® choke tube included
Extended 8-round magazine tube
Crossbolt safety button on trigger guard
Matte black conventional synthetic stock with
checkered gripping surfaces, Steel sling studs.

# SHOOTING
## SCHOOLS

Right is a list of various shooting schools around the country. Typical fees start at about $400 per person for a three- or four-day class and may top out at $2,000 or more depending on the location of the class and the lodging offered.

Most of the people listed here will provide information about firearms and training. If you need a technical advisor for a movie or video project, this is a good place to start. Some folks listed here, like Massad Ayoob of the Lethal Force Institute, also serve as expert witnesses in civil and criminal cases. Some of the better-known schools include the aforementioned Lethal Force Institute, Front Sight, Gunsite, Thunder Ranch and Blackheart International. Some of the instructors listed here have come right from the ranks of the U.S. military Special Operations community.

**Absolute Tactical Training**
2573 Market St.
San Diego, California 92102
619-858-5832
FAX: 619-692-9408
www.absolutetacticaltraining.com
Keiko Arroyo, Chief Instructor

**Academy of Personal Protection and Security**
336 Hill Ave.
Suite 102
Nashville, Tennessee 37210
615-360-6002
FAX: 615-366-7374
www.appstraining.com
J. Buford Tune, Director

**Advanced Training Assoc.**
6136 Mission Gorge Rd #220
San Diego, CA 92120
619-644-1342
Kurt Sawatzky and Lin Henry,
Instructors

**Advanced Tactical Technologies Inc.**
PO Box 51404
Phoenix, AZ 85076
602-706-8010

**Advanced Weapons and Tactics**
PO Box 6258
Napa, CA 94581
707-253-8926
FAX: 707-253-8927
www.awt-co.com
Walt Marshall, Instructor

**Allsafe Defense Systems**
1026 N. Tustin Ave.
Orange, CA 92867-5958
714-744-4485
www.allsafedefense.com
T.J. Johnston, Instructor

**American Pistol & Rifle Association**
(APRA members only)
Firearms Academy Staff
Box USA
Benton, TN 37307
615-338-2328

**American Shooting Academy**
PO Box 54233
Phoenix, AZ 85078-4233
623-825-7317
www.asa-training.com
James Jarrett, Director

**American Small Arms Academy**
PO Box 12111
Prescott, AZ 86304
602-778-5623
Chuck Taylor, Instructor

**Area 52 Smallarms Training Center**
4809 Schley Road
Hillsborough, NC 27278
919-245-0013
area52training@cs.com

**Argenbright International Training Institute**
(law enforcement, military and corporate security)
4845 Old National Highway,
Suite 210
Atlanta, Georgia 30337
800-235-4723

**Arizona Defensive Firearms Training**
PO Box 44302
Phoenix, Arizona 85064
602-279-3770
FAX: 602-279-0333
www.azccw.com
adft@azccw.com
Rick Barkett, Director

**Arkansas Police Trainers**
(law enforcement)
212 West Elm Street
Rogers, Arkansas 72756
501-621-1173 or 501-273-9270
FAX: 501-621-1131
Tim Keck, Executive Director

**Auto Arms**
738 Clearview
San Antonio, TX 78228
512-434-5450

**AWARE**
(Arming Women Against Rape and Endangerment)
PO Box 242
Bedford, MA 01730
781-893-0500
877-672-9273 Toll Free
www.aware.org

**Bay Area Professionals for Firearms Safety & Education**
(Bayprofs)
1600 Saratoga Ave #403-181
San Jose, CA 95129
408-741-5218 (answering machine only)
www.bayprofs.org
Tom Laye, Training Director

**Beretta Training**
17601 Beretta Drive
Accokeek, MD 20607
301-283-2191
Russ Logan and Marcel James, Instructors

**Blackheart International, LLC**
112 Wood Street
Philippi, WV 26416
877-244-8166
FAX: 304-457-1281
support@bhigear.com
www.bhigear.com

**Blackwater Lodge and Training Center**
200 Puddin Ridge Rd. Ext.
Moyock, NC 27958
252-435-2488
FAX: 252-435-6388
training@blackwaterlodge.com
www.blackwaterlodge.com
Ken Viera, General Manager

**Bob's Tactical**
122 Lafayette Road
Salisbury, MA 01952
978-465-5561

**Brantly and Associates, Inc.**
3001 W. 39th St.
Suite 10
Orlando, FL 32839

407-650-1771
FAX: 407-650-8333
jamesbrantly@cs.com
brantlyandassociates.com

**BSR, Inc.**
PO Box 190
Summit Point, WV 25446
304-725-6512
FAX: 304-728-7124
office@bsr-inc.com
www.bsrfirearms-training.com

**Burton's Firearm Instruction**
(for women only)
PO Box 6084
Lynnwood, WA 98036-0084
206-774-7940
Gale Burton, Instructor

**Calibre Press**
(law enforcement and military personnel training)
666 Dundee Road, Ste. 1607
Northbrook, IL 60062-2760
708-498-5680

**California Security & Safety Institute**
706 E. Arrow Hwy, #E
Covina, CA 91722
800-281-1330
Steven Hurd, Director

**Canadian Academy of Practical Shooting**
C.P. 312
Roxboro, Quebec H8Y 3K4
Canada
514-696-8591
FAX: 514-696-2348
www.caps-inc.com
Dave Young, Director

**Canadian Firearms Training**
Ottawa, Ontario
Canada
613-443-0749
www.FirearmsTraining.ca
Dave Bartlett, President

**Chapman Academy of Practical Shooting**
4350 Academy Road
Hallsville, MO 65255-9707
800-847-0588
573-696-5544
FAX: 573-696-2266
www.chapmanacademy.com
John Skaggs, Director

**Chelsea Gun Club of New York City, Inc.**
c/o West Side Range
20 W. 20th Street
New York, NY 10011
212-929-7287
James D. Surdo, Instructor

**Cirillo's Tactical Handgun Training**
1211 Venetian Way
Panama City, FL 32405
Jim Cirillo, Instructor

**CivilShield**
Los Gatos, CA
408-354-1424
FAX: 408-399-2270
www.civilshield.com

**Colorado Firearms Academy**
20 S. Potomac Street
Aurora, Colorado 80012
303-360-5400
John Noble and Michael Schaffer, Instructors

**Colorado Gun Training**
2767 S. Parker Road, #253
Aurora, Colorado 80014
720-435-9964
Rick Vizachero, Director
train@theRange.com
firearmstrainingsite.com

**Colorado Weapons Training**
PO Box 745504
Arvada, Colorado 80006-5504
303-421-8541
ColoradoWeaponsTraining.com

**Combative Concepts**
826 Orange Avenue, #518
Coronado, CA 92118
619-521-2855

**COMTAC, Ltd.**
PO Box 12269
Silver Spring, MD 20908
301-924-4315
FAX: 301-924-3854
comtac@comtac.com
www.comtac.com
Charles A. Davis, Director of Training

**Continental Threat Management**
507 Owen Drive
Fayetteville, NC 28304
910-485-8805
NCLFI@aol.com
Timothy A. Noe, Director

**Cumberland Tactics**
PO Box 1400
Goodlettsville, TN 37070
615-822-7779
Randy@guntactics.com
www.guntactics.com/
Randy Cain, Director

**Dalton's International Shootists Institute**
PO Box 88
Acton, CA 93510
www.isishootists.com
Mike Dalton, Instructor

**Dan Mitchell's Clay Target and Wing Shooting School**
304 Roosevelt
Nampa, ID 83651
208-467-2793
www.idfishnhunt.com/mitchell.htm

**Defense Arts of Texas**
214 N. 16th Suite B-6
McAllen, TX
Robert E. Henry, Director
956-682-0388

**Defense Associates**
PO Box 824
Fairfield, CT 06430
www.defenseassociates.com
203-261-8719

**Defensive Firearms Academy**
PO Box 615
Iselin, New Jersey 08830
www.dfatactics.com
Larry Mraz, Director
732-283-3314

**Defensive Firearms Consultants**
PO Box 27431
Towson, MD 21285
410-321-6522

**Defensive Solutions**
190 Cedar Circle
Powell, TN 37849
865-945-5612
info@defensivesolutions.com
www.defensivesolutions.com

**Defensive Training for the Armed Citizen** (DEFTAC)
5712 Folkstone Lane
Orlando, FL 32822
407-208-0751
deftac03@aol.com
members.aol.com/deftac03
Jon A. Custis, Instructor

**Defense Training International, Inc.**
749 S. Lemay Ste. A3-337
Ft.Collins, Colorado 80301
970-482-2520
FAX: 970-482-0548
dti@frii.com
www.defense-training.com
John S. Farnam, President

**Defensive Use of Firearms**
PO Box 4227
Show Low, AZ 85902-4227
www.spw-duf.info

**Denton County Sports Association, Inc.**
409 Copper Canyon Road
Denton County, TX 76226
940-241-2376
dcsa@airmail.net
www.dentoncountysports.com
Lonnie Ward, Director

**DTOM Enterprises**
PO Box 415
Bloomingdale, MI 49026-0415
616-628-5039
DTOM.us
MTS@DTOM.us

**Executive Security Services International**
Box 5585
Huntsville, Ontario, Canada P1H 2L5
705-788-1957
www.essi.cjb.net

**Farris Firearms Training**
102 Jeremiah Court
Rockvale, Tennessee 37153
615-907-4892
www.farrisfirearms.com
training@farrisfirearms.com

**Federal Law Enforcement Training Center** (FLETC)
(law enforcement training)
FLETC
Glynco, GA 31524
800-743-5382
FAX: 912-267-3144
Gerald Brooks, Program Specialist

**Firearms Academy of Redding**
1530 Market Street
Redding, CA 96001
916-244-2190

**Firearms Academy of Seattle**
PO Box 400
Onalaska, WA 98570
360-978-6100
FAX: 360-978-6102
www.firearmsacademy.com
Marty Hayes, Instructor

**Firearms International Training Academy**
5139 Stanart Street
Norfolk, VA 23502
757-461-9153
FAX: 757-461-9155
Gerry Fockler, Director

**Firearms Research & Instruction, Inc.**
PO Box 732
Abingdon, MD 21009
877-456-5075
www.f-r-i.com
steves02@gte.net
Steven Silverman, President

**Firearms Training Associates**
PO Box 554
Yorba Linda, CA 92885-0554
714-701-9918
FAX: 714-777-9318
Bill Murphy, Instructor
www.ftatv.com

**Firearm Training Center**
The Bullet Hole Range
78 Rutgers St
Belleville, NJ 07109
201-919-0414
Anthony P. Colandro, Director
www.FirearmTrainingCenter.com

**Firearms Training Center**
9555 Blandville Road
West Paducah, KY 42086
502-554-5886

**Firearms Training Institute**
1044 Desert View Dr
Twin Falls, ID 83301
208-735-1469
scoobys@cyberhighway.net

**Firearmz - Firearms Training and Defense**
PO Box 344
Temple, Georgia 30179-0344
770-562-8663
www.firearmz.net

**Front Sight Firearms Training Institute**
PO Box 2619
Aptos, CA 95001
800-987-7719
FAX: 831-684-2137
www.frontsight.com
info@frontsight.com
Dr. Ignatius Piazza, Director

**Global Security Complex**
5750 Herring Road
Arvin, CA 93203
805-845-7011
FAX: 805-845-7945
global@lightspeed.net

**Glock, Inc.**
(law enforcement and military personnel training)
PO Box 369
Smyrna, GA 30081
404-432-1202
Al Bell, Director of Training
Frank DiNuzzo, Assistant
Director of Training

**Guardian Group International**
21 Warren Street, Suite 3E
New York, NY 10007
212-619-2828

**Gunner Joe's Bullseye Academy**
12247 Buckskin Trail
Poway, CA 92964-6005
858-486-6201
Joe Vaineharrison, Instructor

**GunSafety - TampaBay**
PO Box 26393
Tampa, Florida 33623-6393
813-354-2799
Michael Perry, Owner
www.gunsafetytampa.com

**Gunsite Academy, Inc.**
2900 West Gunsite Road
Pauldin, AZ 86334-4301
520-636-4565
FAX: 520-636-1236
Buz Mills, Owner
www.gunsite.net

**Guntek Firearms Training**
4400 A Ambassador Caffery
Parkway #310
Lafayette, LA 70508
337-984-8711
FAX: 337-993-1159
identify@bellsouth.net

**Halo Group, The**
316 California Ave
Suite 748
Reno, NV 89509
888-255-HALO
training@thehalogroup.com

**Handgun Instruction**
Fresno, CA
209-442-8102 or 209-221-9415
Laurie Anderson and Ken Zachary,
Instructors

**Heckler & Koch, Inc.**
International Training Division
(law enforcement and military personnel training)
21480 Pacific Boulevard
Sterling, VA 20166-8903
703-450-1900
FAX: 703-450-8180
John Meyer, Jr., Director

**HomeSafe Protective Training**
5100 Burchette Rd., #3403
Tampa, FL 33647
813-979-7119
Beeper: 813-673-7016
Bret Bartlett, Director

**Illinois Small Arms Institute**
3512 Roxford Drive
Champaign, IL 61821
217-356-0704
John W. Bowman, Director

**Insight Firearms Training Development**
PO Box 12293
Prescott, Arizona 86304-2293
928-708-9208
8662NSIGHT
FAX: 928-776-4668
www.insightfirearmstraining.com

**InSights Training Center, Inc.**
PO Box 3585
Bellevue, WA 98009
425-739-0133
www.insightstraining.com
Greg Hamilton, Instructor

**Institute of Security Services**
(tactical response team training)
1205 Banner Hill Rd.
Erwin, TN 37650-9301
800-441-0081
FAX: 615-743-2361

**International Academy of Tactical Training Systems**
#8 129 2nd Ave. N
Saskatoon, Saskatchewan
Canada S7K 2A9
306-975-1995
Brad Hutchinson, Director
www.attscanada.com
ntc@sk.sympatico.ca

**International Association of Law Enforcement Firearms Instructors, Inc.**
IALEFI
25 Country Club Road, Suite 707
Gilford, NH 03246
603-524-8787
FAX: 603-524-8856
Robert D. Bossey, Executive Director
ialefi@lr.net
www.ialefi.com

**International Rescue and Tactical Consultants** (I.R.T.C.)
(law enforcement and private security training)
PO Box 1128
Westhampton Beach, NY 11978

516-288-0414
Walter Britton and Gary Gross, Instructors

**International Tactical Training Seminars Inc.**
11718 Barrington Court, #506
Los Angeles, CA 90049
310-471-2029
www.intltactical.com
Brett McQueen, Instructor

**ISI** (Instinctive Shooting International)
(law enforcement, military, qualified civilians)
PO Box 6528
Houston, TX 77265-6528
713-666-0269
FAX: 713-666-9791
isi@wt.net
Hanan Yadin, Head Instructor

**James A. Neal Public Safety Training Center**
(law enforcement)
PO Box 579
Toccoa, Georgia 30577
706-282-7012
www.jamesanealtraining.com

**Ladies Handgun Clinics**
2631 New Hope Church Road
Raleigh, NC 27604
919-872-8499

**Lane Community College**
4000 East 30th Ave.
Eugene, OR 97405-0092
503-726-2252
FAX: 503-726-3958
Michael Steen, Instructor

**Law Enforcement Educators**
789 F.M. 1637
Valley Mills, Texas 76689
800-527-2403
Carl C. Chandler, Jr., Instructor
www.carlchandler.com

**Lethal Force Institute (LFI)**
PO Box 122
Concord, NH 03302-0122
603-224-6814

www.ayoob.com
Massad Ayoob, Director

**Loss Prevention Services of New Jersey**
PO Box 15
Mt. Arlington, NJ 07856
973-347-2002
FAX: 973-347-2321
lpsofnjinc@webtv.com

**Malins Defense Systems**
2642 W.Javelina Ave., Stuite 207
Mesa, AZ 85202
602-838-8139
defense_systmems@hotmail.com
Darrell Malin, Instructor

**Marksman's Enterprise**
PO Box 556
Stevensville, Montana 59870
406-777-3557
crews@sprynet.com Jim Crews, Instructor

**Marksmanship Training Group, Inc.**
2549 W. Golf Rd. #217
Hoffman Estates, IL 60194
630-205-1369
www.kapnick.net/mtg.html
Brian Kapnick, Primary Instructor

**Martial Arts Resource**
PO Box 110841
Campbell, CA 95011-0841
408-866-5127
MartialArtsResource.com
Ray Terry, Head Instructor

**Massachusetts Firearms Seminars**
PO Box 881
Lee, MA 01238
413-243-2195
www.mafseminars.com

**Midwest Tactical Training Institute**
11311 S. Skunk Hollow Road
Mt. Carroll, IL 61053
815-244-2815
Andrew Casavant, Instructor

**Midwest Training Group, Inc**
1514 Cortland Drive
Naperville, IL 60565
630-579-0351
andykemp@msn.com
Andy Kemp, Director

**Mid-South Institute of Self-Defense**
(law enforcement and military personnel training)
5582 Blythe Road
Lake Cornorant, MS 38641
www.weaponstraining.com
John Shaw, Instructor

**MINDRICK Security Academy and Shooting School**
Budd Road Box 747
Phillipsport, NY 12769
914-647-4048
www.mindrick.com
Fredrick Vobis, Director

**Modern Warrior Defensive Tactics Institute**
(law enforcement training)
711 N. Wellwood Ave.
Lindenhurst, NY 11757
800-33-WARRIOR
FAX: 516-226-5454
George Demetriou

**National Law Enforcement Training Center**
4948 Westwood Road
Kansas City, MO 64112
800-445-0857
FAX: 816-531-3416
www.odinpress.com

**National Rifle Association**
11250 Waples Mill Road
Fairfax, VA 22030
800-672-3888
www.nra.org

**Northeast Training Institute**
130 N. Fifth Street, Suite 804
Reading, PA 19601
215-872-3433

**NOR-CAL Training Academy**
2016 Oakdale Ave.
San Francisco, CA 94124-2098
415-550-8282
Bob Borissoff, Instructor

**Oceanside Shooting Academy**
618 Airport Road
Oceanside, CA
760-945-8567
Bill Jorgensen, Instructor

**OffShoots Training Institute**
(law enforcement and military personnel training)
119 Cotillion
San Antonio, Texas 78213
210-541-9884
FAX: 210-541-9884
www.offshootstraining.com
Jerry Lane, Instructor

**Operational Support Services, Inc.**
19018 Candleview Drive
Spring, TX 77388
281-288-9190 x205
FAX: 281-288-7019
opsupp@getus.com
David Lee Salmon II,
Law Enforcement Training Director

**Options for Personal Security**
PO Box 489
Sebring, FL 33871-0489
877-636-4677
www.optionsforpersonalsecurity.com
Andy Stanford, Director

**Oregon Firearms Academy**
Brownsville, OR
541-451-5532
oregonfirearms.d2g.com

**Peregrine Corporation, The**
PO Box 170
Bowers, PA 19511
610-682-7147
FAX: 610-682-7158
Emanuel Kapelsohn, President

**Personal Defense Institute**
2603 NW 13th St., #205
Gainesville, FL 32609
904-378-6425
afn01182@afn.org
Jeff Dissell and W.L. Fisher,
Instructors

**Personal Defense Training**
5220 Linnadine Way
Norcross, GA 30092
404-403-5739
david@personaldefensetraining.com
www.personaldefensetraining.com
David Blinder, Director

**Personal Protection Concepts**
PO Box 340485
Dayton, Ohio 45434
937-371-7816
info@ppctraining.com
www.ppctraining.com
Brady Smith, Instructor

**Personal Protection Strategies**
(specializing in women's training)
9903 Santa Monica Blvd., Suite 300
Beverly Hills, CA 90212
310-281-1762
Paxton Quigley, Instructor

**Personal Protection Training**
PO Box 2008
Woodland Park, Colorado
719-687-8226
southeops@hotmail.com
A.C. Bowolick, Instructor

**Personal Responsibility, Inc**
221 Fourth Avenue North Second Floor
Nashville, TN 37219
615-242-3348
FAX: 615-242-6502
John M.L. Brown, President

**Personal Safety Institute**
15 Central Way, Suite 319
Kirkland, WA 98033
206-827-2015
Ginny Lyford, Director

**Personal Security Consulting**
PO Box 8118
Albuquerque, NM 87198-8118
505-255-8610

**Personal Security & Safety Training** (PSST)
PO Box 381
Eagle, ID 83616
208-939-8051
Bruce and Nancy Priddy,
Instructors

**Police Training Institute**
(law enforcement only)
University of Illinois
1004 S. 4th St.
Champaign, IL 61820
217-333-7811
John W. Bowman, Instructor

**Police Training Division**
(law enforcement and military
personnel training)
2 Edgebrook Lane
Monsey, NY 10952
Peter Tarley, Instructor

**Plus P Technology, Inc.**
Minneapolis, MN
612-660-4263
plusp@plusp.com
www.plusp.com/

**Practical Firearms Training**
Covington, VA
540-559-3074
FAX: 540-559-4151
pgpft@cfw.com

**Practical Shooting Academy, The**
PO Box 630
Olathe, Colorado 81425
970-323-6111
www.practicalshootingacad.com
Ron Avery, Instructor

**PRO**
3953 Indianola Ave
Columbus, OH 43214
614-263-1601
www.peoplesrights.org

**Progressive F.O.R.C.E. Concepts**
PO Box 336301
N. Las Vegas, NV 89033
702-647-1126
FAX: 702-647-7325
www.PFCtraining.com
Steve Krystek, Director

**ProTac Glocal Inc**
PMB 233
1208 E. Bethany Dr. Suite 2

Allen, Texas 75002
972-359-0303
www.protacglobal.com
Chris Grollnek, President

**Pro-Tek**
5154 Cemetery Road
Bainbridge, NY 13733
607-343-9999
Tim Roberts, Chief Instructor
tactical@mkl.com

**R & S Protection Services**
4401 N. Dogwood Dr.
Kenai, Alaska 99611
907-283-7001
Raymond Carr, Instructor
alaskaknives@alaskaknives.com
www.alaskaknives.com

**Remington Shooting School**
Remington Arms Company
14 Hoefler Avenue
Ilion, NY 13357
315-895-3574
Dale P. Christie, Director

**Rocky Mountain Combat Applications Training**
PO Box 535
Lake George, Colorado 80827
FAX: 719-748-8557
www.rmcat.com

**Rocky Mountain Gun Safety**
3812 E. Pikes Peak Ave
Suites 207-208
Colorado Springs, Colorado 80916
719-638-7406
rockymountaingunsafety@yahoo.com

**Rogers Shooting School**
1736 Saint Johns Bluff Rd.
Jacksonville, Florida 32246
904-613-1196
rogers-shooting-school.com

**Rural/Urban Tactical Training**
17660 N. 35th Street
Phoenix, AZ 85032
602-701-1614

**Scott, McDougall & Associates**
7950 Redwood Drive
Cotati, CA 94931
707-795-BANG
Mac Scott, Instructor

**Security Awareness & Firearms Education** (SAFE)
PO Box 864
Post Falls, ID 83854-0864
SAFE-LLC.com
staysafe@SAFE-LLC.com
208-773-3624
Robert B. Smith, Director

**Security Training International**
PO Box 492
Vista, CA 92085
760-940-6385
Candace Crawford, Instructor

**Self Defense Firearms Training**
5375 Industrial Drive, Suite 107
Huntington Beach, CA 92649-1545
Greg@firearmstraining.com
714-893-8676
FAX: 714-894-7656
Greg Block

**Serious Sportsman, Inc.**
100 Middletown Road
Pearl River, NY
914-735-7722
John Perkins, Instructor

**Shawnee Hunt Club**
PO Box 10531
Blacksburg, VA 24062
civic.bev.net/shawnee
Betty Strauss, Training Coordinator

**Shoot-N-Iron, Inc.**
17205 Gaddy Road
Shawnee, OK 74801
si-gun@swbell.net
www.shoot-n-iron.com
405-273-4822
FAX: 405-273-4180
Paul Abel, Instructor

**Shooters-Edge**
PO Box 3821
Beverly Hills, CA 90212
info@shooters-edge.com
www.shooters-edge.com
Bruce Krell, Instructor

**Shootrite Firearms Academy**
PO Box 189
Owens Cross Roads
Huntsville, AL 35763
www.shootrite.org
256-721-4602
Ed Aldrich, Instructor
James McKee, Instructor

**Sierra Firearms Academy**
PO Box 9640
Reno, NV 89507
mike@sierrafirearms.com
www.sierrafirearms.com
702-425-1678
Dave Keller and Mike Robbins,
Instructors

**Sierra Firearms Training**
2936 South West Street
Visalia, CA 93277
559-734-6150
559-280-5600 (cell)
Edward F. Peterson, Instructor

**SIGARMS Academy**
233 Exeter Road
Epping, NH 03042
www.sigarmsacademy.com
603-679-2003
Tim Connell, Director

**Smith & Wesson Academy &
Armorers School**
2100 Roosevelt Avenue
Springfield, MA 01102-2208
800-331-0852 extension 255/265
Robert E. Hunt, Director

**Southern Police Institute**
(law enforcement training)
University of Louisville
Louisville, KY 40292
502-852-6561

**South West Association of
Trainers and COMSAT**
PO Box 51510
Amarillo, Texas 79159
www.traintosurvive.com
806-874-1265
FAX: 806-874-1266
Jerry Holland, Director

**Southwest Defensive Shooting
Institute, L.L.C.**
PO Box 190179-266
Dallas, Texas 75219
214-599-0309
A.W. McBee, Instructor

**Southwest Tactical**
4351 Sepulveda Blvd., Suite 450
Culver City, CA 90230
310-838-1275

**Spartan Group LLC**
PO Box 671
Mamers, NC 27552
877-9SPARTA
www.spartangroup.com

**Specialized Training Associates**
(NRA Training Counselor Workshops
and NRA Instructor Certification)
1313 N. Ritchie Ct. Suite 2100
Chicago, IL 60610
312-482-9910
FAX: 312-482-9960
PO Box 453
San Jose, CA 95052
408-985-1311
FAX: 408-985-1311
Lpyle@PaulRevere.org
Leroy Pyle, Director

**Specter Tactical**
60 River Road
East Haddam, Connecticut
06423-1460
860-526-5528
www.spectertactical.com
Chris Adams, Director

**St. James Academy, The**
PO Box 700
Birmingham, MI 48012
810-545-9000
Michael St. James, Instructor

**Storm Mountain Training Center**
Rt. 1 Box 60
Elk Garden, WV 26717
304-446-5526
www.stormmountain.com

**Strategic Weapons
Academy of Texas**
100 N. MacArthur, Suite 120
Irving, TX 75061
972-256-3969
www.weaponsacademy.com
Tim Bulot, Executive Director

**Sturm, Ruger & Company**
Law Enforcement Division
Lacey Place
Southport, CT 06490
203-259-7843

**Suarez International**
2517 Sycamore Drive, #352
Simi Valley, CA 93065
805-582-2499 (Office and Fax)
Gabriel Suarez, President
www.gabesuarez.com

**Surgical Shooting Inc.**
13955 Stowe Drive
Poway, CA 92064
858-668-3453
FAX: 858-668-3457
Gary A. Lakis, COO
www.surgicalshooting.com

**Tac One**
PO Box 3215
Idaho Springs, Colorado 80452
303-698-4566
FAX: 303-582-3655
tacone@juno.com
Gary Cunningham, President

**TACFIRE**
(Tactical Firearms Training Institute)
2426 East Main St.
Ventura, CA 93003
805-652-1345
www.tacfire.com
Dave Manning, Chief Instructor

**Tactical Defense Institute**
2174 Bethany Ridge Road
West Union, OH 45693

937-544-7228
www.tdiohio.com

**Tactical Defense International**
5 Rose Lane
Apalachin, NY 13732
607-625-4488
glhblh@sg23.com
Gary Hellmers, Master Instructor

**Tactical Edge**
Security Consultants
19015 Parthenia Street, Suite 203
Northridge, CA 91324
818-890-3930

**Tactical Firearms Training Team**
16836 Algonquin St, Suite 120
Huntington Beach, CA 92649
714-846-8065
director@tftt.com
www.tftt.com
Max Joseph, Training Director

**Tactical Force Institute**
4231 Kodiak
Casper, WY 82604
307-266-1063
FAX: 307-472-5797
tfi0397@aol.com
Michael J. Wallace, Instructor

**Tactical Gun**
P.O. Box 51404
Phoenix, AZ 85048
480-706-8010

**Tactical Handgun Training**
PO Box 1817
Kingston, NY 12401
845-339-3440
FAX: 845-339-3451
www.tacticalhandguntraining.com
Ken Cooper, President

**Tactical Shooting Academy**
7366 Colonial Trail East
Surry, VA 23883
757-357-9881
www.tacticalshooting.com

**Talon Enterprises**
4 Locust Ave
Exeter, NH

603-772-7981
talon@ultranet.com
Bill Burroughs, Instructor

**Talons Firearms Training, Inc.**
11645 North Highway 287
LaPorte, Colorado 80535
303-493-2221
Ron Phillips and Kyle Caffey,
Instructors

**Team One Network**
Law Enforcement Training Only
620 Richards Ferry Road
Fredericksburg, Virginia 22406
540-752-8190
FAX: 540-752-8192

**Team Virginia**
PO Box 1361
Chesterfield, VA 23832
804-931-4554
teamvirginia.tripod.com
Glenn Blandford, Instructor

**Texas Small Arms Academy**
Houston, TX
713-561-5335
Tim Oxley, Instructor

**The Competitive Edge** (TCE)
PO Box 805
Oakville, Ontario
Canada L6J 5C5
905-849-6960
Nick Alexakos, Instructor

**Threat Management Institute** (TMI)
800 West Napa St.
Sonoma, CA 95476
707-939-0303
FAX: 707-939-8684
tmi@crl.com
Peter Kasler and Peggi Bird,
Instructors

**Thunder Ranch, Inc.**
HCR 1, Box 53
Mountain Home, TX 78058
830-640-3138
FAX: 830-640-3183
www.ThunderRanchInc.com
Clint Smith, Director

**Top Gun Training Centre**
1042 N. Mountain Ave. #B
PMB 303
Upland, CA 91786
800-677-4407
FAX: 888-677-4407
www.1topgun1.com
R.J. Kirschner, Director of
Operations

**Trident Concepts Research Group**
PO Box 11955
Prescott, AZ 86304-1955
928-776-5326
FAX: 928-443-0174
www.tridentconcepts.com
Jeff Gonzales, Instructor

**Tugs 'n' Thugs Defensive Training**
(specializing in, but not limited to,
women's training)
16818 N. 56th St, #220
Scottsdale, AZ 85254
602-788-3609
KateAlex@aol.com

**Turnipseed Stance**
610 N. Alma School Road, #18-213
Chandler, AZ 85224
602-802-0346
www.turnipseedstance.com
Kent Turnipseed, Instructor

**Universal Shooting Academy**
4300 Highway 630 East
Frostpoint, FL 33843
305-688-0262
Frank Garcia, Director

**Vital Options Institute**
503 Trowbridge Street
Allegan MI 49010
616-686-1321
gbadams@datawise.net
Greg Adams and James Bay,
Instructors

**Wallin Video Productions**
Deadly Force Division Videos
950 Highway 10 Northeast, Suite 110
Minneapolis, MN 55432
612-786-1486
Shelly Mydra

**Weigand Shooting Seminars**
685 South Main Road
Mountaintop, PA 18707
www.learntoshootpistol.com
Jack Weigand, Instructor

**Whitten Arms**
2770 Whitten Road
Memphis, TN 38133
901-386-7002
Jim Littlejohn, Director

**Williams Associates
Protective Services, LLC.**
74 Olivia St., Box 164
Derby, CT 06418
203-924-1784
FAX: 203-924-1784
www.wa-protective.com
Brian S. Williams, President

**Wicklander-Zulawski
& Associates**
(law enforcement training)
555 E. Butterfield Rd. Ste. 302
Lombard, IL
800-222-7789

**Yavapai Firearms Academy**
PO Box 27290
Prescott Valley, AZ 86312
520-772-8262
www.yfainc.com
Louis Awerbuck, Instructor

## SCHOOLS, ALPHA SORTED BY STATE

**Alabama**
Shootrite Firearms Academy

**Alaska**
R & S Protection Services

**Arizona**
Advanced Tactical Technologies Inc.
American Shooting Academy
American Small Arms Academy
Arizona Defensive Firearms Training
Defensive Use of Firearms
Gunsite Training Center

Insight Firearms Training
Development
Malins Defense Systems
Marksman's Enterprise
Rural/Urban Tactical Training
Tactical Gun
Trident Concepts Research Group
Tugs 'n' Thugs Defensive Training
Turnipseed Stance
Yavapai Firearms Academy

**Arkansas**
Arkansas Police Trainers

**California**
Absolute Tactical Training
Advanced Training Assoc
Advanced Weapons and Tactics
Allsafe Defense Systems
Bay Area Professionals for Firearms
Safety & Education (Bayprofs)
California Security & Safety Institute
CivilShield
Combative Concepts
Firearms Academy of Redding
Firearms Training Associates
Front Sight Firearms Training Institute
Global Security Complex
Gunner Joe's Bullseye Academy
Handgun Instruction
International Shootists Institute
International Tactical Training
Seminars Inc.
Martial Arts Resource
NOR-CAL
Oceanside Shooting Academy
Personal Protection Strategies
Scott, McDougall & Associates
Self Defense Firearms Training
Security Training International
Sierra Firearms Training
Shooters-Edge
Southwest Tactical
Specialized Training Associates
Suarez International
Surgical Shooting, Inc.
TACFIRE
Tactical Edge
Tactical Firearms Training Team
Threat Management Institute (TMI)
Top Gun Training Centre

## Colorado
Colorado Firearms Academy
Colorado Gun Training
Colorado Weapons Training
Defense Training International, Inc.
Personal Protection Training
Practical Shooting Academy, The
Rocky Mountain Combat
Applications Training
Rocky Mountain Gun Safety
Tac One
Talons Firearms Training, Inc.

## Connecticut
Defense Associates
Specter Tactical
Sturm, Ruger & Company
Williams Associates Protective
Services, LLC.

## Florida
Brantly and Associates, Inc.
Cirillo's Tactical Handgun Training
Defensive Training for the Armed
Citizen
GunSafety - TampaBay
HomeSafe Protective Training
Options for Personal Security
Personal Defense Institute
Rogers Shooting School
Universal Shooting Academy

## Georgia
Argenbright International Training
Institute
Federal Law Enforcement Training
Center (FLETC)
Firearmz
Glock, Inc.
James A. Neal Public Safety Training
Center
Personal Defense Training

## Idaho
Dan Mitchell's Clay Target and Wing
Shooting School
Firearms Training Institute
Personal Security & Safety Training
(PSST)
Security Awareness & Firearms
Education (SAFE)

## Illinois
Calibre Press
Illinois Small Arms Institute
Marksmanship Training Group, Inc.
Midwest Tactical Training Institute
Midwest Training Group
Police Training Institute
Specialized Training Associates
Wicklander-Zulawski & Associates

## Kentucky
Firearms Training Center
Southern Police Institute

## Louisiana
Guntek Firearms Training

## Maryland
Beretta Training
COMTAC
Defensive Firearms Consultants
Firearms Research & Instruction, Inc.

## Massachusetts
AWARE
Bob's Tactical
Massachusetts Firearms Serminars
Smith & Wesson Academy & Armorers
School

## Michigan
DTOM Enterprises
St. James Academy, The
Vital Options Institute

## Minnesota
Plus P Technology, Inc.
Wallin Video Productions

## Missouri
Chapman Academy of Practical
Shooting
National Law Enforcement Training
Center

## Montana
Marksman's Enterprise

## Nevada
Halo Group
Progressive F.O.R.C.E. Concepts
Sierra Firearms Academy

**New Hampshire**
International Association of Law
Enforcement Firearms
Instructors, Inc.
Lethal Force Institute (LFI)
SIGARMS Academy
Talon Enterprises

**New Jersey**
Defensive Firearms Academy
Firearm Training Center
Loss Prevention Serivices of
New Jersey

**New Mexico**
Personal Security Consulting

**New York**
Chelsea Gun Club, Inc.
Guardian Group International
International Rescue and Tactical
Consultants
MINDRICK Security Academy and
Shooting School
Modern Warrior Defensive Tactics
Institute
Police Training Division
Pro-Tek
Remington Shooting School
Serious Sportsman, Inc.
Tactical Defense International
Tactical Handgun Training

**North Carolina**
Area 52 Smallarms Training Center
Blackwater Lodge and Training
Center

Continental Threat Management
Ladies Handgun Clinics
Spartan Group

**Ohio**
Personal Protection Concepts
PRO
Tactical Defense Institute

**Oklahoma**
Shoot-N-Iron, Inc.

**Oregon**
Lane Community College
Oregon Firearms Academy

**Pennsylvania**
Northeast Training Institute
Peregrine Corporation
Weigand Shooting Seminars

**Tennessee**
Academy of Personal Protection
and Security
American Pistol & Rifle Association
Cumberland Tactics
Defensive Solutions
Farris Firearms Training
Institute of Security Services
Mid-South Institute of Self-Defense
Shooting
Personal Responsibility, Inc.
Whitten Arms

**Texas**
Auto Arms
Defensive Arts of Texas

Denton County Sports Association
ISI
Law Enforcement Educators
OffShoots Training Institute
Operational Support Services
ProTac Glocal Inc
South West Association of Trainers
and COMSAT
Southwest Defensive Shooting
Institute
Strategic Weapons Academy of
Texas
Texas Small Arms Academy
Thunder Ranch, Inc.

**Virginia**
Firearms International Training
Academy
Heckler & Koch, Inc.
Practical Firearms Training
Shawnee Hunt Club
Tactical Shooting Academy
Team One Network
Team Virginia

**Washington**
Burton's Firearm Instruction
Firearms Academy of Seattle
InSights Training Center, Inc.
Personal Safety Institute

**Washington, D.C.**
National Rifle Association

**West Virginia**
Blackheart International
BSR, Inc.
Storm Mountain Training Center

**Wyoming**
Tactical Force Institute

**Canada**
Canadian Academy of Practical
Shooting
Canadian Firearms Training
Executive Security Services
International
International Academy of Tactical
Training Systems
The Competitive Edge (TCE)